Teaching
and
Learning
the Democratic Way

PRENTICE-HALL INTERNATIONAL, INC., *London*
PRENTICE-HALL OF AUSTRALIA, PTY., LTD., *Sydney*
PRENTICE-HALL OF CANADA, LTD., *Toronto*
PRENTICE-HALL FRANCE, S.A.R.L., *Paris*
PRENTICE-HALL OF JAPAN, INC., *Tokyo*
PRENTICE-HALL DE MEXICO, S,A., *Mexico City*

GERTRUDE NOAR

Teaching
and
Learning
the Democratic Way

PRENTICE-HALL, INC.
ENGLEWOOD CLIFFS, N.J.

It was not even merely the fulfillment of the child's motivations; it was the fulfillment of the child's need for contact with her peers; the fulfillment of her need for parental support, warmth, and direction; the fulfillment of that discipline which lay in the task itself rather than in external authority; the fullfillment of a role a little harder than she was ready for, so as to constitute a challenge, a forward push into the domain of life that lay ahead. To supply this was the role of the teacher.

Gardner Murphy, Freeing Intelligence Through Teaching. *New York: Harper & Row, Publishers, Inc., 1961.*

Second Printing . . . September, 1963

Foreword

The author of this book has had the advantage of experience as a classroom teacher and junior high school principal in one of our largest cities and has taught at colleges in many sections of the country. More recently, as National Director of Education for the Anti-Defamation League, she has had the opportunity to visit, study, and evaluate public school education in all parts of the United States. This rich background of experience makes it possible for her to write, as she says in the introduction, "about the kind of learning experiences that contribute to the development of effective citizens in our democracy." I am sure she agrees with John Dewey, who wrote, "Only by being true to the full growth of all the individuals who make it up can society by any chance be true to itself."

This book contains many valuable and practical ideas. In the first part the author makes a strong case for unit teaching and describes the various processes involved. The second section of the book deals with the ABC's of human relations—individual and intergroup. Whether or not an instructor is able to use the unit method of teaching to instruct the average child in the routine subjects of the curriculum with even a moderate degree of success depends upon many so-called "extraneous factors." How well is the child physically? How effectively is he adjusted mentally and emotionally to the school, the teacher, his classmates? What sort of relationships exist between and among the children in the school and between teacher and children and teacher and parents? The finest teaching in the world will be ineffective if the young person is physically or mentally ill or if his outlook is characterized by lack of understanding of his fellows or, worse, by fear of them or of the teacher. Good human relations are central to effective teaching of any kind.

v

In this book are to be found facts that every teacher should know, but of which many teachers are unaware. These are facts about the children and their abilities, about the structure of American society, about children of minority groups in the school, about race, about prejudice, discrimination, and religious customs.

Miss Noar believes that teachers are needed who are devoted to good human relations and to the practice of democracy in schools, avoiding both extremes of autocratic and *laissez-faire* methods. Even more important is the need for teachers who recognize the unique opportunity the classroom provides for young people to practice freedom in situations meaningful to them and thus to develop understanding. It can be predicted that the outlines suggested in the book for units of work on race and race relations, cultural pluralism, human rights, and prejudice and discrimination will prove to be of great value to all teachers.

As our nation moves among the more than one hundred countries that now make up the United Nations, young people need to know how to relate themselves to peoples of other cultures, races, and religions on this earth. One out of four people in the world are non-Caucasian—and only one in seven descends from the Judeo-Christian religious tradition. Furthermore, one-third of the people of the world —those in Russian-controlled states and in China—live in regimented authoritarian states where there is no freedom of religion, of information, or of the ballot box. The fortunate one-third living in the West know the meaning of these freedoms. The other one-third are uncommitted. To which ideas will these people of the underdeveloped, disadvantaged countries give their allegiance?

It was once alleged that English battles were won on the playing fields of Eton. If Miss Noar's book has the wide reading it deserves and if its ideas are widely enough practiced, it will not be said in the years to come that freedom was lost in the public schools of America. This volume is an important contribution to education in this country.

DR. FRANCIS C. ROSECRANCE
Dean, College of Education
Wayne State University

Preface

This book is about the kind of learning experiences that contribute to the development of effective citizens in our democracy. It is also about human relations education—an essential part of education for democratic life—and deals with the methods of teaching and learning both human relations and democracy.

Teaching the democratic *way* means helping pupils to understand how people relate to each other as they live and work, and govern themselves and each other in a democratic order.

Teaching the *democratic* way means that the teacher assumes responsibility for showing how American democracy differs from other ways of life and government, such as totalitarianism. He makes sure that pupils understand the basic principle of the worth and significance of the individual in our society, how people share in developing the common good, the value of both competition and cooperation, and the Bill of Rights.

Teaching and learning the democratic way refers to how the teacher performs his task and carries out his responsibilities. It deals with the methods he uses in setting up many and varied learning experiences. Learning on the part of the pupil involves studying facts and finding information from all available sources. It also requires participation with others in the processes which implement the principles of democracy. Skill in living the democratic way and commitment to it are evidences of learning.

The concept of the democratic way in America changes and continues to grow as the meaning of its basic principles becomes clearer, and as it becomes more possible to implement these principles. For example, long before the Civil War people saw that slavery was inconsistent with democracy. The Emancipation Proclamation abolished it, the Civil War was fought, and the long uphill struggle of the Negro to secure the civil rights guaranteed him by the Constitution, began. Study of inter-race relations is essential if pupils are to understand this development, its meaning, and the present state of national affairs with relation to the practice of democracy.

Although many of the people who settled and developed America came to escape religious persecution and discrimination, tension over racial and religious differences and discriminaton still characterizes American life. Realization of the democratic way of life depends upon recognition of the irrationality and injustice of religious bigotry and discrimination. This aspect of intergroup relations must be included in secondary school curricula.

This book proposes that unit teaching provides many opportunities to *teach* democracy through living and learning the democratic way. Since resolution of the problems presented by undemocratic intergroup relations is one of democracy's acute problems, one with which today's youth must grapple in the future, the content, methods, and materials needed to teach about various aspects of this problem are presented in the form of resource unit outlines and reports of classroom work.

The purpose of this book is fourfold: First, it offers a vision of a classroom in which the nonreader and slow learner are just as important as the brilliant, book-minded student. Books become but one of the media and methods of classroom learning. Vicarious and direct experiences are used to ensure that more pupils will learn more about more, more easily. Second, this book gives practical help to the teacher. Answers are provided for his constantly recurring questions —"How shall I begin?" "What shall I say?" "Where can I get materials?" Third, the book includes fundamental facts and concepts about the child and his society which the teacher must have at his command. The teacher who keeps these in mind creates fewer blocks to learning. Fourth, methods of including intergroup relations in curricula are illustrated; information and resources needed to do so are documented.

Unit teaching, in which the values and skills of human relationships play important roles, is not easy, but it is indeed the high road to teaching and learning the democratic way.

GERTRUDE NOAR

Contents

Teaching
and
Learning
the Democratic Way

PART ONE

Unit Teaching

1

First Step: Learning About Freedom
the Democratic Way

BECAUSE THEIRS WAS A RELIGIOUS way of life, the early settlers of America established the public school to equip people to communicate with God by reading the Bible and the hymnals. They accomplished this purpose with a curriculum consisting mainly of reading and reciting.

From this early beginning the schools have always belonged to the people and have served as a tool to preserve the American way of life. When the personal and social lives of the people changed, school curriculum had to keep pace. As life in America became more complicated and new and different people swelled the population, the people's determination to establish civil rights and civil liberties for an increasing number of minority groups was added to the initial goal of religious freedom. Therefore, the school, with its objective of preparing children for the way of life the people desired, was required so to teach its pupils that they in turn would devote their energies to the preservation of those freedoms already won, to the extension of the concept of freedom, and to the practice of freedom as a way of life. Thus, the content of the public school curriculum changed to reflect these enlarged objectives.

Today, in our very complex society, the public school continues to be an instrument dedicated to the preservation of our democratic state and to freedom as our way of life. Thus, American history, civics, and other aspects of the social studies are required areas of learning from kindergarten through senior high school. As the result, when old and young alike are questioned as to what makes life in the United States different from that lived elsewhere, they quickly reply, "our freedom." When they are asked what they value most in our way of life, they answer with conviction, "freedom." The public school has done well to implant this knowledge and value in the minds and hearts of its graduates; but has it done well enough? What more must be done to secure a citizenry willing, determined, and able to give more than lip service to implementing the principles of freedom? True freedom demands action so that all within our borders shall have first-class citizenship.

Teaching the concept of freedom is of particular importance in the secondary school because of the nature of early adolescence. In the span of the adolescent years the individual must accomplish certain developmental tasks to which the concept and practice of freedom are basic. For example, if he is to mature, the adolescent must emancipate himself from his parents. He must learn to exercise freedom as he makes more and more of the decisions by which he governs his life. He must also find his role in our society and learn that living within our fundamental freedoms also means accepting responsibility for individual and group control.

Teaching the concept of freedom and the practice of freedom as a way of life requires content and method. The outcomes to be achieved are information, skills, habits, appreciations, values, and attitudes. Learning must become evident in thought and deed, in speech and behavior. The classrooms in which all of this is to be accomplished must be characterized by order and control, by purpose and industry. Teachers devoted to democracy, eschewing both autocratic and laissez-faire methods, are needed. In their democratic classrooms, license will not be mistaken for freedom.

The content required to teach freedom is extensive. First are the facts of American history: information about the kinds of people who came here and why they left their homelands; about their struggles with the environment, the natives, and with each other. The words and deeds of leaders of minority groups form a significant part of the story of the struggle for liberty in this country. Information about the men and women who led and won and died in the wars must be included. The stories of men and women who pushed back the frontiers of thought as they enlarged the concept of democracy for the world are another part of the heritage to be learned.

The content needed to teach freedom must include understanding of such great principles of democracy as the worth and integrity of every human being and the right to share in policy making. Accompanying these are the great ideas: freedom from want, freedom from fear, freedom to worship as one pleases, freedom to speak one's mind.

School pupils must learn the processes which people use to accomplish their purposes in a free society. Among these processes are conference, discussion, sharing work, pooling findings, competing for excellence, and cooperating to enlarge horizons and ideas and to create products which exceed what the individual could achieve by himself.

Another essential part of the content of the curriculum for freedom is the study and appreciation of the great documents in which our great men and women have set down the structure and guarantees of our freedoms—from the Declaration of Independence to the 1954 Supreme Court decision on segregation.

Dedication to freedom cannot be achieved completely without study of other lands and people. A study of those not yet removed from coercion and persecution, who are at the very moment engaged in fierce struggle for the freedoms enjoyed in America, can heighten an appreciation of what we take for granted. A study of those with differing ideologies and ways of life can be used to establish a base from which to view the democratic way and to realize its advantages. All the resources of radio, television, and the press can be mobilized to bring these realities into the classroom.

Freedom cannot be learned solely through the medium of the printed or even the spoken word. The facts may be grasped by many, but certainly not by all the pupils currently enrolled in secondary school. The use of the word symbol to impart concepts compounds the difficulty which many concrete-minded pupils have when they are confronted with abstractions. Moreover, reading *about* a process is not enough to develop in the individual the skill to use it. The traditional and still commonly used textbook method, best described as lecture-assignment-homestudy-recitation-test, is not adequate to achieve the practice as well as the ideal of freedom.

What teachers teach about freedom often has little connection with the reality of life as the pupils know it. Too often the teaching is devoted to description of what ought to be without mention of what is. To correct this, the teacher must make more use of the community as a laboratory where pupils examine what actually exists there. In most American communities, life as it is lived includes institutions, customs, and people who support less than the full freedom of first-class citizenship for all. This increases the difficulty of teaching the reality of freedom. This difficulty must be overcome by study of the forces and the agencies which are working to correct the abuses and the sins of omission and commission which still remain as part of our social heritage.

The school and society will know that freedom has been successfully taught in the school only when the learning becomes evident in behavior. To accomplish this, the school must allow its pupils to experience freedom and to practice it in situations which are meaningful to them. For example, student organizations through which pupils participate in administration and control are commonly thought of as projects designed to give experience with the democratic processes. However, they need to be carefully examined and evaluated. Too often only a handful of students are involved. Too often their activities are limited to affairs of little importance. Too often all decisions which count are made by faculty.

Extending to all the right to participate in determining classroom work through teacher-pupil planning provides experience in the value and meaning of the right to speak and to be heard. Such planning also involves experience with the principle of sharing in policy making. School pupils practice the democratic processes when they plan together with their teacher and each other and when together they organize their efforts and pool their thoughts and the products of their labor. Thus, they learn to participate in cooperative enterprise designed to achieve the greatest good for all concerned. When such experiences include social action projects, the pupils come to believe in the value of democracy and learn to accept responsibility for making life better.

Because living in our democracy requires understanding and acceptance of all kinds of people, segregation for any reason must be considered undemocratic in the public school. When students who differ from each other in mental ability work together in small and large groups, bent on getting answers they want to questions they raise, and seek solutions to problems of common concern, they are using the democratic processes in a free society. They practice the skills of leading and following, of discussion, and of critical thinking. Preservation of freedom in American thought may in the future rest upon the ability of the common man to gather facts, to weigh them for relative values, to use good judgment, and to make wise decisions.

When boys and girls who differ from each other in color and race, creed and religion, social class and ethnic origin sit side by side, giving help to those who need it, rendering service, utilizing their respective talents for the good of all, they learn to like in each other all that is good and to respect in each other all that is worthy. Then human difference ceases to be a reason for rejection and is recognized as a source of individual creativity that has great significance in our free society. When respect for human differences shows in behavior and becomes a way of life, the teacher and parent know that a great democratic principle has been learned.

Freedom to think and to speak one's thoughts can be learned only when both teachers and pupils know from experience that what they say will not meet with ridicule and sarcasm and that no reprisals will be exercised. Such a climate is not easy to establish. Administrators, counselors, and teachers must be mature enough to accept just criticism, to value difference, and to grant the right to dissent. The adults in the school must also agree that children are people and that they have rights which no individual may deny or abuse. Furthermore, they must govern their relationships with their students in accordance with the principles of freedom. Students who live in a school in which the teachers arrange for them to experience freedom of thought and word, learn to accept it, to value it, not to abuse it, and to grant it to their peers.

If the youth of the land are to learn freedom, the school must help to set them free. They must learn to be free from the pull of childhood; free from the impatient and often unfair control of the father figure demanding obedience; free from the conflict which sets them against law and order and authority; free to assume responsibility commensurate with talent; free from the fear of being dubbed failures by intolerant teachers; free to develop initiative, imagination, creativity, and unknown potentiality; and, in the last analysis, free and proud to be themselves.

2

The Unit: A Method of Teaching the Democratic Way

THE UNIT IS NOT A NEW DEVICE FOR organizing subject matter, nor is it a new teaching-learning method. It appeared some fifty years ago, and, despite variations in form, has never dropped out of sight. Its persistence in education has been accompanied by growing awareness of the unity in life, in society, and in world relationships.

From medicine, psychology, and psychiatry teachers learn that the individual grows, develops, and lives as a total entity. Therefore, they know that he cannot be taught as if his physical, mental, and emotional characteristics and abilities were in separate compartments. From psychiatry and mental hygiene teachers also learn that human behavior is caused—partly from within and partly from without. Therefore, they know that the individual cannot be separated from the environment in which he lives. So, as the teacher's understanding of human growth and development and of the social order increases, he realizes that living and learning in the school must be designed to meet the total needs of the individual. The content and methods must take into account the individual's own background, his immediate family life and the society in which he lives. Moreover, because our world is shrinking, and because of the changes we know will occur in the foreseeable future, the school must also prepare the child with the information and values of internationalism.

Many leading educators have long known that high quality in education requires more than conveying information in tight subject matter compartments. However, in the secondary school department-alization has maintained a strong control over curriculum. In fact, because of the explosion of knowledge in all areas, and the alarm caused by the allegation that in this country the quality of teaching is low, the demand for departmentalization and teachers specialized in subject areas has even reached into the elementary school. One result, in some places, has been rejection of the ungraded school and the self-contained classroom in favor of organizing the school day into subject matter areas presided over by teachers specialized in reading or arithmetic or science or a foreign language. Neverthe-less, and especially in social studies, guides for teachers and textbooks still continue to present subject matter organized into units of work developed around central themes, problems, or questions. However, many teachers fail to use unit teaching methods because they lack the time, previous experience with the method, and clear descrip-tions of how to do unit teaching.

The content in the units of learning needed to teach the demo-cratic way consists of information from several subject areas al-though all the areas may be considered part of social studies. This diversified content is beneficial because one of the objectives of unit teaching is designed to develop the pupil's ability to seek and find the facts needed to answer questions and solve problems regardless of where the search may lead. For example, learning about the democratic *way* may begin with current affairs, but will take the student from there into history, political science, sociology, eco-nomics, literature, and possibly into science. Moreover, the pursuit of information and the necessity of sharing it with others will re-quire learning to read, write, and speak more effectively, skills usually considered the responsibility of the English department.

Educators have long agreed that the school is responsible for developing ability to think, to integrate facts and weigh them for relative values, to formulate principles, and to draw valid conclu-sions. Unit teaching provides maximum opportunity to practice and, therefore, to develop the skills of critical thinking and evalua-tion. Moreover, in unit teaching emphasis shifts from teaching to learning, from listening to doing, from memorizing facts to using them, from copying to creating, from passive acceptance of the teacher's direction to self-direction in learning.

Planning and using unit teaching requires a variety of materials and resources of a wide range of difficulty. Moreover, not only are the talents of the academically able pupils needed but their abilities can be challenged and increased. Creativity is also required, and the highly creative pupils find that their talents and abilities are needed and developed. There is also work for pupils with ordinary or "average" ability to do. Many opportunities exist for those with little academic ability to work under the direction of their more able classmates, and to contribute to class discussions and to decision making. When a teacher understands how to use unit methods and has insight into human growth and development, unit teaching also provides practice in the use of the democratic processes. When students learn the democratic way in school, they acquire the information, attitudes, skills, and values that are linked with the survival of democracy.

Unit Teaching in Elementary Schools

Teaching and learning the democratic way can begin in the elementary school. Where the self-contained classroom is used, the teacher does not have to adhere rigidly to time schedule nor to time bells which separate learning into subjects. At one time an elementary child's day was broken up into ten- or twenty-minute compartments devoted to mental arithmetic, geography, physical exercises, and spelling with half-hour divisions for reading, numbers, history, and singing. Now, in many classrooms, the teacher and children plan together for the learning activities of the morning or afternoon session.

In the early grades, experience forms the basis upon which the reading skills are developed. Social studies is about family life, about people and the work they do, and about the neighborhood. Children begin to learn how people live in the American kind of organized society. Therefore, the teacher plans units of work dealing with shelter, food, transportation, communication, production and distribution of goods and services, and group life and play. Although the immaturity of the pupils requires that content and activities in such units be preplanned, the effective teacher includes more and more opportunities for the children to choose between alternatives and to make suggestions about what to do and how to do it. As fast as children develop the ability, they are admitted to the planning process and eventually even to the selection of the center of interest about which a unit is to be organized.

In the upper elementary grades many teachers make it possible for pupils to work in small sub-groups or committees so they may learn leadership skills and acquire experience with the group processes. Such activities may be limited in the school which uses special teachers for special subjects and a departmental structure. However, one organization plan, which is used in Detroit, Michigan, calls for assigning large groups to the auditorium. The most skillful and creative teachers in the school use that responsibility to provide many opportunities for sub-group work. Very often committees are formed to create, prepare, and produce the programs for the large audience, which assembles once a week. For example, in preparing auditorium programs the less academically gifted pupils work at construction and handling of stage properties. Those with artistic abilities paint scenery and make costumes. Those who read well but cannot write, look up the facts to assist others who need them for their creative writing.

Unit Teaching in Secondary Schools

At the secondary school level, whether or not the school is departmentalized, teachers will be more successful if they are aware of the developmental tasks confronting adolescents. These tasks involve basic problems of human relationships and are common to all persons.

In early adolescence, boys and girls are preoccupied with the changes occurring in their bodies, their minds, and their emotions. They often are as concerned with the trivial as they are with the profound aspects of life and society. They are likely to withdraw at the moment that they reach out. They search and seek but often cannot tell clearly what they want. They begin to turn away from adults and toward their peers whose approval they need. Teachers and parents complain about the girls, and say, "If they'd only let the boys alone!" And, more often than not, this refers to boys at least two or more years older than the girls, because boys of the same age are usually not interested, not ready to dance and date.

In later adolescence, when growth has leveled off and physiological changes are complete, problems of social living move into center stage. Both boys and girls are still preoccupied with sex and think a good bit about marriage and family life. However, what the working world is like and how one measures up to job possibilities are also of great interest and concern. The differences between those students who look toward college and professional careers and those who because of money cannot even remain for graduation, become acute. Tensions and hostilities on the basis of socio-economic class are likely to give rise to human relations problems which too many teachers ignore.

Adolescent developmental tasks fall into the following general categories:

—emancipation from adults
—heterosexual adjustment
—understanding and finding a role in the social culture
—learning about the working world and settling on a course leading toward economic independence.

Unless the school provides an organized program of group guidance, the units of work which deal directly with areas of information, attitudes, and values required to meet the needs and the problems of growing up are likely to be omitted. Of particular importance to adolescents are units dealing with the nature of American society, with minority group culture patterns, with intergroup relations, with discrimination and prejudice in the working world, with race and with civil rights. The content and materials needed for such units can often be gathered from courses of study, text and reference books, and pamphlets published by government and private agencies. Resource units, however, are not teaching plans. From them the teacher must select that content which will answer questions raised by his students and those learning activities that are feasible in his school and community.

Meeting Emotional Needs

All teachers must concern themselves with the emotional needs that are common to all human beings at all age levels. Unless these emotional needs are met in some measure for a pupil, he is likely to be blocked in his mental, emotional, or social development. Minority groups in American society tend to suffer more from unsatisfied emotional needs than do those who belong to the dominant or majority groups. The methods used in unit teaching provide for more satisfaction of emotional needs for more boys and girls, thus insuring that more of them will learn more, more easily.

The first emotional need, first because it appears at birth and remains throughout life, is the need to be liked, to belong, to be wanted and needed for oneself alone. This need for warm, positive relationships with other people is often frustrated by reason of differences in people. Yet, such differences as skin color, the religious affiliation of one's family, the country in which one's ancestors were born are outside the individual's control. He can do nothing to change them.

Therefore, the teacher who wants his pupils to learn the democratic way must recognize the reality of prejudice and discrimination in American society and include in the year's plans units of work dealing with problems of intergroup relations.

Rejection and exclusion, which deprive people of satisfaction of the need to feel worthy of affection, is often based upon differences not only in race, but also in color; not only in religion, but also in creed and also in social class and ethnic origins. For example, light skinned Negroes often prefer not to associate with dark skinned Negroes and vice versa. Dark skinned Caucasians are likely to be rejected by white Caucasians who may not even know that they are similar in race. Difference in race itself is the most obvious cause of prejudice and discriminatory behavior.

An example of exclusion because of difference in creed within the Christian religion is anti-Catholicism. Another is rejection by many Christian sects of such fundamentalist groups as Jehovah's Witnesses. Rejection and exclusion based upon religion itself is common. Anti-Semitism is one example. Buddhists, Mohammedans, and Indians (if they have not been converted) are also far from feeling liked and wanted in American life.

Social class, which is based largely upon economics and differing values and patterns of behavior, often causes pupils of the lower classes to be rejected by their middle-class peers and teachers. Nationality background sometimes operates to exclude some groups from membership in prestige clubs and activities. Pupils of Polish and Italian families are likely to suffer most.

Pupils who are not accepted and who feel that they are not wanted by teachers and peers see themselves as unlovable people and therefore they have trouble liking themselves. This will probably make it hard for them to like others. Maintaining good human relations within and across group lines becomes almost impossible for them.

Unit teaching provides opportunity to include information and understanding of basic human differences. Acceptance of difference as a positive value in American life is a desired outcome of such units. The ability to relate across group lines grows when pupils who differ identify common problems, set up their mutual goals, and work together to achieve their objectives. Then they see that group differences are not valid reasons for rejection of groups or individuals within the groups.

Another emotional need that has great intensity in human life is the need for achievement and accomplishment. When it is satisfied, the individual feels of ever greater worth. His success increases his effort and releases his energy. When a pupil is deprived of satisfaction of this need, which happens every time he "fails" in school, he feels inferior, inadequate, and unworthy. Because people behave largely as they perceive themselves to be, the pupil who continually fails, by reason of that failure, is likely to become unable to try, unable to work, unable to learn. In other words, lack of success itself serves to block learning.

Minority group children, especially Negroes, Puerto Ricans, Indians, and those of Mexican ancestry, suffer from feelings of inferiority because, in the total social structure of American life, the groups to which they belong are unable to achieve in the same degree as the dominant whites do. When to the depression and despair they often acquire from adults, these children must add failure to achieve in school, learning is blocked.

Probably the most frequent question American school teachers ask, is, "How can I possibly adjust my teaching to meet the needs of individuals who differ so widely?" Unit teaching provides the following answers to that question: (1) Successful committee work depends upon a variety of abilities. (2) The use of vicarious and especially of direct learning experiences in and out of the school enables those to learn who have difficulty in using word symbols without depriving the verbally gifted of equal opportunity to learn from the most difficult books and materials that are available. (3) Successful participation with peers enhances interest and increases effort. (4) Content close to the reality of life motivates learning at all levels of ability.

Rejection, failure, feelings of inferiority and inadequacy in themselves block learning. Moreover, they create anxiety which, if chronically excessive, also blocks learning. And, once again, minority group pupils suffer most. This is due to the conditions which American society imposes upon them: the various forms of discrimination and segregation; the consequent low levels of aspiration many of their adults have for them; and the despair with which they view their own vocational futures. Anxiety levels become unendurable when to these group anxieties, the school adds anxiety connected with mastering unrealistic content, so-called standards, punishment by failure, encouragement to leave, marks and report cards.

Unit teaching affords a way of living and learning which is free of artificial tensions. Moreover, units of work can be developed to afford insight into the nature and causes of anxieties connected with minority group membership and intergroup relations. Through knowledge of success in the struggle for civil rights, through personal contact and investigation, through films and speakers, hope for the future can be expected to replace despair, and anxiety will be reduced.

On all counts, teaching and learning the democratic way results in greater satisfaction of emotional needs for all of the children of all the people.

3

Scope and Sequence:
Content and Timing

TWO PROBLEMS ARISE BECAUSE SCHOOL administrators and teachers must continually reconstruct curriculum to meet the needs of our rapidly changing society: first to decide what to include, and second to decide the best arrangement of the several elements. In pedagogical literature the word "scope" is used to designate the "what," and "sequence" becomes the technical term for the "when." Uppermost in the minds of those who think about these problems are the fears that to omit important factual materials is dangerous and that unless preventative care is exercised wasteful repetitions will occur.

Teachers are often limited to the scope and sequence outlined in courses of study. They fear criticism if they do not cover the syllabus, and they may be very insecure when they are confronted with the responsibility for planning units of learning with their students. A different concept of scope and sequence is needed, to which such significant publications as the Harvard Report on "General Education"[1] and the Educational Policies Commission's book *Education for All American Youth*[2] make important contributions.

[1] Paul H. Buck *et al.*, *General Education in a Free Society*, report of the Harvard Committee (Cambridge, Mass.: Harvard University Press, 1945).

[2] Educational Policies Commission of the NEA, *Education for All American Youth* (Washington, D.C.: 1944).

16

The scope or content of the program designed to prepare the young for life in our democracy includes information about both the social processes and human relations. Youth must learn the way in which people organize and control themselves and others. At each school level the special needs which are peculiar to the ages of the pupils affect content. Thus, in the elementary school the emotional as well as the mental and physical needs of childhood impose certain limitations. In the junior high school the needs created by adolescent tasks require additional attention. In the senior high school, impending adulthood and economic independence add elements to the scope of the program. In both elementary and secondary schools, a part of the program is dictated by the fact that the students are living in this physical world which they must understand and interpret, and to which they must make personal adjustments. A third part of the curriculum grows out of the fact that children and adolescents, alike, must learn to communicate ever more effectively in English.

The broad areas of need are reflected in traditional subject matter courses. Problems of development and relationship are studied in group guidance. Knowledge, understanding, and control over the natural environment are learned in nature study, general science, biology, physics, chemistry, anthropology, psychology (mental health), health, and astronomy. Effective and pleasurable communication is dependent upon increased ability to read, write, and talk, which also includes the study of literature and creative writing—in other words all that usually constitutes the courses called language arts or English. Human relations and organized living in a democracy are essential parts of social studies—a composite of history, geography, civics, economics, political science, and problems of democracy.

The teacher who has freedom to depart from the completely departmentalized program needs to look at scope from a different point of view. His problem is to survey the pupil's life in our society. When he does so, he sees that the needs to be met arise out of life. The pupil is a member of a family, he belongs to a school group, and he lives in a gradually enlarging community. In both, he not only is developing as an individual but is also learning to live with others who are different from himself. He is already a consumer of goods and services. He is a potential producer of goods and is already involved in the distribution of goods and services. He is ready to increase and enlarge his concepts of spiritual, moral, ethical, and aesthetic values. He must accept the role of citizen and learn to live within and to participate in the American way of organizing and controlling life in the democratic tradition.

No lines or walls separate one area of living from another or divide the dynamic processes which go on within them. For example, production cannot be understood apart from consumption. History cannot be separated from geography or economics. Nothing can be studied without the use of English. Effective learning experiences cannot remain solely inside of one or another subject matter course.

Clearly, too, few interests and needs can be identified as belonging to only one grade level. For example, people are concerned with the home, with food and clothing, with work and law and order at all ages. However, the maturity level and the social conditions surrounding the pupils both impose limitations and determine specific needs. Learning experiences, therefore, ought to be planned and developed by the teacher and pupils on the basis of their own immediate needs, their common concerns, and the problems confronting society. Because all such problems and questions cannot be predetermined, scope and sequence should have no hard and fast boundaries within which a teacher is required to operate. Sequence is really a matter of relevance and of readiness to learn. This places upon the teacher and his students responsibility for determining the next job to be done. One way to do so is to seek answers to such questions as:

—What *have* we done?
—What is there still to be done?
—In the light of the strength and weakness of our past performance and of our present position on the road to becoming mature people and intelligent citizens, what must we do next?

If these questions are discussed with sincerity and honesty, little dangerous omission or wasteful repetition will occur. To further insure against both, an adequate system of record keeping is required. The individual teacher insures continuity and critical evaluation from day to day by keeping a log or diary in which he enters the day's accomplishments. These notes may be organized in outline form for ready reference at the close of the unit. Copies of such outlines, filed with the principal or supervisor, or in the school library, provide succeeding teachers of any group, first-hand knowledge of the pupil's previous experiences. If a chart is devised for recording the names of the units studied by all classes, the learning experiences of every group can be followed as long as they remain together.

Athough such record keeping decreases the chance of repetition, little wasted or dangerous repetition is apt to occur anyway. In the first place, the curiosities and needs of the young are legion. They resent repetition because it is boring. Secondly, the teacher is the responsible agent in the planning process, and he must insist on the necessity for exploring new fields. And finally, if for some reason pupils are eager to do a unit with which they have had previous experience, the teacher must find out what they actually know about it before planning begins. Then the very nature of the growth process as well as the fact that no subject, question, or problem is likely ever to be completely explored, answered, or solved at any school level will insure that new ground is covered and that time is not wasted on needless repetition.

No system of organized education ever assured to anyone complete knowledge. Omission is a fact of life and of education. By far the largest part of the population in former years did not remain in school long enough to get even half of that which was planned for a twelve-year program. Nearly half of those who enter first grade still do not graduate from twelfth grade. Today the explosion of knowledge makes it impossible to "cover," let alone master, any field in the elementary and secondary grades. Every unit a class undertakes must be delimited by reason of time, maturity, and available materials. Omission of some facts is, therefore, inevitable. What essentials are to be included must always be redetermined in the light of the time available and the learning abilities of the pupils. Moreover, since abilities differ, obviously the academically able will omit less than those whose rate of learning is slower, and whose mental complexities are less.

If, on the other hand, we stop to consider what omission is dangerous, we are confronted with an age-old question that has many answers: What learning is of most worth? The modern teacher realizes that most facts by and of themselves are of little importance because isolated facts are quickly forgotten. He knows that human relations, the way to find facts, the skill of critical thinking, and the habits of acceptable and effective behavior are of enduring worth. He also knows that the values, principles, and processes needed to live effectively the democratic way do not come out of reading texts about them. They are developed when pupils have suitable, meaningful, and satisfying experiences in which these values, principles, and processes are used.

4

Second Step: Getting Acquainted

BEFORE A TEACHER CAN APPROACH
the development of a unit of work, he should know many things
about the individuals and the group he is to teach. In the elementary school where the teacher is with his class most of the day, time to
study individuals is available. Obviously, the secondary school teacher
will not have the time if he meets a class for only one period a day
and has four or more classes to teach. In some secondary schools,
however, ways are being found to change the organization pattern so
that at least one teacher is with a group of pupils more than one
period a day and can remain their teacher for at least a year. That
teacher usually discovers the value of studying the individuals in the
group and of learning about their interpersonal relationships. So informed, he can plan more effectively for both instruction and guidance.

Individual Differences

All that we know about the nature of learning indicates that an
individual can progress only from where he *is* at the moment. The
teacher must, therefore, plan to teach in such a way that he meets the
individuals in the group at their learning levels. Mass instruction
must be abandoned because it is ineffective; for if it aims at the least

21

complicated minds and the slowest learners, the more able are likely to be bored. Boredom and its consequent fatigue block learning. On the other hand, if the teacher aims at a hypothetical middle or average pupil, those who function below that level will be out of luck, for they can neither jump or reach up to that level. They become frustrated, aggressive, hostile, or apathetic. Those emotions also block learning. A few teachers in the secondary schools still seem to feel justified in aiming their instruction at their most able pupils, the college-bound. When they do so, to the failure and frustration of the rest are apt to be added jealousy and hatred of classmates. The poor interpersonal relations that result in the group also block learning.

For the most part, American teachers are middle-class people. They often teach as if all their pupils also lived in middle-class homes where grammatical, cultured, middle-class English is spoken; where privacy, conveniences, and some luxuries are provided; and where relationships and learning are motivated by middle-class values. When there are lower-class and culturally deprived pupils in the class, they are likely to become confused by the teacher's demands. Then deep-seated value conflicts may be created. Confusion and conflict block learning.

Teachers must understand that no home life *can* exist for some pupils; that to talk good English in their homes and neighborhoods might ostracize some; that vulgar, obscene and profane words are part of all conversations for others; and that few, if any, universal values on which they can count actually exist. If, therefore, profound conflicts are to be avoided, the teacher must find out about the neighborhoods from which his pupils come. Until he knows about his pupils' roots and culture patterns and values, he will be unable to understand them, and until he understands them, he will have difficulty teaching them.

For many pupils, learning is both difficult and slow because they are in poor physical condition. It is of little use for the teacher to demand concentration, attention, obedience, punctuality and regular attendance from boys and girls who have too low metabolism, glandular disturbance which creates obesity or under development, malnutrition, anemia, decayed teeth, festering tonsils, impaired vision or hearing, or brain damage. All of these handicaps block learning.

As the teacher looks at an ordinary eighth-grade group, for example, he is likely to see not only thirteen year olds but fourteen and fifteen year olds as well. However, even boys and girls of the same chronological age differ in many other respects. They vary in height, weight, color, nationality, religion, health, ability, social background, economic advantage, achievement levels, name, hobbies, activity, interests, family pattern, number of parents, physical and emotional maturity.

The teacher should know which girls have reached puberty and what boy-girl relationships and attitudes exist, and the degree to which each child has succeeded in emancipating himself from the control of his parents, which is a major factor in determining attitudes toward teachers and authority. Much of the disturbing classroom behavior directed at the teacher is the result of perfectly natural conflicts in the home.

Adolescent Relationships

To nearly all elementary school children, the most important person in the classroom is the teacher. In adolescence this changes rapidly. What the teacher, the parents, and all other adults say, think, and want becomes much less important. At this point in development, the child joins his group. From then on, his peers are of supreme importance. He seeks in every way to gain security, attention and status among them.

The interplay of boy-girl relationships results in the development of a pattern of social life in the group itself. This child society begins to get organized as soon as the group meets in the classroom. Without some knowledge of it the teacher is lost. He must know which pupils are centers or stars of attraction. The politician in the group may be with him or against him in planning units of learning. The presence of hostile cliques may prevent the success of group work. If planning and committee work are to be successful, elements of the code which governs life in the child society must be known and used. This code is quite subtle. It changes from year to year as the values given to certain characteristics and actions assume different proportions. Teachers catch glimpses of it as they watch groups at work and at play, as they get the confidences of a few individuals, and as they learn to interpret behavior patterns. Successful discussions depend upon strategic use of key students and of the more hostile leaders.

The actions of the class clown, the bully, and the scapegoat need to be interpreted to those individuals themselves and to the group. Pitfalls await the teacher's pet, the "perfect" boy, and the isolates. The child who is rejected by the group needs much help from the teacher.

Necessary Facts About the Pupils

During the first few weeks of the school year the teacher must accept responsibility for setting up many different kinds of experiences. The purpose is twofold: (1) The pupils need to develop a sense of security in his leadership and in their own continuing accomplishment. (2) The teacher needs to assemble concrete evidences of performance levels, learning potentialities and group relationships. These constitute a real basis for new learning experiences to develop social skills and the tool subjects.

Figure 4-1 will help the teacher to do the necessary planning.

Planning for Long Periods

Secondary school teachers often have trouble learning what to do with time as they plan the daily and weekly program during the early weeks of the year. The time schedule evolved should depend upon the maturity level, emotional stability, concentration and attention spans, and the needs for physical activity, manipulative expression, and rest periods observed in the pupils.

The schedule [1] on pages 27-28 illustrates how activities help the teacher to discover such things about the pupils as their use of language, reading abilities, concentration and attention spans. It also provides for movement of the group toward participation in identification of common interests and selection of a center of interest for a unit. Presumably, the teacher will have clarified the reasons for browsing and how to do it.

The class (in the junior high school) would have its first pre-

[1] Gertrude Noar, *Freedom to Live and Learn* (Philadelphia: Franklin Publishing Co., 1948), pp. 22-23.

What the teacher needs to know about the pupils	Experiences that reveal the facts	Records to be consulted
Level of performance in tool subjects.	Reading lessons. Audience reading. Silent reading. Standardized tests in spelling, reading, English usage, and English grammar. Group and individual tests on current events, history, geography, literature. Games, quizzes, group contests.	Records from previous grades.
Scholastic and social abilities and interests. Ability to follow directions.	Standardized tests, inventories, questionnaires, interviews. Creative writing (Autobiography, Three Wishes, My Gripes, What I Would Do with $100, My Favorite Person). Games. Library periods. Spontaneous assignments to do things, get information as needs arise and questions are asked. Errands. Parties, picnics, and trips.	
Past experiences, home conditions, economic level, affectional security.	Intimate writings (as above). Conferences with previous teachers and counselors. Making a community survey. Party for parents. Home visits.	Clinical records about adjustment to adults. Individual and group records of units previously studied. Any available community surveys.

Fig. 4-1. Preliminary Work During Orientation Period. Gertrude Noar, *Freedom to Live and Learn* (Philadelphia: Franklin Publishing Co., 1948), pp. 20-21.

What the teacher needs to know about the pupils	Experiences that reveal the facts	Records to be consulted
Maturity levels—physical, social, emotional. Levels of emancipation from adults.	Discussions of fun, beauty, home life, neighborhood problems, friendships. Interviews with individuals. Conferences with parents. Observation of work and play.	Clinical records.
Health problems.	Questionnaires. Interviews. Observation.	Records of medical and dental examinations. Cumulative records. Records made from parental interview when child first entered school.
Nicknames, hobbies, after school and in school activities.	Hobby show. Intimate writings (as above). Oral presentations. Interviews. Questionnaires.	
Group social pattern (sociometrics), group code, leaders, special roles (bully, clown), pattern of attractions and rejections.	Observation in and out of classroom. Conversation periods. Setting up of committees as needed for incidental jobs. Games. "Guess Who" questionnaires. Setting up of experiences. Trips. Sorting pictures for room decoration. Elections. Dramatizations. Browsing periods.	

Fig. 4-1 (cont.)

liminary experiences with pupil-teacher planning on Tuesday when they organize and commission their first committee. Planning for the use of time does not occur until Thursday.

MONDAY

9:00- 9:15   Conversation: "What I did on Saturday and Sunday."
"What I saw happening in nature over the weekend."

9:15- 9:50   Creative writing growing out of the conversation: stories, poems, radio skits.
For those who cannot write, drawing, clay modeling, looking for pictures.

9:50-10:00   (Or as pupils show need.) Rest period to walk around, get a drink, visit the lavatory.

10:00-10:15   Reporting to the class about the book being read.

10:15-11:00   Exchanging finished books for new ones.
Individual reading.
Reading instruction for those who have reading difficulties.

TUESDAY

9:00- 9:30   Discussion of health problems such as: visit to dentist, securing eye glasses, faithfulness in doing posture exercises, rest and recreation schedules, diets for the thin and overweight (not suitable above grade 8).

9:30-10:00   Browsing in science books, pamphlets, magazines, and newspapers brought to class by the pupils and teacher in response to questions raised in Monday's conversations about weekend outdoor activities. Discussion of what to look for, the use of table of content and index, and, for some, review of key words and terms to assist in reading must precede use of the materials.

10:00-10:05   Rest break.

10:05-10:30   Discussion of answers to science questions raised on Monday.

10:30-11:00   Setting up and commissioning a committee to go to school library after school to get more material on the subject which seemed to be of greatest interest to the class.
Use of dictionaries to find meaning of new words.
Recording the day's work in individual diaries and class log.

WEDNESDAY

9:00- 9:30   Record keeping (each pupil has his own folder in which he keeps all written work such as his record of current reading, the list of words he is studying, his unfinished and completed creative writing, and his diary.

9:30-10:00   Corrective teaching in field of language arts based on group needs as revealed by conversation, discussion, written work.

10:00-10:15   Written exercises.

10:15-10:30   Rest and physical exercises.

10:30-11:00   Reading for fun (pupils have free access to book shelves from which they select new books as they finish old ones).

Setting up bulletin board committee.

THURSDAY

9:00- 9:30   Discussion of current affairs: Questions which indicate need for information are written on the chalk board.

9:30- 9:45   Committees are set up to seek the answers.

9:45-10:00   Selecting and commissioning committee to plan for a nature trip to follow up the discussion of science questions earlier in the week.

10:00-10:10   Rest period.

10:10-10:25   Pupil-teacher planning of what to do during the remainder of the period. Decision reached: trip committee to meet with teacher while others read, write, look for pictures in magazines (related to discussions and questions raised), arrange bulletin board, file articles clipped from newspapers.

10:25-11:00   Activities as planned.

FRIDAY

9:00- 9:30   Browsing for materials on questions raised the previous day during discussion of current affairs.

9:30- 9:50   Reporting new subjects to consider as possible centers of interest.

9:50-10:00   Rest break and conversation in preparation for discussion.

10:00-10:30   Discussion of the relative importance of main interests pointed up thus far (some were in the area of science,

some in history, others in current events and still others
had to do with personal problems of living).

10:30-11:00   Written work to clarify thinking, "What I would like to
study next."

The purpose of the above schedule is not to give the teacher a
ready-made plan for use in his classroom. Rather, it should be examined critically to see how variation of activity is arranged, how
various levels of ability and performance are taken care of, what
facts about pupils can be obtained during such a week, how time is
distributed, and what elements are omitted (for example, guidance
and student organization). The allocation of time to each activity
is merely suggestive. The sensitive teacher knows when to stop an
activity because pupils become restless, bored, or tired. He also
learns when to disregard his time schedule in order to capitalize on
eager enthusiasm and willing participation.

5

Third Step: Selecting
the Unit

PUPIL-TEACHER COOPERATION IN SE-
lection of a center of interest for a unit is not likely to be the method
used by teachers who have been given courses of study which they
are required to accept and follow without deviation. Very often,
however, modern guides for teachers list a variety of alternative
units. In some guides, two-thirds of the units are required, and the
remaining third are left for the teacher and his class to decide. Pupil-
teacher planning then is the method to be used for part of the time.
Moreover, when he makes his preplanning survey of any unit,
prescribed or otherwise, the teacher can and should look for places
at which alternatives are possible. In connection with these, opportunities can be created for choice, decision-making, and practice
of the planning processes.

If unit teaching in a social studies course is restricted to a single
period each day, probably nothing other than work on the unit can
be undertaken by the class. However, if the class is scheduled for
more than one period each day and the teacher is responsible for
more than one subject (frequently language arts and social studies
are combined, or English and history), then time must be set aside
for learning activities outside of the unit itself. For example, in
many unified, general education or core type classes, the teacher
designates specific periods during the week to be reserved for litera-

ture study, reading for fun, and creative writing. When the teacher is also the class adviser and responsible for guidance, on some days during the week when, possibly, the class meets more than two periods, time is taken for group discussion of their problems of living and for the work of the student organization. These and other activities, such as participation in drives for Red Cross and Community Chest, may be required by the school. Time must also be allotted to programs for special events, such as patriotic holidays. Activities apart from the unit are often referred to as "parallel activities."

Because this is a book about unit teaching, its special applicability to intergroup relations education, and the opportunities it provides for experience with the democratic processes, description of parallel activities and the many other things that go on in the classroom in addition to the unit are omitted. This is not to denigrate their importance.

The democratic classroom is not the place for "busy work," following of idle whims, or purposeless play. The teacher does not confront children with such cold questions as, "What are you interested in?" or "What do you want to learn?" or "What shall we do today?" At no time does the teacher abdicate or give up his role as guide, leader, director, or initiator of thought and of activities. He makes careful plans to probe for interests and concerns, to push thinking, to set up stimulating experiences, and to make his students stretch themselves by work. Moreover, the responsible teacher makes clear to his class the behavior limits in the room and the consequences of infractions of the rules they and the teacher set up during their first week together. Students also need to understand that official school codes and laws place specific responsibilities on teachers and duly constituted administrative authorities.

Orientation and Approach

During the orientation period, which is full of teacher planned and directed activities, the teacher makes a conscious effort to catalogue whatever deep or sharply pointed interests and needs are disclosed. Experiences from which to gather these must be deliberately planned.

For example, the pupils are encouraged to bring in all kinds of books, pictures, objects, and collections. The teacher also brings rich and varied browsing materials of his own or from the library. These materials help develop the skills required to browse for general interest and to answer questions that have been raised. Those materials belonging to the school are changed every few days so that other classrooms are not deprived. Pictures, charts, maps, and articles are organized, mounted, and placed on bulletin boards by pupils who are already able to work independently.

At the beginning of a semester, the teacher may have to do most of the planning himself. When he knows enough about the pupils from his study of their records and from the results of classroom life and work, he can draw them into the planning process. He does this by offering alternatives whenever he can. For example, he asks: "Would you like to all read together today, or would you rather go on with your own books?" "We can take one trip this week, shall it be to the art museum or the science exhibit?" As the pupils answer such questions as, "Why?" "Why not?" "What for?" "How?", "With what materials?" "When?" "Where?" and "Who shall be responsible?" the habit is established of delaying choice until careful consideration has been given to facts and their relative values, to conditions, and to consequences. The habit and skill of evaluating are also developed by using these questions: "What was good about our experience?" "Where were we weak?" "What did we learn?" "In the light of what we know and need to know, what must we do next?" All of these discussions are exercises in critical thinking.

A film, currently showing in the local theatre, may provide the stimulus for a unit of work. A special morning show can sometimes be arranged at reduced rates. Much of the arranging for the trip can be delegated to pupils. If relevant, or if the class is not yet focused on any one area of interest, other trips will help. These may be to an historical museum or to industrial exhibits or plants. The destination depends upon what the teacher wants to bring to the attention of his class.

Films, recordings, radio broadcasts, and TV programs can be used to stimulate interest in race relations, the United Nations, and foreign lands. A speaker or an interview, provided the teacher briefs people beforehand, may raise questions about money and economics, or the relationship between peace and aid to Asian nations.

When an event of world-wide importance occurs, students will probably need information about history, which will require appropriate learning experiences. For example, a special meeting of the United Nations is called to deal with an emergency situation in Africa, a continent about which most young people know very little. On the other hand, the spark needed may come from an incident in the life of one of the pupils. For example, the apprehension and conviction of a classmate for a crime he has committed could very well result in a unit on juvenile delinquency.

Occasionally at the beginning of the year, or later when it is time to take account of stock, the teacher may need to plan a frontal attack to develop a background from which students can look directly at their own educational program and at what, up to the moment, they have accomplished. Several hours of purposeful, critical thinking can be provided by discussion of such questions as "Why are we here?" "What are the characteristics of the intelligent, democratic citizen?" "Where are we now on the road that leads to that end?" "What, in the light of all this, do we need to do next to carry us farther along toward our goals?"

At the conclusion of a unit of learning, time is needed for evaluation of past experiences. Questions are raised: "What were our goals?" "How far did we get in accomplishing them?" "What holes did we leave?" "What did we do well?" "What were our mistakes?" "In the light of these facts what should we consider for our next unit?" From such considerations, for example, in one school a class which had been studying the threats to democracy became keenly interested in and found they knew too little about Russia. Another, after a study of juvenile delinquency, went into the study of family relationships. A unit on foreign policy, in one class, was followed by one on atomic energy.

Discovering Needs and Interests

Pupils express their interests and needs in different ways depending largely on their maturity and previous experience with the process of pupil-teacher planning. Sometimes, especially with younger and less sophisticated students, the teacher can begin by asking, "What do you *wish* to know or to know more about?" Then, of course, wishes expressed by individual pupils have to be explored to find out if they are of concern or interest to the rest of the class. Those of general concern can be listed as possible centers of interest for units to be studied.

Questions arise when pupils feel free to express their desires for action. They ask, "Could we do . . . ?" Desires for new information are stated simply: "We want to learn about . . ." Occasionally they get into problems of values with, "Is it right or wrong to . . . ?" The pupils with little experience in planning use single words to indicate areas of information they wish to probe. They say, "Let's study: Africa, or plastics, or astronomy, or atomic energy."

In some cases every expressed interest should be listed. In others, after discrimination is developed, only a few which have real possibilities and in which there is widespread interest need to be listed. Selection of one, in any case, is a difficult and exciting experience for both teachers and pupils. The following outline suggests seven useful approaches to selection of a unit:

Activities to Determine Needs and Interests

1. Browsing through rich, colorful, varied material brought into the classroom by teacher and pupils from library and homes. These should be books, pamphlets, pictures, newspapers, exhibits, and collections. Browsing can be done before school, between lessons, and during periods set aside for the purpose.
2. Arranging a specific experience. For example, to take a trip; see a film; see a TV broadcast; listen to a radio program (or recording); invite, listen to, and question a speaker; interview a veteran, a famous person, a visitor to school, people in the community, parents, teachers.
3. Discussing events of immediate significance to a pupil, the teacher, the nation, the city, the world.
4. Surveying interests, concerns, problems.
5. Providing manipulative experiences, such as science experiments, sorting collections, mounting pictures.
6. Building a background of purpose by discussing such questions as:
   Why are we here?
   What is an educated person?
   Where are you now in the process of becoming effective citizens?
   What shall we do next?

7. Evaluating past experiences by discussing such questions as:
   What were our goals?
   How far did we go in that direction?
   What holes are there?
   What did we do well?
   What were our mistakes, weaknesses?
   In the light of the answers to those questions, what shall we do next?

Decision-making

Before choosing a unit the pupils should determine the character-istics of a *good* unit. An inexperienced group is likely to refer back to a teacher-planned unit which they enjoyed. As they come to believe in their freedom and to know that their suggestions will be accepted, they eagerly add things they would like to do and for which they never dared to hope. Even younger pupils enjoy learning and using the word "criteria" to indicate the standards they will use in making decisions. Older students may use more adult terms. The following are usually identified as standards to be used in deciding what makes a good unit:

—Will it be interesting to all of us?
—Will it be useful now and later on when we are adult?
—Will we learn new things that are important for us to know?
—Will it be too difficult or too easy?
—Can we do something about it now?
—Will we have time for it?
—Does it offer opportunity for art work or play production?
—Will we be able to take trips, see movies, hear radio programs, make things, make scrap books, invite speakers, interview people, have bulle-tin boards?
—Do we have appropriate reading materials (books, newspapers, maga-zines, pamphlets), and can we get more?
—Will there be opportunities for discussions?
—Will we be able to work in committees?
—Will we be able to make and hear reports?
—Will it cost anything?
—How long will it take?

After the pupils set up criteria to help them choose units, atten-tion can be given to the suggested list of words, or ideas, or questions to which they are seeking answers and to the problems for which they want to find some solutions. Immediately some can be eliminated on the basis of lack of appeal or unimportance. Others can be postponed if materials and equipment are not available. At this point, rejection of a topic is not taken as a personal affront by the pupil who originally made that suggestion; in fact, the name of that individual is likely not to be remembered.

The next step toward decision-making is to find if suggestions are related. For example, one group saw that the subject "Freedom from want" was related to the question, "Are there jobs enough for all?" Most lists will also have ideas that can be grouped together. For example, "How can people learn to live together?" goes with "Why do the Negroes in the South have so much trouble?" Simple questions can become double-barrelled when, as in one class, "Are we in the United States still struggling for liberty?" was joined to "How will the outcome of the struggle for freedom affect me?" Single words or simple statements can be turned into questions when the reasons for studying a subject are more fully explored. For example, "China" may become "Why do people say the next war will begin in China?" The use of questions rather than titles helps not only to point direction but also to delimit the undertaking.

The process of setting up criteria, of measuring suggested units against them, and finally of making a decision are experiences in critical thinking. Practice in that process develops the habit of making thoughtful, wise choices, and it provides insight into the scientific method of inquiry. Moreover, the experience is essentially practice in the use of the democratic process.

The next step in selecting the unit is to crystallize opinions which are already partly formed. In all likelihood, much talking back and forth will be done outside of the classroom. Gradually pupils begin to group themselves around one or another of the several possibilities being considered. Sometimes they engage in heated arguments in the cafeteria or on the way to and from school. Often they seek the opinions and advice of their parents.

Where time permits, each subject may be briefly explored by the entire class with the teacher acting as discussion leader. On the other hand, the teacher might request three or four pupils who are particularly interested in one of the topics to present their ideas in a panel discussion. Sometimes conversation circles are useful. Browsing to find more reasons and more information in support of one or another of the areas can be done constantly. Sometimes written statements help. Occasionally, a group interested in a special subject may select an able spokesman to speak to the class about it.

At some time during the interval which occurs before making a decision, the teacher must help the class to examine various methods that can be used to decide issues. The method best known to students is voting, and they are likely to believe that it is the most democratic process to use. (Whenever a ballot is used, for example, in election of representatives to the student council, care must be taken to make it secret. This will serve to minimize the use of undue influence by the powerful members of the child society.) However, the pupils need to understand that voting is not the best way to make group decisions regarding the work to be done during the following weeks. Decision on a vote usually requires a simple majority which could be only one more than half. Then just one less than half of the class would be dissatisfied with the choice of unit. Developing consensus is preferable in this situation. Even though it may be a difficult and time-consuming process, it pays high dividends in the consequent contentment of all; and it also helps to weld divergent elements into a unified group.

The teacher has a definite role to play during these discussions. However, he must refrain from exerting too direct an influence and certainly from imposing his will upon the class. If he does so, the pupils will probably become cynical and frustrated. If they doubt the teacher's sincerity, some may even become aggressive and hostile, others passive or apathetic. Active interest and participation in discussion will sink to a low level.

Equally important, however, is that the teacher never lose sight of his responsibility for postponing choice until all the facts are before the class. He must lead and guide thought and discussion. His task is to be sure that the class sees the triviality of one problem as contrasted with the serious nature of another. He is responsible for explaining that some members of the group have already had experience in one suggested area but that another will be new to all.

At times pupils ask the teacher directly for his opinion or even for his preference. A direct answer from him may be possible if his rapport with the group is very good, but it exposes him to the necessity of accepting a decision contrary to his stated choice if strong pupil leaders are not entirely on his side. Should such a situation arise, the teacher's stature increases when he accepts defeat without rancor or resentment.

Often after a center of interest has been selected and the unit of work has been planned, a few children intensely interested in an alternative problem remain dissatisfied and rebellious. Under such circumstances, the class should discuss the problem. With the teacher's help, a plan can be made to have them pursue their topic, accepting responsibility for keeping the class informed, for joining the class in such activities as trips, and for listening to all committee reports. At other times the antagonism will disappear if the teacher makes a special effort to give the dissenters interesting or prestige things to do.

Occasionally it is advisable to give the entire class an opportunity to explore briefly a subject which seems to interest them but which, to the teacher's mind, is not a suitable unit. For example, the subject matter may be too difficult. This would become evident when the pupils attempt to read the available material. Or, usable materials may not be available, and instead of searching for facts the class would have to depend upon the teacher for information.

The development of a single question of enough significance and of sufficiently general concern, upon which a whole group wants to work, is a difficult but exciting experience. To help the reader to visualize the selection of a center of interest and the use of pupil-teacher planning, a day-by-day account of what could happen in a classroom will be used to illustrate methods as they are described. The story is based upon personal classroom teaching, observations, teachers' reports, and talks with teachers in many places. The unit deals with intergroup relations and their connection with democracy. The scene is a ninth-grade classroom. Ninth grade was selected because of the importance of placing such a unit where nearly all boys and girls are still in school. (Especially in a three-year junior high school, most of the pupils remain through the ninth year, and the heavy drop out sets in afterwards.) Any such study, however, cannot be completed at the ninth-year level. It should come again as part of American history in the eleventh year and cannot be omitted from good twelfth-year courses in problems of democracy.

At each succeeding grade level, the teacher must begin by finding out what students *know* and how they feel about democracy rather than with what a previous teacher may have taught. It is a truism that pupils do not learn what the teacher teaches. The new unit must be planned in accordance with what information, attitudes, and skills the boys and girls have at the moment.[1] Among the devices that can be used to reveal them are social distance questionaires, open-end questions, and role-playing. They uncover stereotyped thinking, negative and hostile attitudes, and name-calling.

UNIT TEACHING IN A NINTH-GRADE CLASS

The boys and girls in 9B5, combined English-Social Studies, were an enthusiastic group, tremendously interested in each other. The teacher was somewhat worried about how to get them to choose a center of interest around which to build their first unit. The only needs he had heard them express were to learn more English, and to look at the future by talking about careers. In discussion of those two things, he had explained to the class that English would not be a suitable unit because the study of the English language was part of all school work. He assured them that he would stress English throughout the term whenever necessary. He also pointed out that careers, and more properly, jobs and the working world would be discussed in connection with the self-appraisal program, shop work, and the guidance program. It was now time to make a direct approach to identification of a suitable unit, and the teacher saw that he must play a positive role.

Stimulating Interests

The many problems of orientation, class organization, and testing had consumed so much time that little thought and attention had been given to the world-shaking events making the headlines in the daily newspapers. The teacher planned, therefore, to devote the following Monday to them,

[1] See the resource units on prejudice and discrimination, race and race relations, and human rights in Part Three for preplanning surveys of content, learning activities, and available materials on many aspects of intergroup relations as democratic problems.

and over the weekend he gathered pictures, maps, science books, and history texts for browsing to stimulate interest. When the class arrived, the boys and girls clustered around the bulletin boards which were filled with big newspaper headlines and pictures about the Congo, Laos, conflicts in the South, Russia, missiles, and satellites. On the way to their desks, they picked up copies of news magazines and the day's newspapers.

The class was to spend two hours with him that day, so the teacher let the pupils read for the first half-hour. By then, a little restlessness was apparent, so he suggested that the windows be opened and that the pupils might walk around a bit and stretch their muscles. As he wandered among them, he knew by their conversations that the next hour of discussion would be lively.

Human Relations as Common Concerns

Attention was directed first to the latest reports on Khrushchev. Presently the teacher asked, "But isn't that only rumor?" A student answered, "Yes, it's part of the cold war." The teacher countered, "Can anyone really know what *is* fact?" A girl added, "It's all propaganda," and the teacher asked, "Is propaganda only bad?" Then a boy asked, "How can a person find out whether a statement is intended for propaganda or not?" Discussion continued, moving from Russia to the pupils' own concerns with the questions: "Is the problem of propaganda of concern to all of us?" "What phases of our own lives does it touch?" "Do we need knowledge of this kind now as well as later when we will be adults?" The first possible center of interest, propaganda, had emerged and was written on the board.

Some of the boys were vitally interested in missile warfare and our competition with Russia, so as soon as they could, they brought discussion back by way of Khrushchev's ambitions. The question arose, "What is life like in Russia as contrasted with America that would make communism so attractive?" Various opinions were expressed, and the need for information and facts that no one had soon became evident. Khrushchev's character was compared with Kennedy's. The differences in power of the two positions were explored.

The period was nearly over when one student said, "Before we get too excited about life in other countries, we ought to take a good look at ourselves." "What does that mean?" the teacher asked. "Well," a girl spoke up, "shouldn't we look at the violence now going on in the South?" Another added, "And how about the row in this city over our Christmas celebration last month?" And a third said, "Look at our slums." As the teacher asked, "Are these questions vital to every American?" the bell rang, but he wrote on the board "Human Relations in America." A number of children said on their way out, "Yes, that is it." Others were unwilling to accept human relations so fast. They wanted time to discuss other matters which seemed of equal importance.

WHAT HAPPENED ON THE SECOND DAY

Many of the pupils brought pictures to class, which raised the problem of how to use them to the best advantage. Someone suggested that a bulletin board committee take care of them. There were enough enthusiastic volunteers to eliminate the necessity of selection. The class, however, wanted to tell the committee what to do. They said that the pictures must be changed twice a week, separate displays were to be organized for various subjects, and class time was to be requested to call attention to new pictures. Members of the class promised to bring much additional material. The teacher reminded them of the picture-lending file available in the library.

The first new topic proposed for consideration was missile warfare. They soon realized that information about fuels and combustion, metals, and the structure of matter would be needed. The use of atomic energy for civilian purposes was suggested. Speculation as to the nature of future wars began. To crystallize discussion the teacher suggested that although it would be very difficult, atomic warfare should be listed as a possible unit.

The possibility of war was beginning to cause fear and excitement. The teacher, who felt that still other aspects of the problem should be placed before the class, said, "Are you very sure that nothing should be changed about democracy? Do we have all the answers?" Minutes of silence followed. Then one of the girls said, "I guess what you mean is that we need to examine how we really feel about democracy. Then, maybe we will discover that we are not all equally satisfied with how it works for everybody." "Yes," agreed the teacher, "and then I am sure we will find our own responsibilities for improving how we operate the democratic way." He turned to the board and wrote the fourth possible unit: "Democracy in America: Can It Be Improved?" Before class was dismissed, the teacher assigned for homework that each pupil write questions to be answered in connection with each of the possible units. He explained that this would make each student do some critical thinking. The units suggested now were: Propaganda; Human Relations in America; Atomic Warfare; and Democracy in America. Can It Be Improved?

WHAT HAPPENED ON THE THIRD DAY

Questions Formulated

Many boys and girls had their questions ready when the teacher entered the room. Hands were up and the first volunteers went to the board to write their questions. The class offered additions, eliminations, combinations, and corrections. They finally arrived at the following:

Are human relations vital to each person's life?

—Does this mean between individual people, or among different groups in our society or among the nations of the world?
—How do children get their attitudes toward people different from themselves?
—What is prejudice and how does it affect people?
—What is discrimination? Who discriminates against whom, why and how?
—Do bad human relations affect our classroom, our school, our neighborhood?
—Do the problems of race relations in our country affect our relations with other countries?

Atomic warfare

—What is a missile, how is it constructed?
—What is meant by missile-gap?
—What is the connection between missiles and atomic bombs?
—What is atomic energy, and how does it work?
—Will nuclear warfare destroy our civilization?

What is right and wrong with democracy in American life?

—What is meant by the worth and dignity of every human being?
—Do Americans live by the Bill of Rights?
—Does everyone have equal opportunity to choose what he wants to be? If not, why?
—Do all our people have a high standard of living? If not, why?

The period was drawing to a close, and the area of propaganda had not been outlined or discussed. The teacher suggested that since no one had worked on it, interest was evidently lacking and the subject should be eliminated. No one disagreed.

WHAT HAPPENED ON THE FOURTH DAY

Criteria for Choosing Unit

As soon as the class was ready after examining the new bulletin board displays, the teacher suggested that since they would soon choose a unit, they should review the factors to be considered. This was not a new exercise for the students, so with little waste of time the following criteria were listed on the board:

What makes a good unit

1. The possibility of accomplishment, not too hard or too easy.
2. General interest and concern.
3. Opportunity to get new information.
4. Information must be available, including reading matter, films, speakers, places to go.
5. It must be the most important unit *now*.

The class then turned to consideration of the three possibilities presented the previous day which were still on the chalk board.

Eliminating and Combining Ideas

The first pupil to speak said: "Atomic warfare belongs in science rather than in this class." Discussion revealed that the science teacher had said that his course would include such things as fuels, metals, combustion, and atomic energy. Pupils pointed out that nuclear warfare had to do with people and societies and civilization and asked if these aspects would be discussed in science. Some students reminded the class that they were not taking science at present.

After considerable argument on both sides, the class decided that a unit on the social studies aspects of nuclear warfare could be postponed until those who were in science classes had completed their work on it.

The class then considered the teacher's suggestion that the other two possible units were related to each other and that a combination might be possible. Instead of involving the entire group in the task, he then suggested that a committee could work on combining the two while the others were completing their creative writing assignment for the week. (One hour each week was devoted to writing apart from the unit.

This week pupils were writing their autobiographies.) Realizing that high ability was required for the combination and synthesis of ideas, the teacher appointed the committee instead of asking for volunteers.

WHAT HAPPENED ON THE FIFTH DAY

Decision-making

While the creative writing papers of the previous week were being distributed, re-read, and rewritten by some, the teacher circulated among the pupils giving individual assistance. The chairman of the special committee appointed the previous day, since his paper needed no change, went to the board and wrote, for the class to consider, the following subject and questions. During their meeting the committee had added new questions to those already raised when the suggestions for units on human relations and democracy were discussed.

Unit subject:

Democracy requires good relationships among individuals and among the many groups in our society.

Questions to which we need answers:

—How do children learn about human relations?

—What is an attitude? Do attitudes affect relationships?

—What is prejudice? Are children born with prejudices? How do they get them? Why are people prejudiced against other religions and races? Can prejudice be changed? How?

—Are members of our class prejudiced against each other? For what reasons? How do our prejudices make us act?

—How do prejudiced people act in our school, in our city, in the nation? Is discrimination democratic?

—Do prejudice and discrimination interfere with carrying out the Bill of Rights?

—Do prejudice and discrimination have anything to do with a high standard of living?

—How do prejudice and discrimination measure up to our democratic ideals, principles, and values?

—How will prejudice and discrimination affect each of us later on?

—Do race relations in America affect our relations with other nations?

—What should we do about intergroup relations in view of our responsibilities to the future of democracy?

As soon as the questions were on the board, the teacher asked the class to put aside whatever they were doing and give attention to the committee's ideas. The committee chairman read the subject and questions to the class and pointed out which ones were reworded from previous class work and which were added by his committee. Some questions were raised about the meanings of terms which could not be fully answered. The teacher asked the committee to be sure to get the information needed. He then called attention to the next to last question on international relations. After a brief discussion, the pupils saw that it included too much for this unit. A girl suggested that it become the next unit, and the class agreed. Before leaving the matter, the teacher suggested that those interested could begin to gather material about it. Two of the very able pupils said they would do so.

The chairman of the committee then suggested that the class test the proposed unit against the criteria which had been set up the previous day. This helped the pupils to see the immediate value and importance of the unit. They also agreed that the subject matter would be valuable to them in the future as citizens and as parents. In other words, they not only identified the importance of the subject matter but identified themselves *with* it. There was no need to vote. The class had come to their decision by the process of consensus.[2]

[2] This case study account is continued in the following chapters to illustrate techniques of content planning, committee work, vicarious and direct learning experiences, learning by word symbols, and evaluation.

6

Fourth Step: Pupil-Teacher
Planning of Content

AS SOON AS THE CENTER OF INTEREST for a unit has been selected, pupils want to tackle the job of planning it. Before he meets with the class for this purpose, the teacher should survey the learning possibilities presented by the subject the class has chosen. In addition to surveying the subject matter, the teacher should also review what he knows about the interpersonal and the intergroup relationships which exist in the class. These are significant forces in the pupil society. They may facilitate or block progress in decision-making and in organizing committees.

The teacher has a specific role to play. He is responsible for requiring pupils to include essential parts of the content which they may forget or do not know. He is equally responsible for ruling out what he knows to be beyond the possibilities of the group and for delimiting in view of available time. Also, after giving previous thought to possible culminating activities, he must alert the class to clues for these activities as they arise in the discussion of content and learning activities.

The teacher is responsible for knowing and telling the pupils what materials and equipment are available, where they are located, how to get them, and where additional source publications can be secured. In addition, he must have some source material on hand so that pupils can begin to work as soon as they have made some plans.

46

This kind of readiness for his role in pupil-teacher planning gives a teacher security and prevents him from allowing the class to make mistakes. If he fumbles in the planning process, it will amuse the boys and girls and may cause them to doubt their teacher's adequacy and sincerity. It may even undermine their faith in the unit method and in the democratic process.

Clarifying and Accepting Goals

The first step in planning is to clarify both teacher and pupil purposes. If the teacher begins by announcing his own objectives and does not permit pupils to state theirs, some doubt about the reality of the cooperative, democratic process may arise. Goals are identified when pupils answer the question of why they want to do the job (or find the answer to this question, or solve this problem). Younger pupils and those with little previous experience in planning are likely to answer that they want to improve themselves or that they wish to learn to read better or to spell, to talk or to write better. Very often pupils recognize their need to learn to live together. They always want new information. With greater maturity and experience, students express a desire to share their work with each other. When no fear of disapproval exists, boys and girls admit that they want to have some fun.

In the class whose work is being described, objectives were identified in the following way:

WHAT HAPPENED ON THE SIXTH DAY

Establishing Goals

The teacher began discussion by saying: "We have spent a good bit of time deciding on our unit. Let us see if we can put our objectives into words. What do you want to accomplish in this unit?" Immediately one boy said, "I want to find out about my own prejudices." A girl added: "I want to know where mine came from. I know what they are." A third said, "Is there anything I can do about it when I don't like a person 'just because'?"

The teacher said, "Are you going to be satisfied with each one learning only about himself?" "Oh no," several answered at once. Then one said, "This has to do with all of us, and others too." The teacher said: "Can we generalize? Can someone make a generalization that applies to all people?" After some minutes of silent thought, a girl said: "Is this it? We want to learn the facts about prejudice and discrimination in our classroom, our school, our city and our nation." There was much nodding of heads, so the teacher wrote the statement on the board as the first objective. He then reminded the class that the unit was to include democracy. After a few minutes of silence, a pupil offered, "We want to know what is the effect of prejudice and discrimination on democratic life in America." Again general agreement occurred, so the teacher wrote it down as the second objective.

In similar fashion, and by interaction among the pupils and the teacher, the following other objectives were added:

We want to understand our responsibilities with respect to democracy.

We want to add new words to our vocabularies.

We want to improve in reading, writing, discussing and doing group work.

We want to increase our ability to think.

The teacher then said that the pupils should keep these objectives in mind while browsing in the newspapers, magazines, books, and pictures for the remainder of the period, so that they would be ready to plan the content of the unit the next day. He reminded the pupils to look for reports of conflict between people and groups and for articles on discrimination, race relations, religion, and civil rights.

Three students requested permission to go to the library for additional books. The teacher said that one should go to see if there would be room for them. He returned and said that the librarian was glad to have them come.

When the period was nearly over, the teacher called the class to attention and said: "Please get any additional material you can from the newspapers and magazines you have at home. What your parents think you ought to learn in this unit would also be helpful. If any of you want to do additional reading tonight, please check with the class librarian whatever books you take and bring them back tomorrow." Then the bell rang and he dismissed the group.

The Need for a Planning Guide

Many junior high school boys and girls may not have had formal, in-school, pupil-teacher planning experiences. In that event, the teacher may have to call upon their memories of out of school planning experiences for them to discover the basic elements to include. For example, he may say: "Did you ever plan a party? How did you begin? What had to be determined next?" As pupils answer such questions, the teacher can write the words "how," "when," "where" on the board. Next they can be arranged in an orderly time sequence. Once such guide words are established, they can be placed permanently on a bulletin board or on a poster and copied into individual notebooks and class logs. If guide lines to planning are readily accessible, committees can turn to them later when planning their work. The following outline for planning is a suggestion, but not the only possible arrangement. The class can develop its own formula and determine for itself the relative position of the several parts of the planning job.

Basic elements in planning

1. Why? Why not?
2. What? What for?
3. Where?
4. When?
5. With what materials?
6. How? By what method?
7. Who and by whom?
8. Shall we tell others? Who? How? When? Who shall do what?

Once goals are determined, content planning can continue. This should be done as soon as possible so as to reassure pupils and their parents that facts, reading, and writing are to be emphasized. The process begins when the teacher asks, "What do you need to know to answer the questions you have raised? (or solve the problem that confronts you)." He writes the given answers on the board. From time to time he may ask, "Is it necessary for everyone in the class to find that answer?" This paves the way for sharing in committee work and identifies those things that must be considered minimum essentials to be learned by all.

As soon as the minimum essentials to be learned are determined, all can get to work on them without waiting for content to be completely planned or committees to be formed. Most groups want to have both time limits for the accomplishment of these essentials and tests on the factual material learned. They usually suggest short answer tests, long essay type tests, and quiz programs.

A plan for common learning of minimum essentials gives the teacher a breathing spell while everyone is working quietly on his own. However, during such a period, as well as during planning, the teacher should be sensitive to signs of fatigue. Rapidly growing adolescents tire of sitting, listening, and the intense mental activity that is required by cooperative planning. Activity must be stopped in time to avoid boredom and restlessness. Sometimes a break can be permitted during which the students are free to leave the room for a walk in the corridors, to walk around the room, or to chat with friends. Some may want to look out the windows. After this, if enthusiasm is still high, planning can be successfully resumed. At other times an entirely different type of activity, possibly handwork, drawing, writing, or reading should be arranged.

As the planning of content moves forward, the teacher must take an active part in it. If, as previously stated, he has made a pre-planning survey, he can suggest arrangement of elements in the planning outline. He should make sure that the boys and girls see the relationships among the questions that are raised. He will be aware that time requires holding the main topics down to a reasonable number. This will also simplify committee organization.

As content is being outlined, the teacher exercises his responsibility for introducing important phases of the subject of which pupils may not be aware. For example, when relevant, he makes sure that the historical approach and/or background is not overlooked, and that both social and scientific implications are included. He also knows when suggestions made by pupils are not feasible. If he does not say so, the success of the unit and of the planning process may be endangered.

Opinions differ as to what should be done about issues, questions, or problems that seem too difficult. Some teachers believe that constant deferring because of difficulty tends to develop feelings of inferiority and frustration. Other teachers believe that such difficulties must be avoided and questions beyond the ability of the class must not be permitted because consequent failure produces feelings of incompetence and insecurity and inhibits growth. However, the range of ability in every group is so large that what might be too difficult for some will be well within the capabilities of others. Adolescents have greater capabilities than most people give them credit for. Moreover, a group is able to go beyond what an individual can do when they are given the chance to think and work together. If the students have had sufficient experience and are secure enough to accept the idea that all will not learn the same things at the same time, then topics too difficult for some can be assigned to others. The teacher also keeps in mind that arrangement of groups and learning experiences must be such that the able students will be challenged and interested; that slower and less capable students will have jobs to do in which they, too, can succeed; and that all will benefit from the inspiration of the most able in the peer group.

The teacher who does not have an adequate background of information on the unit deserves consideration. If he has rapport with his class, he can, if necessary, go into any unit with them from scratch, recognizing that it will require a good bit of homework on his part. If he and the pupils are insecure, it would be better to postpone a unit with which he is entirely unfamiliar.

The case study continued below shows how planning proceeds in a classroom.

WHAT HAPPENED ON THE SEVENTH DAY

Content Planning

The class assembled promptly. The teacher reminded the pupils of the goals they set up the previous day and gave them a little time to assemble and look over the articles and newspaper reports they had found while browsing. Then the boys and girls were ready for planning. The teacher knew that an exhaustive study of the subject was not possible. The class began with what the special committee had prepared two days before. The teacher, who led the class, accepted all suggestions that were made and wrote them on the board. Later, these were examined for overlapping and feasibility. Some were then combined, others eliminated. At times the teacher helped to refine and express what individuals offered. The following content outline was the result of group thinking.

Unit subject:

Intergroup relationships must be improved if democracy is to be really achieved in the United States.

Goals:

Those listed on the fifth day remained unchanged.

Content:

What we want to learn:

—The meaning and spelling of words: democracy, prejudice, discrimination, stereotype, exclusion, rejection, employment, civil rights, race relations.
— About prejudice: its causes, how children learn it, what it does to people, how people show that they are prejudiced, our own individual prejudices, what we can do about them.
—About discrimination: in our school, in employment, in housing and education; its effects on the individual, on the nation; what we as individuals can do about it.
—About race relations: what is race, the kind of race relations we have in the school, community, and nation, what we can do as individuals to improve them.
—About the effect of prejudice, discrimination, and race relations on American history.
—The relation of all of this to democracy?
—Our responsibilities with respect to improvement of our own lives and life in our school and community?

The teacher requested the pupils to begin the study of new words as homework. A plan was made for recording the words, defining them, and using them in sentences in the unit-record book which every pupil was to keep. While waiting for dismissal, the boys and girls talked with each other about the way to divide up the work.

7

Commitee Work: Practicing
the Democratic Way

EVEN AT THE SECONDARY SCHOOL
level, teachers often meet pupils who have had no previous experience
with committee work. Such pupils may not see the value of dividing
up the work to be done by the class. In that case, the teacher should
take time to explain the reasons for sharing the fact-finding job and
for allocating responsibilities connected with this and other kinds of
learning experiences to specific individuals. This is also a good point
at which to discuss the democratic processes involved in committee
work. The teacher should emphasize that committee work experience
develops skills needed for living the democratic way.

There is no single best way to organize a class for effective, cooperative work. Every group presents different social patterns. Every
unit offers different possibilities for learning activities. Every teacher
must find, from among the many different methods, those which
work best in each particular situation. In all probability mistakes will
occur, but they should be treated as learning experiences, which they
will in fact become if the class and the teacher evaluate them properly. No experience has failed if from it both teacher and pupils make
progress in developing positive attitudes toward the democratic way
of life.

Before proceeding with organization, the class should discuss the
various ways committees can be formed and decide which method to
use. Immature and inexperienced pupils may suggest that a row of

53

pupils can be a committee. Those who think of committees as competing teams may want leaders picked first, by either the teacher or the class, and then have each leader pick his own committee. Such suggestions may indicate preoccupation with intragroup or peer relationships. The class may have to be told that each one has the right and privilege of identifying his own special interests and that those who have similar interests then become a committee. Such a discussion is, of course, unnecessary with older and more experienced students.

Most likely when making a choice of interests, some pupils will act consciously or subconsciously on the basis of relationships. Sometimes for some purposes, since people do work well with others they know and like, this method can be used. The danger lies in exclusion or rejection of unpopular or of minority group students.

In order that friendship may not exert undue influence in choices, a method other than raising hands should be used. One alternative is written requests addressed to the teacher. This may be a brief note, but the pupil should be asked to include in it his reasons. In all cases the individual's second choice should be indicated to facilitate making adjustments should one committee be over subscribed. Should this be necessary, the teacher must be careful either to call for volunteers or to use a device that will make the decision possible on an objective basis. Otherwise, students will question the validity of their participation in making decisions.

Membership in both research and activity committees, then, can be decided in several different ways. Sometimes students will volunteer for one or another task on the basis of their abilities, interests, desire to undertake a new experience, need for recognition, or their friends who are volunteering. Sometimes the teacher should appoint people to committees on the basis of what he knows are the special abilities required and possessed by individual pupils. Sometimes the class may decide which of its members should undertake a specific task and may also tell them what to do.

Sociometric groupings are also desirable for some purposes. This method, however, is time consuming and requires the teacher to be familiar with social distance questions and with how to construct and interpret a sociogram. The questions used may be as simple as, "With which three classmates would you like to sit, to work on a committee, to visit, to invite to your home?" From the chart on which he plots the choices and indicates the relationships, the teacher can discover cliques, pairs, loose friendships, opposing forces, and isolates. This information may be useful in planning strategy, allocating responsibilities, organizing committees, and guiding individuals. Sociometry, however, is not an essential part of unit teaching.

The class log which we are using to illustrate methods shows how committees can be quickly organized.

WHAT HAPPENED ON THE EIGHTH DAY

By the time the class assembled, each pupil had made up his mind on which section of the content he wished to concentrate. They agreed that new words were to be studied by everyone. They also felt that the entire group should get information about the final question: the connection between intergroup relations and democracy. That left four general areas for committee work: prejudice, discrimination, race relations, and history. These were called committee one, two, three, four.

The teacher distributed 3x5 cards and asked the pupils to write their names on one side and to mark their first and second choices on the other by simply putting down the number of the committees. Then, using a very simple technique, he called for the cards of those wanting to be on committee one. These were quickly handed to him and he counted them. In turn, each of the other committees were called, collected, and counted. Had there been great imbalance, he would have looked for the second choices and rearranged a few cards without reference to the names of the pupils on the other side of the cards. In this case, there was no great difference, so he handed each pack to a pupil and asked them to write the committee lists on the board while the rest of the class copied the lists into their unit-record books.

After the rest-break which followed, the class discussed the qualifications for committee officers. The teacher then designated a corner of the room for each committee and asked each committee to select a chairman, secretary, and an alternate to serve in the absence of an officer. Before the period closed, brief progress reports were given by all committees in which they announced their selections. The teacher told the class for homework to write down their ideas for their committee work, so as to be ready to meet with him for planning on the next day.

Committees should be organized on the basis of needs. The need to get the information required to answer the content questions usually arises first in planning a unit. Groups formed to get information are generally called research committees, and everyone in the class should belong to one such committee. Other needs, however, not connected with the unit itself, may require earlier committee work. For example, a committee can be formed to organize the classroom library; another sub-group might take over the housekeeping duties. A third could be commissioned to interview certain staff members, such as nurse, counselor, or dietitian, about their responsibilities and the services they could provide. A fourth might be needed to arrange a special activity—a party, a hike, a play.

The need to make contacts with people who can bring new points of view and personal experience into the classroom is another reason for a committee. This type of committee is called an activity committee. Other examples of activity committees are sub-groups to secure films, recordings, and projectors, to plan trips and social activities, to make file boxes, posters, and scrapbooks, to take care of bulletin boards, collections, and displays, and to write and present plays, programs, and quizzes. Obviously, all these do not come into being at the same time.

A steering committee may be needed to help the teacher plan the daily and weekly programs. This group should be made up of the best thinkers in the class, for the leadership training and experience it offers will be invaluable to them. The steering committee can consist of the leaders of the research committees, or it can be selected for the purpose from the class at large. The teacher may prefer to appoint this group which he will need to meet frequently. Steering committee meetings depend upon the job to be done at the moment. They can be arranged before or after school, during study periods, or in the teacher's unassigned time. While the rest of the class is writing or reading or studying, the teacher can also work with the steering committee.

Without much previous experience, boys and girls do not know how to lead, how to participate in small group discussion, how to pool information, how to record committee meetings, or how to formulate and give reports of their process, their plans, and their findings.

In some cases, *demonstration* of how to conduct a meeting will help the entire class. In all cases, the teacher will need to observe leaders and arrange to meet with them for special training. The teacher should be with each committee when it meets for its first planning session. Therefore, very seldom, and never at the beginning of unit teaching, should all committees meet at the same time.

Information for Committee Consideration

By the time a class is ready to organize committees, they have before them the content outline of the unit. Each pupil knows on which specific section of it he wants to work. Work cannot begin, however, until they know about materials and equipment: what is available in the room, in the library, in other parts of the building, and in their homes; what more can be obtained, from whom, and how. Magazines, pamphlets, newspapers, and pictures are usually suggested in addition to books. The teacher is responsible for making available, at this point, lists of references which will be most helpful to the various committees. It is not enough to simply tell the students to go to the library and look up books on the subject.

Boys and girls whose previous school experiences have been almost entirely with reading may be unable to think of other sources of information. Then the teacher must be ready to suggest films, recordings, radio and TV programs, and people, both in and out of the school. He should have at hand lists of available films, agencies, and resource persons and advance notices of relevant radio and TV programs. Although this general discussion takes place with the class as a whole, specific plans are to be made later by each committee for itself.

At this point some teachers like to set up learning-activity committees, which cut across the research committees. Thus, one pupil from each content committee becomes a member of a second committee for TV, radio, films, resource persons, or trips.

Gathering new materials and using human resources will necessitate the study and practice of letter writing, telephoning, and interview techniques. Although such activities require very few persons, the class can discuss the procedures and what is to be said. Dramatizing and role-playing are helpful ways to demonstrate and practice these techniques.

Guiding Committee Meetings

The next question to be decided is where and when the work is to be done. Discussion should clarify that learning goes on in and out of the classroom; in the afternoons and evenings as well as the school day; that school and public libraries are to be used; that people at home and in the community are sources of information; that museums, stores, factories, and public buildings are places to be visited in search of knowledge.

Research committees should be organized as soon as content outline has been sufficiently planned but not necessarily completed, so that pupils can get to work, and begin the unit while interest is high. When this is done, the groups can hold their first meetings to select their officers. A chairman, a secretary, and an alternate to serve in the absence of an officer are all that each group needs for efficient operation. Before this first meeting is adjourned, plans should be made; officers should know how to get and distribute materials; pupils who have reading difficulties should know where and how they are to get information; progress reports to the class should be prepared, and pupils selected to present them. The report of the first meeting should contain the names of elected officers, the questions on which the group will work, and the plan they intend to follow.

Committee work requires skills which secondary school students do not often have. The teacher is called upon to give assistance and training. His task requires courage and patience. A committee meeting should be held only when the group has work to do. The leader plans for it, announces it, and adjourns it when the task has been completed. Between meetings committee members need not sit together since each one will be working by himself. Sitting together can produce a discipline problem for the teacher and deter accomplishment.

In his preplanning survey, the teacher gives some thought to where committees can meet and when. Rarely should four or five of them meet at the same time in the same room. If the furniture lends itself, and he can endure the noise of many pupils talking at once, and the pupils have learned to control themselves and each other, simultaneous meetings may be successful. Classes often devise a signal to be used when voices get too loud. Flashing the electric lights is effective although some teachers prefer to tap a small bell. A better arrangement, however, is to plan for one or two groups to meet while the rest of the class are doing individual writing or reading. Occasionally a committee can take chairs into the corridor for a brief meeting. Nearby conference rooms, empty classrooms, and the library can be used. However, a committee meeting held away from the supervision of the teacher is likely to be successful only when the group has a specific task to accomplish and is required to show results when they return. The personnel of the group and the skill of its leader should determine which committee may work outside of the classroom.

Whenever committees are in session, the teacher should move from group to group to determine which of them need help. One or more may not be able to function at all because of conflict among the pupils involved or because of the inadequacies of their leaders. If the teacher cannot correct the trouble, reorganization or even disbanding the committee may be necessary. In that case the pupils can be distributed among the other groups, or the work to be done may be held up until another committee has finished its original assignment and can take on another. Observation of the groups at work reveals to the teacher strength which can be used and weakness which needs to be eliminated. When the pupils are able to work without much help from the teacher, he continues to watch them, to participate in their discussions and planning sessions, to praise and encourage, and to record progress and individual growth.

How Committees Work

Sometimes a committee has difficulty because the pupils in it do not fully understand what they are expected to do. Their concept of committee work may be at fault. For example, if, when the content of the unit was planned, it was divided into sections for the several committees, the students may use the same method of outlining content and then dividing it into small bits which they apportion to each committee member. That results in fragmentation and small, insignificant assignments. Moreover, it defeats the objectives of committee work, which include the experience of mobilizing facts from many sources, finding that authorities do not always agree, discovering that a single source rarely produces all the facts, and learning that when work is shared and findings are pooled, the results are better than most persons can produce by themselves.

One of the teacher's responsibilities is to show each committee that they must first redefine their problem until their task is quite clear. Next, the group must explore their problem by formulating sub-questions and try to get closer to what the class needs to know about the subject. Then, all the members must accept responsibility for getting as much information as they can about the total problem from all available printed materials, pictures, films, radio, TV, places, and people. The sources to which each pupil goes depend upon how he learns best. Some on each committee should choose reference books and encyclopedias. The teacher may help them to make that choice on the basis of their abilities. Those for whom sufficiently easy reading material is not available, should be encouraged to gets facts from people. Many pupils will use a variety of sources.

After a suitable time has elapsed, the committee chairman calls a meeting at which he asks each member to tell what he has learned and to name the sources be used. As the pupils respond and pool their facts, differences in information may be discovered and have to be reconciled. The teacher's help is often needed to integrate learnings and find underlying meanings. Especially in the early part of a unit, group chairmen need help in finding materials, organizing facts, securing the participation of all members, and summarizing progress reports.

In all likelihood, the teacher will find that one or more of the groups do not have enough skill to proceed with their work. For example, some may need remedial reading or new reading skills. Others may not know how to use a book's index or table of contents. Many will not know how to make outlines and take notes. Skills in spelling, writing, talking, organizing display materials, conducting meetings, and presenting reports are required for effective living and learning the democratic way. Whenever the teacher discovers a need, he must meet it. This means that he takes time out, if necessary, to teach, drill, demonstrate, correct, praise, reward, and encourage.

In most classes a schedule for meetings and a rhythm of activities can be set up so that pupils will know when to meet and for what purposes. These plans should be worked out so that while one committee is meeting with the teacher, the others work quietly by themselves. Sometimes all but one group should be studying or writing or reading, depending upon their several plans. While pupils are busy at their desks, the teacher can call to the front of the room any committee which needs his help or on whose work he wishes to check. When the sequence of activities is determined, it can be printed on a large poster and placed where all can see it. Pupils should also copy it into their unit-record books. When this is done, pupils do not need to ask, "What shall we do next?" or complain, "We don't know what to do," or say, "I haven't anything to do." The following sequence shows the rhythm of committee work:

1. The committee is formed to get some of the information called for in the content outline or to carry on a specific learning activity.
2. It meets to elect officers, to distribute reading materials and other resources, to clarify its problem, and to decide what each member shall do first.
3. The members work as individuals while waiting for the first planning meeting with the teacher.
4. The committee meets with teacher to:
   a. Plan its content outline.
   b. Assign specific jobs to members.
   c. Develop progress report.
5. The first progress report is given to class. It contains names of officers, plan of work, questions raised.
   The class records the report, raises additional questions, and offers suggestions.
6. Members work as individuals for a day or two.
7. Committee meets, preferably with the teacher, to:
   a. Pool information.
   b. Plan for further work and activities.
   c. Develop second progress report containing:
      1. New words and terms to be learned by class.
      2. Information.
      3. Plans for class activities, such as trips, broadcasts, films.
8. Members work as individuals (teacher direction may be needed).
9. Committee meets to pool and plan activities and report.
10. Progress report is given—and so on until the committee has completed its work and plans its final report.
11. Final report may take different forms, such as:
    a. Discussion panels, round tables, symposiums, forum of the air, town meeting.

   b. Organized factual material, which should not be merely that copied from books.

   c. Quiz.

   d. Exhibition of collections, constructions, original illustrations, posters, pictures (avoid showing tiny pictures), charts.

   e. Entertainment—skits, dramatization, broadcasts.

The chart in Figure 7-1 shows how the teacher arranges to meet with each committee in turn, and what the other committees do at that time.

Committee Reports

Committees must be required to make frequent progress reports. The first of these may be merely announcement of purposes and plans. It may also include statements about the difficulties encountered with respect to members and materials. These can be discussed by the class to get general reactions and suggestions. Later on, progress reports must include information of importance in the unit. The teacher is responsible for developing relationships among the several committee reports. He also sees that materials are shared by all committees.

In addition to training leaders, the teacher must train all the students to listen to reports and to participate constructively in discussion of factual material and controversial issues. Some students will be unable to do this at first, but practice develops skills. For practice, the class can be directed to tabulate new ideas in the reports and discuss their relative values. The teacher must also be alert to opportunities to develop critical thought by challenging statements for accuracy and authority.

After the committee has given its report, the class members should be encouraged to add information, give other examples from their own experience, state associated ideas, and ask appropriate questions. Pupils should record factual material in their unit-record books. In order that such records may be complete and accurate, the teacher or the committee secretary can write the facts on the board. After all committees have completed their research, discussion must return to the original questions and objectives which prompted the unit, and the class must determine how close they have come to their goals and what more is still to be done.

Sequence of activity	Committees			
	1	*2*	*3*	*4*
1	All committees meet to elect officers and distribute materials.			
2	Every child works as an individual in the general area assigned to his own committee or at essentials for which all are to be held responsible. This is preparation for the first planning meeting.			
3	Meets with teacher to plan content, allocate jobs, develop progress report.	Teacher gives directions for individual work to continue.		
4	Gives report to class; notes suggestions.	Listen to the report of Committee No. 1, make records, raise questions, make suggestions.		
5	Teacher gives directions for work as individuals.	Meets with teacher for first planning.	Teacher gives directions for work as individuals.	
6	Listens to and records report of Committee No. 2.	Makes first progress report.	Listen to and record progress report of Committee No. 2.	
7	Meets to pool information, plan activities, develop progress report (teacher help may be needed).	Teacher gives directions for work as individuals.	Meets with teacher for first planning.	Teacher gives directions for work as individuals.

Fig. 7-1. Chart of Committee Activity.

Sequence of activity	Committees			
	1	2	3	4
8	Gives second progress report.	Listen to and record progress report of Committee No. 1.		
9	Listen to and record report of Committee No. 3.		Gives first progress report.	Listen to and record report of Committee No. 3.
10	Teacher directs work as individuals.	Meets to pool and plan and develop report. Teacher help may be needed.	Teacher directs work as individuals.	Meets with teacher for first planning.
11	Hear and record first progress report of Committee No. 4.			Gives progress report.
12	Listens to and records report.	Gives second progress report.	Listen to and record progress report of Committee No. 2.	
13	Meets to pool, etc.	Work as individuals.	Meets to pool, etc.	Work as individuals.

Fig. 7-1 (cont.)

Each research committee must present a final report to the class. At the appropriate time, the teacher discusses the various forms such reports can take. Pupils will be bored if reports lack variety. The final report should be presented when it is ready, and this will vary among the groups. Some have smaller tasks and so finish first. Some people work more successfully together and so complete larger jobs more rapidly. If all reports are delayed until all are ready, idling, procrastination, and boredom are likely to result.

Certainly one committee will finish first, and the teacher must be ready to help them to plan something useful and interesting to do while they wait for the other groups to give their final reports. Among the things the teacher can suggest are:

—Read more extensively on other aspects of the unit.
—Make a brief study of a new topic of interest to them.
—Pursue an individual interest.
—Begin work on a culminating activity.
—Write for, collect, or organize material at hand, to be presented when suggestions for the next unit are discussed.
—Prepare bibliographies on one or more subjects.
—Help other individuals in the class or other committees.

In the class whose work is being described to illustrate methods, the teacher's log contained the following report of one committee's work.

LOG RECORD OF A COMMITTEE'S ACTIVITY

The large committee working on the historical aspects of the subject found that the textbooks on American history gave little or no space to it. The students with sufficient reading ability consulted history books from the public library and their own homes, as well as encyclopedias.

They also found that historical novels and plays reflected intergroup conflicts, prejudice, and the struggle for equality. Among them were *To Kill A Mockingbird* by Harper Lee, *Blessed Is the Land* by Louis Zara, *The Crucible* by Arthur Miller, and *A Raisin in the Sun* by Lorraine Hansberry. Individual students told the class about the books they were reading. Before the unit was over, many of the students went to see the film of *A Raisin in the Sun*.

Reports on the effects of prejudice on American history were given at intervals by the committee. They described the religious conflicts which brought both Quakers and Puritans to the Colonies. The persecution of witches in New England was seen to have a relationship to the struggle for academic freedom and the persecution of people believed to be Communists in the McCarthy era. New insight was revealed in the report dealing with the struggle of the Jews in New Amsterdam for the right to bear their share of responsibilities as well as for the right to have synagogues and to worship in their own way.

Of course, race prejudice during slavery, the Civil War, the development of Jim Crowism in the South, and the denial to Negroes of the right to vote and of other rights connected with first-class citizenship led to discussion of the immediate present. The class became aware of the meaning of the nonviolent resistance movements. They came to understand the international implications of bad intergroup relations in America.

Another of the committee's reports dealt with prejudice against Orientals in the early history of the far western states, its violence during World War II, and the abatement of it since 1950.

Prejudices against the "Okies," against Mexicans, against migrant families, and against the American Indians were mentioned, but there was not sufficient time to get all the facts. However, as the result of the excellent work done by many boys and girls, the class became aware of the extent and dangers of intergroup hostilities and conflicts throughout American history.

How prejudice has prevented complete personal fulfillment of important people was discussed in connection with the failure of Al Smith to be elected to the presidency of the United States because of his religion. The 1960 election campaign in which another Catholic, John F. Kennedy, was elected showed them that progress has been made in eliminating religious prejudice.

Keeping Records

In unit teaching, every pupil should be required to keep records of what goes on during the unit. These should include the factual material reported by the committees and other relevant information. The teacher may have to help pupils learn to organize their records. For example, under the heading *Speakers*, should go name, position, facts I (the student) got about the subject, questions asked and answers given, how I felt about the speaker and his presentation.

Under the heading *Films*, should go name, title, the story (or the subject), evaluation of it as a film, and the information I got from it.

Under the heading *Trips*, should go place, date, reason for going, what I saw, important experiences I had, what I learned.

Committee work should be recorded as follows: the names of committee members and its officers; the content questions on which the committee worked and answers they got as the result of pooling their findings; and any notes the individual wishes to make about his own participation and research.

Factual material presented by all committees should be recorded by every child. The teacher must help the class to determine what to record when progress and final reports are made.

Some teachers prefer that records be kept in a unit-record book. Others are willing to have them placed on loose sheets of paper which are kept in individual folders. Creative writing and book reports are also kept in those folders. Records may be in the continuous possession of the child or filed in the classroom where they will remain safe, in good condition, and available at all times. When the pupil's written work is thus accessible to the teacher, he can mark papers at his convenience. On the other hand, a teacher may prefer to have pupils hand written work directly to him. Then he marks and returns the papers to the pupils, who place them in their folders. The teacher reviews the contents of each folder when he makes up marks for report cards. He can also use a folder at any time to write a personal note to a parent about a student's work. Another important use of these folders is for review of the contents by teacher and pupil, together, when self-evaluation is underway. The following lists include the kinds of records that a teacher and class may want to make and the methods of making them:

Records of Unit Activity

Books read (use of folder recommended, with data of interest to pupil recorded on outside and creative written work kept in it)
Magazines read
Newspapers read or a clipping file on one special subject
Movies attended, comments
Radio programs heard
Visits paid
Trips taken
Interviews

Meetings attended
Speakers heard
Letters written
Phone calls made
Problems solved
Papers written
Reports given
Participation in class work, committee work
Plans made: "Today I did . . ."
           "Tomorrow I will try . . ."
New words learned and used
Spelling to be studied
Errors in speech to be corrected

Records of Skills and Their Evaluation by Pupils and Teacher

Tools needed for learning and communicating:

1. Reading
2. Use of books for information
3. Use of library
4. Speech
5. Spelling
6. Written expression

Social skills:

1. Attitudes toward:
    democratic processes
    natural resources
    welfare
    health
    consumer issues
2. Behaviors
3. Interests
4. Abilities to:
    converse
    make honest reports
    do committee work
    participate in discussion
    follow directions
    direct others
    answer questions
    plan

organize—materials, activities, groups
concentrate
observe
evaluate—work, self, and others
decide
5. Appreciations of:
   people
   things
   processes

Values and attitudes:

1. Toward self
2. Toward others
3. Toward work and play
4. Toward human differences
5. Toward freedoms
6. Toward civil rights

Methods of Recording

By individuals—for own use, for teacher's use, for parents' use
By class as class book, diary, or log
On classroom chart—committee areas, dates of progress reports, evaluation given by class
On individual cards—self-evaluation, teacher evaluation
Files kept by teacher: for each child, for class
Folders kept by pupils: used by teacher

Problems of Participation

We must not assume that committee work provides the solution to all problems of participation on any grade level. Pupil leaders in secondary school, as well as in the lower grades, will have much trouble with many pupils who are so often wrongly described as "just sitters." No child is by nature inactive, lacking in curiosity, and indifferent to the peer group. Specific causes lie behind each one's refusal to take part in group work. Pupil leaders are unable to find these and cannot cope with them. The study of such pupils and the application of remedial measures is another of the teacher's tasks.

Enumeration of a few of the causes and possible remedics may serve at this point. Personality clash may point to the necessity for reorganization of a group, for training of the leader, or for the referral of a maladjusted pupil to a counselor.

If a pupil cannot read the material provided, he may require simpler material or special reading instruction, or he may need to be directed to other sources of information such as TV, radio, films, and people. Perhaps he might serve the group and receive recognition by collecting pictures they need and clipping articles from newspapers and magazines, or if he has the ability, doing art work to make committee reports more understandable and enjoyable.

A pupil who is preoccupied with other matters may need to be referred for case study by a counselor. An interview may reveal a consuming interest in another subject or hobby or emotional problems connected with sex or family relationships. If strong outside interests are the case, the teacher may allow such a pupil to pursue his own hobby or drive during class time if by so doing he can also make some contribution to and receive attention from the class.

Some children, by reason of their own previous authoritarian classroom experiences and the lack of understanding on the part of parents and siblings, have difficulty in adapting themselves to the pattern of work in unit teaching. They may even resent it and feel that without textbook-recitation teaching they will not be well prepared for the next grade. Development of the habit of self-appraisal, attention to keeping individual records of achievement, frequent class discussion of the values of democratic practices and processes, provision of opportunities for these children to learn facts and apply them to the problem under discussion, constant pushing of their thinking by adroit questioning, all will further their growth and acceptance of the new way of working.

Lack of knowledge of how to use books, how to study, how to organize factual material will be at the root of much seeming unwillingness to participate. Many hours can well be spent on improving these skills for all the children in the class.

Apparent laziness may call for medical examination, correction of physical defects, investigation of habits of personal hygiene, a discussion of nutrition, sleep, and recreation habits with a pupil and/or his parents.

Unwillingness to accept any out of school responsibility may point to socio-economic problems in the home, living conditions that make study impossible, indifferent or hostile parents, or the necessity for the child to earn money at a job which consumes all his leisure and energy.

Occasionally a teacher raises the question, "Why should the time of these pupils be wasted working so inefficiently when under my leadership they would learn so much more?" The answer lies in a second question: Learn more of what? This calls for thoughtful study and discussion of the characteristics of the democratic personality, the methods by which those traits can be developed, and the school's responsibility to society. One of the most important elements in democracy is leadership. Inherent in these techniques is the opportunity of training the future generations in the art and practice of leadership. This is a difficult task and one which will take years to accomplish. A single teacher plays but a small part in it and must be content with small signs of growth in the desired direction.

Some of the elements involved in leadership will receive attention in Chapter 8, which deals with materials and discussion techniques. A teacher who wants to assist pupils who are potential leaders must examine and study the following problems: what to do with authority; how to delegate authority; how to give directions; how to check on assignments; how to speak to followers; how to talk *with* people rather than *at* them; from whom, how, and when to seek help; the relation of time to work; how to recognize and reward all contributions whether they be little or big; and how to deal with inattentive and recalcitrant classmates. Complete answers to these leadership problems are not yet known.

SUMMARY OF CLASS ORGANIZATION

Types of Committees	*Methods of determining membership*
1. Research	Organized on the basis of content
	Appointed by teacher or class
	Elected by class
	Volunteered for on basis of interest or ability
	Applied for by letter
2. Steering	Made up of chairmen previously elected by committees
	Selected by teacher
	Elected by class for this purpose

3. Activity ....Appointed by class or teacher as need arises
                         Elected by class
                         Volunteered
                         Made up of representatives from each re-
                         search committee

Activities for which committees may be needed:

Fact-finding
Bulletin board displays
Collecting specimens, art objects, pictures, or other relevant items
Interviewing in and out of school
Keeping track of radio and TV programs in and out of school
Securing, previewing, and showing films
Securing and taking care of speakers
Planning and arranging for assembly programs
Getting new material
Writing letters of invitation and thanks for speakers or material
Making scrapbooks
Constructing equipment
Planning trips
Doing art work
Securing relevant music, recordings, and songs
Planning, taking part in, and producing dramatics
Planning social activities

How committees work: Committees do many different things, of which research or bookwork is only one. The teacher must help pupils to understand when and how committees do the following:

1. Organize themselves.
2. Plan—why, what, how, when, where, who.
3. Delegate individual fact-finding tasks.
4. Have meetings to pool findings and plan reports.
5. Report on progress, difficulties, speeches, broadcasts, plans underway, information gained, reading done.
6. Ask and answer questions.
7. Arrange for, conduct class on, and take trips.
8. Direct class to listen to radio and TV broadcasts and arrange for in-school listening and viewing.
9. Plan and conduct interviews in and out of school.
10. Collect pictures, printed materials, and other relevant items.
11. Secure and show films.
12. Write:
        Creative stories, poems, plays.
        Quiz programs.

       Letters to invite and thank speakers, to plan interviews and trips, for materials.
13. Make plans for speakers.
14. Do construction and experiments.
15. Dramatize (rehearse and produce).
16. Secure and use recordings.
17. Draw—friezes, murals, posters, illustrations, cartoons.
18. Keep records—individual and class (outlines, diaries, logs).
19. Evaluate processes and results in light of goals and plans.
20. Plan and carry out culminating activities.

8

Learning from the Printed and Spoken Word

IN MANY SCHOOLS A SINGLE TEXT, written to follow the course of study, is used by both teacher and students. The teacher sometimes holds it in his hands as he conducts a recitation on the chapters assigned for homestudy on the preceding night. Sometimes teachers require students to answer the questions at the end of each chapter and write them in notebooks. Doing that assignment often means just copying from the book or, for those who cannot read the book, not doing home work. In fact, some teachers permit no variation between what the books says and the answers students give. In many such classrooms no one ever challenges the statements made by the author; no one ever doubts the completeness of the descriptions he gives of history and present life or the soundness of the conclusions he draws. The textbook writer dominates the minds of the students. The use of a single text, even when a few supplementary books are available, will not solve the reading problem which exists in almost every classroom where reading levels may spread over four to six grades.

A teacher accustomed to using a single text is apt to be frustrated when confronted with the demand that unit teaching makes for many kinds of publications. His first question is likely to be, "Where can I get the materials I would need?" That problem is not too difficult to solve. The following are some things a teacher can do with little or no financial expenditure by himself or the school.

First, the teacher will need to determine the required range of difficulty. He can do this quickly without the use of reading tests. (Of course, he will need to use tests later to help him to analyze the nature of individual reading needs.) With a stack of graded books before him, he can ask a pupil whose reading level is not evident, to read from each book in turn. When there is no evidence of strain, and questions reveal comprehension, the level is enjoyment. When comprehension is not easy, but within reach, and recognition of some words requires thought, the *learning* level is indicated. When the pupil becomes tense, perspires, squirms, and does not understand what the book says, the *frustration* level has been reached. If lessons are assigned at that level, the pupil is doomed to failure. He may forget or lose his book, and his homework will not be done.

Since there is probably a span of four grade levels of reading in every ordinary class group, two above and two below grade level, a ninth-grade teacher, for example, can swap single copies of every set of books he has for single copies of the texts used by teachers of seventh, eighth, tenth, and eleventh grades. These would include history books, science books, literature books, civics books, and even spelling books. His classroom library is thereby enriched fourfold and made useable to many more students.

A second method of adding books for a wide range of reading abilities is to secure from the school library, for a period of two weeks at a time, all the books on the unit being studied. The public library will also lend many books on a given subject for as long as four weeks if the teacher explains and takes them out in his name. The librarian there is usually glad to buy materials for use in unit teaching if she has sufficient notice. More over, many pupils have some books at home which they are willing to share with classmates. They, and the teacher himself, can give or lend books from their personal libraries.

Every classroom should also be supplied with newspapers. Sometimes the local publisher is willing to donate a package of papers left over each evening. If not, the teacher can bring his and so can a number of pupils. A committee of pupils who do not read easily, having learned the important words to look for, can read headlines and clip articles and pictures to be filed for use by all content committees. The material may be on the sixth to eighth-grade reading level, but the content will be on the adult level. This is a third way to secure much needed material.

Every classroom in which unit teaching is being done needs a magazine corner. Back issues of many publications can be brought in from home, from friends, and from the offices of doctors and dentists by the teacher and students. Again the pupils with reading difficulties can clip both articles and pictures to be filed and ready for use. The use of magazines is a fourth way to meet the need for material on a wide range of reading levels.

A fifth method makes use of a constellation of activities for the more able pupils. It consists of writing letters to the many organizations and associations from which free and inexpensive materials can be secured. The contents of the letters can be discussed by all the students, but the best writers and spellers should be entrusted with the writing task. School stationery should be used. A clear indication of the use to which the material will be put by the class (not by the writer alone) should be included. The teacher should countersign the letter. Not more than one student should write to any one place.

When this material arrives, a committee of the most able students should have responsibility for reading it, sorting it into three groups (for teacher use, for class use, to be discarded), and marking that material to be retained whose purpose is propaganda. The following guide lines will help the committee to do a satisfactory job:

—Content should not be out of date. The copyright date on a publication should be reasonably recent.
—The value of content which is historical in nature cannot always be determined by looking at the date of publication.
—Content of lasting value is desirable.
—Content should be free from blatant or objectionable advertising.
—Many publications which deal with the same subject but come from different organizations are needed.
—Propaganda material should be clearly marked by the committee.
—Content should be free from name-calling and stereotyping of minority groups.
—Religious literature should not be retained.
—Illustrations help to make a publication useable.

Guides to free and inexpensive curriculum materials should be purchased by the school librarian and made available to the classroom teacher. Business and industrial organizations and human relations agencies will send catalogues on request. Many educational periodicals such as the *NEA Journal* and *The Bulletin* of the National Association of Secondary-School Principals publish lists of available materials. The Superintendent of Documents, Washington, D.C. and the Federal Office of Education are also sources from which publications can be obtained. Most of these publications are pamphlets in which the vocabulary is not too difficult for secondary school use.

A return to the classroom, the work of which is being used to illustrate methods, will help the reader to see how much reading material can be obtained.

WHAT HAPPENED ON THE NINTH DAY

Exploring Sources of Materials

When the class was ready, the teacher opened discussion by saying, "Before you begin to plan your committee work, we must make a list of the source materials you need and where you can get them." Many pupils were ready to name some of the reference books, encyclopedias, dictionaries, textbooks, supplementary books, magazines, newspapers, and pamphlets in which they browsed before the unit had been selected. Some of the books were in the classroom library, others in the school library. Two pupils offered to get the library books after school. Some pupils named books they had at home and promised to bring them. Several students volunteered to go together to see what the public library would lend to the class.

Some magazines were available in the school library, but these could not be clipped; so pupils agreed to bring what they had at home. *Crisis,* published by NAACP, *Ebony, Life, Look, Time,* and *Newsweek* were promised. A table was set aside for magazine reading. The classroom regularly received one newspaper from which several pupils promised to clip relevant articles. Everyone also agreed that reading newspapers at home was to be daily homework. Two boys promised to make a file box in the shop, and several able readers said they would scan and file all incoming clippings.

The teacher said that pupils could go to or write for materials from the human relations agencies in the community. The addresses of the local Urban League, NCCJ, ADL, and the Committee Against Discrimination were written on the board. Some pupils volunteered to visit them after school hours. Others said they would be responsible for writing letters during the next few days.

The teacher also had several annotated film catalogues. One boy said he would look through them for any that could be used. Two boys promised to read the radio and TV schedules and to alert the class to relevant programs. One boy, who had schedules in his pocket, said that a panel on desegregation in the North would be on the radio at 9:00 P.M.

The period was nearly over, and the teacher announced that he would meet with Committee One first thing the next day. Pupils were reminded that homework consisted of vocabulary study, bringing unit-record books up-to-date, listening to the radio panel, reading the newspaper for pertinent items and editorials, and giving thought to the planning of committee work.

Nearly two weeks had been consumed in the selection and planning of the unit. Emphasis during this time was on process and practice. The teacher took the time remaining before the bell rang to review the processes that had been used and to relate them to effective living in a democratic society. The class recalled that they had engaged in all aspects of planning, all kinds of discussion, and in evaluation. Much critical thinking had been needed. Pupils said they appreciated that they had a part in making most of the decisions. They remembered that both voting and consensus had been used to arrive at decisions, and they understood the purposes of both processes. The teacher emphasized the importance of good judgment and wise choice and complimented his class on their increasing skills. He also clarified that although experience with process would continue to be provided, getting factual information was the main objective for the next week.

Discussion Techniques

Unit teaching makes much use of discussion. In the pupil-teacher planning periods, when committee planning and pooling of findings goes on, in evaluation experiences, and whenever ideas need to be clarified and meanings discovered, the method to be used is discussion. Some critics of modern methods say that pupils become glib. Some teachers complain that children are ready to talk about anything. They feel that such talk is merely use of words, expression of fantasies, suppositions, and wishes without reference to facts. Teachers are justly dismayed when pupils express opinions without information to back them up or when they cannot tell the sources of "facts" stated with conviction. Teachers are also alarmed at the tenacity with

which some boys and girls cling to mistaken ideas even when confronted with contrary evidence.

Many adults have those same characteristics. Traditional methods
of learning from single-subject textbooks did not correct their glib-
ness, superstitions, and stereotypic thinking.

Inherent in the techniques of unit teaching *are* the possibilities of
teaching children how to think, how to use the scientific method of
inquiry, how to keep open minds, how to reserve judgment, and how
to choose wisely from among alternative ideas and actions. The
teacher is called upon today to learn how to teach his pupils to do
critical thinking and to set up experiences in which to practice and
develop thought skills.

Methods of exploring backgrounds, of seeking interests and needs,
of setting up criteria and goals, of planning, of evaluating, all involve
talking, exchanging ideas, and collective thinking. Every such experience involves both the teacher and the group. Both of them need to
have not only skill but also specific preparation for each discussion
experience.

Discussions in which either adults or students participate, whether
they be in small or large groups, often fail to be satisfactory experiences because the *leader* is inadequately prepared for his task. Also, a
discussion can fall flat when the members of the group have not previously been told what is to be discussed and where to get some information about it. Teachers themselves, find it hard to be both
leaders and participants in faculty discussions and committee work
without previous experience or training. They, therefore, should not
expect, let alone require, perfection from pupils unless and until they
provide the necessary teaching and opportunity for drill and practice.
In schools where administrators give teachers opportunity to develop
their own skills and abilities as discussion leaders and participants in
committee work, teachers become more successful in the use of discussion techniques in their own classrooms.

Leadership Roles

A discussion group requires several people who can fill leadership
positions: a discussion leader, a recorder or secretary, and a reporter
(someone who can tell others what the discussion was about and

what decisions or conclusions were reached). The leader, whether he is the teacher or a pupil, must have previous knowledge of the subject to be discussed. This will enable him to challenge stereotypes and superstition, insist on facts, supply needed information, and direct the pupils to do new research. Therefore, the teacher must meet with pupil discussion leaders to help them to be prepared.

After preliminary reading and thinking a well prepared leader often develops a series of key questions. He uses these to steer the discussion and to insure the exploration of important areas. If a copy of them is given to the recorder, he will be able to make notes under each question as ideas and facts are presented by the group. Then, when the group is ready for it, or because discussion of a point has come to a dead end, the leader or recorder, using his notes, can give a quick summary of what has been said. He can then pose the next question and so move the group forward. Participants find it helpful to have guiding questions either duplicated and distributed, or written on the chalkboard, either as they arise or before discussion begins. They help pupils to take notes.

If a very able student is available, he can be asked to write on the board facts and ideas as they are presented, and preferably to organize them in some form. This is a difficult task requiring maturity and a highly organized mind. A slow or even average pupil should not be assigned to such a task. A pupil who has difficulty writing on the board or spelling would seriously interfere with the progress of discussion. If the teacher must stop to dictate, or the class is asked to correct what has been written on the board, discussion will be sidetracked and will be difficult to resume.

To be an effective discussion leader a person must know something about the other people in the group. The teacher usually gets this information during the orientation week and adds to it every day. For example, he learns which students can be relied upon to get and produce facts. He makes a note of those who are timid and shy so he can seize every opportunity to include them. To do so, he watches their facial expressions and bodily movements, which may reveal their readiness to participate, and asks them questions or asks for their opinions or agreement. He also remembers to praise their contributions by both look and word.

The teacher-leader usually knows who is a "show off," whose personality tends to be destructive, who blocks, and who wastes time. He learns how to keep the ball out of their hands and has skill in taking the ball away, without displaying anger or personal dislike. Good leadership requires control of self when someone in the group throws a verbal bomb shell. The good leader also knows how to permit and how to stop laughter and how to teach pupils not to laugh at mistakes.

The teacher gradually learns about the attitudes of his pupils towards authority, adult leadership, personal freedom, and peer relationships. He also discovers how to use this knowledge in group discussion strategy.

To be successful with discussion, a teacher needs to know the rates of speed with which various members of the group think. Unless he keeps this in mind, a few pupils are likely to carry the discussion too far too fast, while the majority are left behind. At times, the fast thinkers and talkers may have to be held in check. This can be compensated for if, from time to time, they are asked to review what has been said so far, to formulate new questions, to lead the group forward into a new phase of the subject, or to summarize. Able pupils should be helped to regard such opportunities as part of their training for leadership.

One of the most difficult things for a leader to learn is how to deal with the pupil who talks irrelevantly or too long, or who drags the discussion off on a tangent. Just what to say requires tact and firmness and sometimes quick thinking. After a while the pupils themselves learn how to quell their obstreperous classmates. They do it by squirming as soon as those with no terminal facilities arise to speak, or they say, "That is off the subject, let's get back." Sometimes they groan. The teacher uses such situations to teach children how to control themselves and each other.

Another problem the teacher faces is learning to accept everything that is offered without fear, anger, or surprise. Unless he can do this, pupils will remain insecure and afraid to express themselves. Fear of being different or of reprisal should not be allowed to block boys and girls from saying what they honestly think. Later, when facts are being organized, opinions are being scrutinized, and judgments are being formed, the group itself will be able to discard whatever is unworthy or irrelevant. By then no one is likely to remember who was responsible for what has to be discarded, and so feelings will not be hurt by rejection nor will inferiorities be intensified.

Preparing for a Discussion Group

We hardly need to say that the first step in preparing pupils for a discussion is to announce the subject, question, or problem to be explored. Then, to prevent the pupils from an exchange of ignorance, the teacher must tell them the sources from which facts can be gathered. Students must be made to understand that they need a background from which to talk. They also need to know that opinions should be based upon thought as well as facts. Since printed materials are usually used to get facts, it may be necessary to study the words likely to be found in them. And, since many pupils have difficulty with reading, people, pictures, radio, and TV must also be considered as respectable sources of information.

In preparing for discussion, pupils should learn how to express their opinions and how to indicate the difference between statements of fact and of opinion. For example, they need practice in when to say, "in my opinion," "to my mind," "I believe," "it seems to me," "in my reading I found," "some people say," "the fact has been established," "rumor has it," "my father thinks," "the expert suggested," "public opinion polls reveal," "the book says," "I heard on the radio," and so on.

Pupils do not know the difference between arguing without fact or reason and presenting arguments although in discussions they do both. This, too, can be learned through practice. Boys, particularly, also want to debate issues. The place, limitations, and dangers of debate and the difference between the objectives of debate and discussion should be clarified.

Although most secondary school pupils often engage in classroom discussions, little time is given to study of some of the aspects of democratic group thinking. One is freedom to exercise the right to conform, and another, of great importance, is exercise of the right to dissent. Although by the time they reach secondary school students may have some understanding of group thinking, more must be purposefully done if its values are to be fully realized. Some time may be required before the freedoms to speak, to be heard, and to differ without anger can be fully exercised in classroom discussion. Until by their actions, the students show that they have learned how to use these freedoms, the teacher must regard their review and study as a necessary part of preparation for discussion experiences.

A class group will not be fully prepared for discussion until freedom from fear is also understood. The goal to be achieved is elimination of fear of the leader, of peers, and of criticism. Success in reaching that goal comes when the pupils stop using ridicule, jeers, and reprisals to inhibit some classmates. Fear of inadequacy will also be reduced and creativity will be increased when everyone develops and shows respect for the worth and integrity of every individual in the class, no matter how different he or his ideas may be.

Many years ago, then Secretary of the Treasury Fred Vinson, on his return from the World Monetary Conference, said in his first radio report to the nation, "Upon the ability of the people to participate in conference and discussion lies the hope for world peace." The teacher faces no greater challenge and responsibility than that of learning both how to be a discussion leader and participant, and how to teach these skills to the youth of America.

Types and Purpose of Discussion

The kind of discussion to be used at any one time depends upon the purposes for which it is planned. When the whole class is the discussion group, the teacher acts as leader unless a very able student is available and trained. General discussions are usually held for the purpose of exploring a subject, increasing general information about a subject, changing opinions, creating new insight, clarifying thought, planning, giving opportunity for self-expression, and demonstrating the values of collective thinking. They also provide opportunities to practice leadership.

Committees may undertake discussions for their own group purposes, in which case the chairmen are the leaders. If the teacher wishes to have more participation in a given discussion than can be accomplished by a class discussion, and if pupil-leaders are available, he can divide the class into three or four parts. Sometimes these can be called conversation groups. The ability to converse is not too prevalent in adult life and might be restored if students were given the opportunity to practice it in school. The forum of the air, the symposium, the panel, and the round table are other types of discussion which require able, well-prepared participants and leaders. In addition to the purposes already stated, those discussions demonstrate techniques and enrich experience for the gifted students.

The first task confronting a discussion group and its leader is to determine the purposes for which they are meeting and the goals they want to accomplish. When the time at their disposal is coming to an end, the leader has the task of summarizing. Before the group disbands, or moves into a different kind of activity, they need to review the objectives with which they began. Then, in the light of those goals, the final task is to evaluate their experience. This judging of strength and weakness should deal with leadership, process, participation, roles played by various persons, new ideas gained, conclusions drawn, and decisions reached. Discussion provides excellent opportunities to develop the habit of evaluation.

9

Learning from Direct and Vicarious Experience

ALTHOUGH WORD-SYMBOL LEARNING
is the most frequently used method in all classrooms, teachers know
that a considerable portion of their pupils cannot learn readily from
the printed page. However, all of them can learn from direct experience, and most can learn from vicarious experience. The vicarious
experience of pictures, both moving and still, maps, and charts are
most commonly used to supplement the printed and written word
symbols. Thus, illustrated magazines and books are important, and
both filmstrips and films should be used in the course of every unit.
Nearly all schools now have audio-visual libraries, but teachers have
difficulty securing what they need at the time of need. Moreover, few
film libraries are yet equipped with material dealing with intergroup
relations. However, national and local agencies (listed in the Appen-
dix), university film libraries, and commercial film distribution agencies do have them and will furnish catalogues on request. No such
film should be used without previewing, presentation, and follow-up
discussion. They are tools for learning, not for recreation or entertainment. Even those students who learn readily from word symbols,
also learn readily from these vicarious experiences.

Radio and television also provide vicarious learning experience,
and most school systems now make these available. Many daytime
programs fit into units dealing with the democratic way of life. Small

committees or one or two members of each content or research committee can be given responsibility for keeping the class informed
about schedules and for securing equipment or space for in-school
listening and viewing. Listening to and seeing appropriate and relevant programs can be included in home assignments for all the pupils
or for appropriate committees. In the former case, class discussion
should follow the next day. In the latter case, the committee can
either report to the class or incorporate what they learned into their
own discussion and study and report it at a later date.

Direct Experiences with People

All students, bright and slow learners alike, learn when they have
direct experiences. Among these are face-to-face interactions with
people in and out of the classroom—with teachers, of course, but
with many others as well. Thus adults, especially qualified by reason
of their backgrounds, training, employment, professions, and experiences, can be secured as speakers, consultants, and resource persons.
Teachers, working together, can develop a list of those willing to
serve. From such a list, appropriate people can be selected for the
class by a small special committee or by one or two members of each
research committee. Using people as sources of information provides
for many related activities: letter writing, telephoning, preparing
questions, preparing introductions and thank-you remarks, note taking, summary writing, role-playing, and dramatization. Some of these
can be class activities; others can be the responsibility of sub-groups
or committees formed for the purpose, whose members are selected
because of their special abilities or needs.

Interviewing people to get facts and opinions needed for discussion
and committee work is also direct experience. Pupils who cannot read
the available material can be assigned to talk to people from whom
they too can get information and thus be prepared for participation
in discussion or committee meetings. Sometimes those to be interviewed are experts. Other teachers, students, parents, neighbors, and
friends should be included. Interviews also provide pupils with opportunities to converse with adults—an experience quite strange even
to many young adolescents, especially those who are in the culturally
deprived third of the population.

When an interview with an important person in the community is projected, the class may wish to select a committee to go to see him. The class can then commission their representatives as to what they are to bring back. Once chosen, the committee must organize itself: who is to be the leader and what notes are to be taken must be decided. After the interview, they will need to organize their findings and report to the class. The person to be interviewed will appreciate some preliminary information. The teacher is responsible for telling him what the unit is about, the questions students are likely to ask, and what he, the teacher, would like to have brought out in the interview.

Careful planning for a speaker is also required. Care must be taken to secure an adequate room. If the auditorium is to be used and other classes invited, someone must be given responsibility for setting up the amplifier. Letters of invitation should be sent to interested classes and possibly to parents. A committee should be delegated to act as hosts to receive and seat guests. The speaker should be informed by letter about the unit of learning so that he can plan his talk to suit the needs of the class. The letter can be planned by a committee, written by one pupil on school stationery, and countersigned by the teacher. Questions to be used after the main address should be prepared by one or all of the several research committees. Letters of thanks can be written by every pupil or by one for the class. If the latter device is used, the entire group should hear the first draft and, if necessary, make suggestions for its improvement.

Value of Trips

Trips are direct, multiple-learning experiences which are essential in teaching and learning about the democratic way of life and of government in large and small communities and in rural areas. Reading and hearing about democracy, films, radio and TV programs all help, but nothing is quite so effective as going outside of the school for first-hand experience with democracy in action.

At the secondary school level, departmental organization (the use of single subject periods of forty-five or fifty minutes) creates difficulty for teachers wishing to take classes on trips. However, the multiple values that are involved in such an experience make it so worth while that teachers do find ways of overcoming obstacles. One method is for English and social studies teachers to cooperate with each other and rearrange their schedules. For example, Miss A has English[1] and English[2], each to meet first and second periods. At the same time Mr. B has Social Studies[1] and Social Studies[2], each also to meet first and second periods. Ordinarily their schedules would be as follows:

M	Eng[1]	Eng[2]		M	Soc St[1]	Soc St[2]
Tu	Eng[1]	Eng[2]		Tu	Soc St[1]	Soc St[2]
W	Eng[1]	Eng[2]		W	Soc St[1]	Soc St[2]
Th	Eng[1]	Eng[2]		Th	Soc St[1]	Soc St[2]
Fr	Eng[1]	Eng[2]		Fr	Soc St[1]	Soc St[2]

Miss A   Mr. B

In order to get periods long enough for trips (for which, at the beginning of the day pupils could also leave before first period), Miss A and Mr. B and their classes could be scheduled as follows:

M	Eng[1]	Eng[1]		M	Soc St[2]	Soc St[2]
Tu	Eng[2]	Eng[2]		Tu	Soc St[1]	Soc St[1]
W	Eng[1]	Eng[1]		W	Soc St[2]	Soc St[2]
Th	Eng[2]	Eng[2]		Th	Soc St[1]	Soc St[1]
Fr	Eng[1]	Eng[2]		Fr	Soc St[2]	Soc St[1]

Miss A   Mr. B

In the middle periods of the day, lunch time can be included. At the end of the day, the trip need not end with the ringing of the dismissal bell. Such an arrangement permits both the English teacher and the social studies teacher to take their classes out of the building, and if they wish, they can go together.

Careful planning for a trip is essential if maximum learning is to result. The details of preparation for going and returning and patterns of behavior during the trips need to be discussed by the students. They can decide beforehand about the kinds of clothing to be worn, smoking on the street, control of voices and manners; then, the teacher's fears, safety hazards, annoyances to other classes and teachers in the building when leaving and returning, and disciplinary problems are reduced to a minimum.

Much depends upon the purposes which the teacher and pupils wish to accomplish. For example, a trip may be used as an approach to a unit and may, therefore, be an exploratory experience. It will motivate and stimulate interest in a proposed topic and help to bring consensus of opinion required to make a decision. In that case, the entire class should participate in the general planning. Specific details, such as telephone calls, letter writing, collection of money for transportation, can be delegated to student committees selected for the purpose by the teacher or by the class.

During the course of a unit one or more committees may plan trips for themselves. They may want to get some special information not found in books, or to interview a local official, or to secure materials they need, or to see art or historical collections, or to see a business or industry in operation. In that case, committee members may do their own planning and make their own arrangements. They will probably need help from the teacher and must in all events be required to tell him their plans and experiences and, eventually, to report to the class. Sometimes a committee may think it a good idea for the entire class to go on a particular trip. In that event, the committee takes responsibility for the plans and arrangements, makes sure the class is adequately prepared, and conducts the trip as well as whatever follow-up activity they envision.

The first thing to be done in planning a trip is to discuss its purposes and to set up the goals to be accomplished. Questions need to be answered: "Why are we going?" "What do we want to find out?"

"How are we going to get the information?" "What records shall we need to make on the spot?" Contact with the people and place to be visited is essential. This can be done by phone or mail. People to be visited and those in charge of the place need to have information concerning the pupil purposes and what they want to see and do.

Specific details of transportation have to be planned—what vehicles are to be used, the cost if any, where pupils are to board subways, busses, or automobiles, where they alight, where they again board them for the return journey. The exact cost must be determined and plans made to secure the money. Usually pupils pay their own way. Provision must be made for those who cannot afford the cost, and this must be done without publicity. Some classes raise the required money. Some school systems arrange for the use of school buses during the day.

As soon as the planning committee has all the facts at hand, they can be presented to the class. In some schools and especially with younger pupils, letters written to the parents describing the trip and its purposes are a good idea. Although this seems unnecessary if trip taking is to be considered an extension of the classroom, courtesy to parents and consideration of their concern for the safety of their children dictate the wisdom of this procedure. Moreover, such letters are effective means of informing parents about the school's program. Some parents may be sufficiently interested to offer to go along. Such help will often be welcomed by junior high school teachers.

Teachers should keep in mind the fact that pupils do get tired and that rest periods should be planned. A count of pupils before, while en route, and again before transportation vehicles leave for home may prevent mishaps. The teacher may need to make a preliminary visit to the place. However, if the faculty have developed a plan for recording and sharing their experiences, review of these records may serve the same purpose. Sometimes classes want to go to see a commercial film. Before permitting this, the teacher should see the film himself.

In the senior high school, if the teacher does not plan to return in time to meet his next class, he must arrange for a colleague to take his place. Also, the other teachers of the class he is taking out must be notified if they are not to return in time. These arrangements should be done as far in advance as possible.

Junior high school pupils and, in some cases, older adolescents will not be ready to go until they have discussed the responsibility of the individual to the teacher, the group, and the school. They will need careful directions for getting outdoor clothing from lockers, how, when, and where to leave the building, and methods of keeping together on the street. Disciplinary problems can be avoided if the teacher insists that "difficult" pupils remain near him. Discussion of manners and behavior on the street, in public vehicles, and at the place of interest is essential. The school's policy on the question of smoking while on trips should be clearly defined. Consequences to follow infractions of the rules of conduct the class sets up must be determined, and they should be applied if necessary. If lunch in a restaurant is to be included, menus, attitudes toward waitresses, the use of table utensils, and table manners might have to be studied, demonstrated, or role-played. Bulletin board displays, question boxes, and mimeographed material are useful devices in preparing for the trip.

People enjoy reliving a meaningful experience. Students should be given the chance to do this in as many ways as they and the teacher can devise. An evaluation discussion should come as soon as possible after a trip. The goals that were set up by the group should be reviewed. Answers to such questions as: "Did we accomplish our plans? Why not?" are needed. Transportation should be evaluated, and behavior recalled. The learnings should be listed, and any new problems and questions raised should be answered.

A very common method of crystallizing learnings is to require written reports. This is often a bore to some and too difficult for others. It may even spoil the trip in some measure. If the teacher feels that writing is essential, the pupils should be given individual choice of several different ways of doing it. A letter to parents, friends, or other relatives can be a virtual report, but it is more easily motivated especially if it is really mailed. Some student may be moved to write a poem. Another may write a story. A group may write a skit to dramatize some especially funny or thrilling experience.

Talking is as valuable as writing. The class as a whole may exchange experiences, or conversation groups can be set up. Artistically talented students may choose to do painting, clay modeling, or construction in wood or metal. Some pupils may be stimulated to make a collection of pictures, a scrapbook, or a nature collection.

A letter of thanks, written to the key person at the place visited, is a fitting close.

Trips and speakers, films and TV programs are part of the Higher Horizons and other enrichment programs being used, especially in the large cities, to give cultural and social experiences to culturally deprived pupils. Use of vicarious and direct learning experiences enables these pupils to make higher scores on I.Q. and other tests and to raise their aspiration levels. They come to believe in their own worth and in education, and they see good in the democratic way.

Organizing Community Resources for Effective Use

In a school where many teachers are making extensive use of community resources, pooling of information about them is both interesting and useful. A committee of teachers may have the responsibility for doing that job. Lists of consultants who are willing to come to the school to speak to the students should be compiled, duplicated, and distributed to all teachers. The lists should include, in addition to names, addresses and telephone numbers. Most helpful is to group the people according to their usefulness, under headings related to units, topics, areas of interest, and subject matter. The list should also include the members of the faculty and other adults connected with the school and school system, such as custodian, janitor, secretary, doctor, nurse, dietitian, superintendent and supervisors.

Most communities, whether large or small, are able to furnish speakers, consultants, and resource persons engaged in a wide variety of activities. The following are typical sources for such persons:

Art schools and associations
Broadcasting companies
Business and industry
Crime prevention agencies
Dramatic groups
Economic enterprises
Exchange students and teachers
Government service agencies
Health agencies

Historical associations
Human relations agencies
International groups
Labor organizations
Men's fraternal organizations
Museums—art, commercial, scientific, historical
Music clubs and music schools
Nationality associations

Political groups
Professional associations—medical,
    dental, legal, pedagogical
Race relations organizations
Religious organizations
Social service agencies
Sports leagues and clubs

Transportation companies—rail,
    subway, aviation, bus lines
Travel agencies
Universities and colleges
Welfare agencies
Women's clubs
Youth groups

The many individuals who reside in the immediate neighborhood
of the school can also be enlisted as resource persons. Use of them
and of the students' parents will increase their knowledge of and
interest in the school. A letter soliciting their help can carry an
important message of interpretation of the school to the community. A bridge is thus created over which pleasant public relations may flow.

Teachers engaged in unit teaching can also help each other by
compiling information needed when trips are being planned. Places
to visit can be listed in any fashion convenient to the teachers. In
addition to the location, the name of the person to contact, telephone
numbers, hints about the nature of the experience and values to be
derived, costs, transportation problems, and dangers to be avoided
will all be helpful to colleagues. Communities have many of the
following places of interest to which trips can be taken:

Airports
Bakeries
Banks
Broadcasting studios
Business enterprises
Churches
Colleges and universities
Construction sites
Courts
Dairies
Farms
Filtration plants
Government buildings and offices
Historical sites
Hospitals
Housing projects
Industrial plants
Lecture halls
Libraries
Lumber yards

Museums—art, scientific,
    commercial, historical
Nationality settlements
Newspaper plants
Nurseries
Other schools
Packing houses
Parks
Playgrounds
Public meeting places
Publishing companies
Railroad stations and yards
Recreation facilities
Slum areas
Stores
Theatres—legitimate and moving
    picture
Telephone companies
Water fronts

The following summary of vicarious and direct learning experiences appeared in the teacher's log of the unit being used to illustrate teaching and learning the democratic way.

Use of printed material

Many kinds of learning experiences were cooperatively planned and carried out by pupils and teacher. Some of them were initiated and directed by one of the research committees. For others, special committees were required which the class selected and commissioned. The unit underway offered the possibility of learning facts from many printed sources. In addition to our local newspapers, we used *Crisis* (NAACP), *Ebony, Life, Look, Time, Newsweek,* and *The New York Times.* Most of them were brought in by the pupils. A committee of pupils with reading difficulties (after I had made sure they could recognize key words) clipped articles of importance on all aspects of the unit. Another special committee, this time of very able readers, scanned the clippings, articles, and pamphlets and filed them under appropriate headings. Thus, we always had more material than was in any of the books.

The daily newspapers furnished articles and editorials on the progress of desegregation of schools. Information about the freedom riders, who protested discrimination in transportation buses and bus terminals, came from both newspapers and magazines. A panel from one committee reported on and led the class in discussion about the freedom riders and the sit-in demonstrations at lunch counters.

Community agencies

One day early in the planning, I brought to the attention of the class the human relations agencies in the city and suggested that material could be obtained from them. I had previously secured catalogues from the American Friends Service Committee, National Conference of Christians and Jews, Anti-Defamation League, Urban League, and the Federal Office of Education. Content committee leaders looked these over and checked those items which seemed to be relevant to their work. Several pupils immediately offered to write the necessary letters. They obtained school stationary from the main office and drafted the letters that night at home. Next day these were read to the class. Several changes and new ideas were suggested. When the letters were in their final form, I countersigned them, and they were mailed. When the new material arrived, I appointed a committee of my most able students to scan the pamphlets and, with my help, distribute them to appropriate committees.

One of the pieces of material most useful for our unit was a pamphlet by Dr. William Van Til, published by ADL, called *Prejudiced: How Do People Get That Way?* Another, also from ADL, was Ashley Montagu's *What We Know About "Race."* The UNESCO pamphlet on *Race* was excellent. ADL's *Prejudice and Society* by Earl Raab and Seymour Lipset and *Prejudice and Politics* by Charles P. Taft and Bruce L. Felknor were read by several very able pupils who made special reports on them to the class. Although it was difficult, the committee especially interested in the historical approach, read Oscar Handlin's *Race and Nationality in American Life* published by Anchor Books, paperback, in 1957.

A pamphlet called *Discrimination In Housing* by Eunice and George Grier was used by the advanced readers in the committee concerned with the subject; most of the others studied *FEP and the Cost of Discrimination.*

Speaker

Several students suggested that if they, as a committee, visited an agency and told the staff there about the unit underway, they might be able to get a speaker, consultant, or resource person to visit the class. General discussion of this proposal resulted in arrangements to visit the Committee Against Discrimination. One of the pupils made a 'phone call to set a late afternoon visit. I promised to go along. We were most graciously received at C.A.D. The director there was delighted with our unit. He promised to send a well-qualified speaker on the subject of discrimination in housing.

The day before the speaker was to come, the committee asked for time to have the class help them to complete their plans and set up questions for the speaker. The chairman agreed to be responsible for introducing the speaker and thanking him at the end of the period. The speech we heard was excellent, and the discussion which followed helped the students very much. Many of them that night wrote thank-you letters, which I inspected and which we mailed next day.

After school visits

The pupils working on discrimination in employment, instead of having a speaker, made plans for after-school interviews with employers who had businesses in their neighborhoods. This required deciding what questions were to be asked and allocating various aspects of the subject to the several members of the group. To alleviate some degree of nervousness about the experience, I suggested role-playing the situation. The class observed the role-play and helped the committee members to get additional insight into the task they had before them. Two days later the committee met with me to pool their experiences and the facts they had learned and to decide how to report to the class. Their report included dramatization, some of which was done with much humor.

Films

One of the persons interviewed, in talking about the difficulty non-white students had in getting part-time jobs, suggested that the Urban League's film A Morning for Jimmy would be an important experience for the class. The committee reported this, and the audio-visual committee offered to secure the film and a projector, to preview the film, present it to the class, and lead the discussion. I arranged to be present at the preview and helped the committee to set up the leading questions to guide discussion after the screening.

During the course of the unit, other films were secured and shown. Among them was ADL's High Wall, which deals with the way parents unwittingly pass their prejudices on to children. It also shows how seriously prejudice and hatred interfere with development of character and prevent good family living. The class also had a good discussion of the NEA's filmstrip All of Us, the People of the World, which emphasizes both the unity and diversity of mankind.

Trips

When the committee which was studying interreligious prejudices came to the question of why, they found that none of them knew anything about Judaism. They decided that ignorance affected their attitudes. They asked a Jewish classmate, working in another committee, to meet with them. During their discussion the next day, he suggested that a visit to a synagogue would be the best learning experience for the whole class to have, and he promised to make all the arrangements. The suggestion was placed before the teacher and the class. There was general agreement.

The rabbi of the synagogue met the class at the door. He took them for a tour of the building and when they were finally in the Temple, he showed and explained the Scrolls containing the Ten Commandments, the Eternal Light suspended from the ceiling, and the Menorah. They had many questions to ask and came away with information with which to replace myth, superstition, and ignorance. Holiday observances were especially interesting to many pupils.

Small groups went on their own, after school and on weekends, to visit other kinds of churches. This, in some cases, meant interfaith sharing as pupils of different faiths visited Sunday schools and churches with their friends. After each such experience the individuals involved shared their findings and new insights with their classmates.

We also took a trip to see the new interracial housing developments and one of the most depressed areas of the city.

Resource persons

Speakers, resource persons, interviews, films, trips, role-playing, dramatizations, and much reading went on in connection with all the problems included in the unit. Many pupils talked with their parents about family values and how children learn to like or dislike people, things, and ideas. History teachers were called upon for help with the Bill of Rights, so too was my friend who is a lawyer. Letters were written, phone calls were made, and interviews were arranged in half a dozen agencies. Among them were the Anti-Defamation League, the National Conference of Christians and Jews, the Urban League, the Mayor's Committee on Civil Rights, the Commission Against Discrimination, the Race Relations Council, and the local United Nations Council.

10

Last Step: Evaluating the Pupils and the Unit

IN MANY SCHOOLS THE MOST IM-
portant tools the teacher uses to evaluate the achievement levels of
each student are the standardized objective tests secured from test
publishers. Testing programs are often believed to measure the
effectiveness of teaching as well as the extent of learning. Most
teachers also use frequent or periodical, unannounced or announced
tests, reviews, and quizzes to measure factual knowledge. But testing is only one part of evaluation. Evaluation, to be valid, must
include the concept of growth and should take into consideration
all that goes on in the classroom. Moreover, evaluation should be
done in terms of objectives.

Growth in the use of the tools of learning can probably be
measured objectively, so can the acquisition of given facts. Comparison of an individual's performance with that which has been
established by means of standardized tests as normal for his age
group is considered necessary in many school systems. There are,
however, many more areas of human growth and development with
which the teacher must be concerned and for which most measuring
devices are inadequate. To evaluate them the teacher records, from
time to time, in brief, descriptive, factual terms, exactly what a pupil
says and does. These indicate the pupil's progress—his change or
lack of change, his failure to grow or his development of thought

and feeling, as well as his ability to match beliefs and values with behavior.

The pupil's skill in evaluating himself and his work and other people and their work also needs to be developed and appraised by himself and by the teacher. This skill grows with practice of the process itself. Such practice is afforded when criteria and goals are discussed. Then pupils have opportunity to examine and judge their motives in choosing a unit as well as the merits of the proposed unit. Further experience in evaluating self and work is provided by testing facts learned, skill in reading, and writing ability.

When, at the end of a report period, marks must be determined, the teacher who is concerned about a pupil's ability to evaluate himself and his work confers with him. He may then ask that student, "What mark do you think you should have?" If the pupil rates himself below or above the teacher's judgment, they examine together the pupil's folder of work and the teacher's records of daily responses and participation; and together, they discuss quality, quantity, effort, and growth.

When a person has skill in critical thinking and the habit of evaluation, he is able to ask and answer such questions as: "What is good or strong about myself (us), the way I (we) work, and my (our) product? What is poor or weak about me (us), my (our) process, what I (we) produce?" "In the light of my (our) strength and weakness, what must I (we) do next; how shall I (we) proceed to capitalize strength and correct weakness?"

To develop these skills and habits further, the teacher arranges for committees to practice the process. He sits with each group at intervals, and he may, after they have given their final report, discuss the way they worked, the qualities of leadership and followership, and what they produced. Moreover, the entire class engages in a similar evaluation session when the unit is finished. This also provides experience in reexamining goals and in judging how much progress was made toward their accomplishment.

Many and varied types of standardized evaluation instruments are available for all grade levels and all purposes. There are also inventories of interests, questionnaires, and social distance scales to uncover attitudes and the possibility of discriminatory behavior. The teacher who is concerned with teaching the democratic way will want to be familiar with them. When units on minority groups, prejudice and discrimination, or intergroup relations are underway, older secondary school students could be given the opportunity to examine them and to help select those suitable for their use. Tests of aptitudes, potentialities, and skills measure ability to study, social behavior, social sensitivity, social maturity, communication, judgment, health, and safety. Other testing instruments reveal needs, social group structure, and ability to engage in critical thinking and to interpret data.

Tests designed to reveal the acquisition of information and skills must be carefully prepared. Such facts as who, what, when, and where are quickly forgotten. Of greater importance is acquiring skill in mobilizing facts, yet this skill is rarely tested. Growth in ability to find and use sources of information to formulate and apply general principles, and to make use of the scientific method of inquiry should also be determined.

Marks and Report Cards

Methods of reporting growth and development to parents are usually determined by the school system. The teacher who is using modern techniques may be hampered and embarrassed by the necessity of using antiquated reports. The student and his parents are helped if report cards are supplemented with individual letters and interviews during which the pupil's record book and folder, the class records, and the teacher's records are used.

Marks and marking systems have long been sources of acute anxiety to teachers, students and parents. Too often marks on report cards are regarded as facts; whereas, at best, they are merely evidences of teachers' judgments, which can be wrong. Moreover, a single symbol cannot possibly represent what a student knows about a subject, what he learned during the previous six weeks, what skills he now possesses, what his growth, attitudes and effort have been, and how he stacks up in relation to a mythical norm for the grade level.

When the teacher, at the end of a four- or six-week period, sits down to make up the marks for all his individual students, he is likely to be consciously or unconsciously influenced by many factors, some of which are not at all related to the individual's achievement, growth, present level of performance, or relative place among his peers. Teachers, themselves, say they are influenced by the following:

—Factual information possessed regardless of whether it was learned in a previous grade or outside of school
—Behavior (a mixture of action, speech, and attitude)
—Promptness (some teachers reduce the mark when a paper comes in late)
—Effort
—Cooperation (which too often means only obedience)
—Cleanliness (of the work *or* the student)
—What church the student attends, if any (often a subconscious prejudice)
—Social class of the student (also a subconscious attitude of the middle-class teacher to lower-class people)
—Race (some teachers are conditioned by ideas of racial inferiority)
—Position of the student's parents (influential parents sometimes exert pressures)
—Reading ability
—Recitations (some of which were easy questions, others hard ones)
—Short-answer tests
—Objective tests and standardized tests
—Essay-type tests
—Spelling
—Grammar
—Participation in discussion
—Participation in Committee work
—Leadership
—Attitude toward authority (of the teacher, the principal, and other adults)
—Attitude toward peers
—Independent study ability (ability to be self-directed in learning)
—Ability (too often judged on the basis of I.Q. tests which measure only a few of the fifty-odd elements which are known to comprise intelligence)
—Time of year (whether it is the beginning or end of the year or semester)

Objectives for which to work	Methods of evaluating progress

1. Orientation to the school
2. Adjustment of the child to his peers in the group
3. Adjustment to teachers
4. Development of democratic habits, abilities, attitudes:
    ability to work with a group
    respect for rights of others
    respect for opinions of others
    class spirit
    support of chosen officers
    intelligent, active school citizenship
    participation in discussion and planning
    ideals of service
    ability to express own opinions
	1. Observe individuals
	2. Observe group life
	3. Make anecdotal records
	4. Study and interpret anecdotal records
	5. Observe and record:
	    offices held
	    services volunteered
	    participation in group work, discussions
	6. Judge growth as revealed in creative writing on topics concerned with self and interpersonal relationships
	7. Observe group judgments
	8. Study attendance records

5. Development of thought habits:
    clear thinking
    resisting influence of others
    making own decisions
    attacking problem intelligently
    setting up own and group goals
    planning work
    adhering to plan
    evaluating progress
    insisting on fact and authority
	1. Observe and record anecdotes and comments made by peers
	2. Study records made by group secretaries and leaders
	3. Use standard and homemade tests designed to reveal ability to judge data, choose wisely, plan effectively

6. Development of work habits:
    neatness
    ability to gather information
    thoroughness
    ability to follow directions
    promptness
    accuracy
    ability to observe
    ability to keep honest, useful records
    ability to correct own errors
    ability to carry task through to completion
    ability to appraise own work fairly
	1. Evaluate written work
	2. Record promptness in getting to school, to class, and in getting jobs done
	3. Use standard and homemade test to reveal:
	    ability to gather information
	    ability to follow directions
	    ability to observe
	4. Inspect and evaluate records kept by pupils
	5. Engage in pupil-teacher evaluation discussions

7. Establish good health habits and correction of physical defects	1. Observe—daily inspection 2. Study records of attendance 3. Examine medical records and determine child's attitude toward correction of defects

Fig. 10-1. Pupils and Teacher Take Account of Stock. Gertrude Noar, *Freedom*

Objectives for which to work	*Methods of evaluating progress*

8. Development of personal character-istics:
    self-reliance
    responsibility
    self-control
    habit of obedience
    creativeness, originality
    becoming less egocentric
    courtesy
    appreciation of work
    aesthetic appreciations
	1. Observe and make anecdotal records
	2. Judge creative writings and artistic efforts
	3. Observe and record group judgments of individuals

9. Development of skills in:
    reading
    writing
    speaking
    spelling
    listening to radio
    looking at films
    social living
    use of democratic practices
	1. Use standard and homemade tests, games, contests
	2. Examine individual records kept by children
	3. Observe and record growth as evidenced in participation and contributions to discussions, planning, group activities

10. Development of standards in reading and appreciation of reading as a leisure-time activity	1. Survey leisure-time activities 2. Judge records kept by child 3. Judge written work 4. Judge discussion of books read

11. Knowledge of:
    current affairs
    people and life in immediate and remote communities in America and other lands
    how food, shelter, clothing are provided and obtained
    processes of consumption and distribution
    own abilities and possibilities
    human development, nutrition, first aid, hygiene
    value of museums—art, science, history
    how to use charts, maps, graphs
    history, American institutions—home, church, school
    American freedoms and way of life
    American government
    how to employ leisure time
	1. Test
	2. Inspect, evaluate, record work done by each child
	3. Judge quality and quantity of reports made to class

to Live and Learn (Philadelphia: Franklin Publishing Company, 1948), pp. 81-82.

What can a teacher do about this problem of marks? Relatively little can be done so long as a school system holds on to letter (A,B,C,D,E or G,E,F,P) or number grades (1,2,3,4,5). Relatively little can be done so long as parents, especially those who are pressuring both pupil and teacher about college entrance, demand A's. Relatively little can be done so long as colleges seem to place heavy emphasis on the applicant's high school marks and rank in his graduating class. Some hope exists that this situation may be alleviated in the future. College admissions officers are admitting candidates from all quartiles. Studies of success and failure in college show that some admitted from the lower ranks of their high school classes graduate from college with honors, while some from the top quartile fail and drop out of college. Also some state colleges must accept all applicants who have completed high school.

Every teacher should examine his own attitudes and feelings, discover his own prejudices, and bring into consciousness the factors which influence his judgments of the potentiality, achievements, and efforts of his students. Moreover, and possibly more important, he can accept the idea that the marks he records are *judgmental, not factual.* Once he does so, he can bring both students and parents closer to reality about them.

The teacher's reactions and judgments of many things the pupils do—both written and oral—can be recorded in words rather than letters or numbers. Remarks such as: "This is good," "I like what you say," "Your thought is fine, but you must correct the punctuation," "I know you can do better; please try this again," "I'm afraid this was too difficult for you; see me about using another subject (or test)," "You are showing great improvement," express the teacher's interest, desire to help, approbation, concern, and judgment. Such remarks are also meaningful to parents.

Objectives of teaching and learning the democratic way and methods of evaluating progress toward attaining them are summarized in Figure 10-1, pages 102-103.

Evaluating Attitudes and Behavior

In a unit dealing with the democratic way, or with any aspect of intergroup relations, the individual must at some time be confronted with his own attitudes and probable behavior. Social distance scales are helpful. The following final chapter of the story used to illustrate methods will help the reader to see how attitude and behavioral studies might be undertaken. In it, the teacher comments briefly, on some of the values of the total experience.

Self-examination of attitudes

In connection with the study of their own attitudes, those of their classmates, and those of the other pupils in the school, measures for finding out about negative attitudes, stereotypic thinking, and discriminatory behavior had to be devised. In the early planning of learning activities, the boys and girls decided that each one should write a letter to himself, describing as best he could his own feelings and thoughts. Some decided, for example, to write how they would behave if new neighbors, different in color or religion from their own families, moved in next door. Some of the pupils planned to write descriptions of Jews, Negroes, English people, Catholics, Italians. In other words, they would define the stereotypes they then believed to be true. The letters were to be sealed and not looked at again until the end of the unit. Then, on reading them again, each student could decide for himself whether he had changed.

Planning action

Then the students agreed to listen to each other for stereotypes. When they heard one, they planned to challenge it with such questions as: "How do you know?" "What is your source of information?" "Let's test that against the facts." They also agreed to watch for scapegoating. Two such incidents were brought to the class for discussion. The class talked about the use of stories and dialect jokes and what to do when confronted with evidences of prejudice, name-calling, insulting remarks, hatred, and bigotry. Some role-playing was tried, but no easy answers were found to those questions.

Other classes involved

After much discussion and several attempts on the part of a small committee of very gifted students to write a questionnaire to sample school-wide opinion, a request for such an instrument was taken to a professor of psychology in the local college. He helped them to formulate the simplified social distance scale in Figure 10-2, page 106.

Tabulation of the results of this brief unsigned poll, which was administered with the help of several other teachers, revealed that a considerable amount of racial and religious prejudice existed in the

Check the column which shows how you feel about each of the following:

Having as a dinner guest in your home:

	Would like	Would not like	Not sure
An Italian			
A Catholic			
A Jew			
A Negro			
An Oriental			

Working with:

	Would like	Would not like	Not sure
An Italian			
A Catholic			
A Jew			
A Negro			
An Oriental			

Having as a neighbor:

	Would like	Would not like	Not sure
An Italian			
A Catholic			
A Jew			
A Negro			
An Oriental			

Fig. 10-2. Simplified Social Distance Scale.

school. The teacher said he would bring the information to the attention of the principal for discussion at the next faculty meeting.

Study of the community[1]

As the result of reading and interviewing people in the community, one committee, which devoted its time largely to discrimination, came to the conclusion that people who easily condemn the South for its treatment of Negroes are not looking at what is happening in the North. They decided to investigate housing discrimination. They wrote to the American Institute of Public Opinion to get information on how to conduct a poll on the question: "Do you approve or disapprove of a Negro moving into your neighborhood?" Following the advice they received, a map of the town was divided into areas, each of which was assigned to several members of the committee. The task was to interview at least 100 adults in the town and to get reasons for the answers given.

The committee reported that 48% of those interviewed approved of having Negroes move into their neighborhoods; 39% did not; and 13% refused to answer. The remarks made showed all degrees of opinion. Among them were: "These polls make trouble." "As long as he was an agreeable, decent chap, he could come sit at my table, and I would welcome him as a brother." "I wouldn't sell my house to one, but I play bridge with a Negro couple." "I'd give equal rights but separate areas." "I would approve, myself, but go along with the majority if they disapprove."

The committee also went to see four local real estate agents. They asked the question, "Would you sell a house to a Negro?" The answers they got ranged from yes to no. One said that buyers had to be "fitted into environments where they would be accepted." Another talked about evaluating "compatibility" before selling to a Negro. The students were told that Negroes would have difficulty buying in all but five neighborhoods.

Another question to which the committee sought answers from realtors was, "If you sell, do you expect pressure against you, and from what group?" They were told that individuals rather than organizations raise objections.

The committee reported that realtors and others think that the state laws against discrimination in housing are adequate. (The class had

[1] This report is based on a project undertaken in the fall of 1961 by an 11th grade class in the Verona High School, Verona, New Jersey, and reported in their school newspaper, *The Fairviewer*, 11/22/61.

already been informed about the laws.) However, they found that many houses in the town were one- and two-family dwellings, which are exempt from the law. They also talked to one real estate agent who frankly said he would break the law.

The class heard this report with keen interest and discussed it at length. Among their conclusions was that stronger laws and greater understanding are needed to correct discrimination in the town.

Evaluating Success of Unit

Judging individuals is only part of the task of evaluation. The value of the unit itself needs to be judged in terms of the objectives set up by the class. In the case study, the teacher evaluated the unit as follows:

All the committee reports had been given, new materials had been classified and filed, and posters and pictures had been removed from the bulletin boards. Nothing was left to be done except the final evaluation discussion. To guide it, the teacher wrote on the board: "Did we accomplish our objectives? What was weak? What did we do poorly? What did we do well?"

During discussion students were earnest, sincere, and honest in their efforts to evaluate themselves as individuals, the processes used in committee work, their skills, their leaders, and their gains.

The teacher wrote in his log the following statement of what, to his mind, were some of the most important outcomes of the unit:

Some of the objectives of the unit, for example, development of skills needed in the practice of democracy, were achieved as the result of the processes used. Thus, committee work required pupils to learn to work together, to cooperate. At the same time, committees competed with each other in presenting interesting and challenging reports.

Students learned how to give and take, how to negotiate, and how to compromise. They found that implementation of the principles of democracy added to the well-being of all. Experience proved to the pupils that exercise of their right to share in making decisions and policy resulted in better feeling on the part of all concerned about those decisions. This decision-making experience also increased their stature and self-respect as individuals. Their need to feel of greater worth was met when I and their classmates accepted their ideas and suggestions and praised them for the quality of service, processes, and products.

I found that when I provided many learning experiences and much encouragement and reenforcement, many students performed more ably than I had thought they could. Moreover, many of them made a real effort to do their best and so become more competent. Although competence is required to achieve excellence, competence is also produced in the pursuit of excellence.

Among the by-products of the methods I used in unit teaching was the increasing faith of the boys and girls in themselves, in their classmates, and in me, their teacher. Moreover, we all soon began to pull together in striving for the same end—the full development of each individual pupil's potentiality.

Outcomes to Be Expected

If the methods of unit teaching and learning are used consistently in teaching about democracy, more boys and girls will have maximum opportunity to learn more, more easily. More of them should, therefore, be enabled to function more effectively in adult life. They will have acquired the following essentials for living the democratic way:

INFORMATION *about the facts, ideas, concepts, and general principles of American government and way of life.*

VALUES *that motivate the good life in the democratic tradition: of the individual person, of human similarity, of human difference, of law and order, of dissent without anger, of honesty and integrity in thought and action, of responsibility, of education.*

PROCESSES *used to carry on democracy: cooperation, competition, goal-setting, planning, work, study, discussion, decision-making, evaluation.*

SKILLS *needed to live the democratic way: leadership, voting for leaders on the basis of qualifications, ability to follow, making wise decisions as individuals and through the process of consensus, participating in discussion, and critical thinking—gathering facts from many sources, weighing them for relative values, challenging stereotypes and superstitions and testing them for reality, recognizing and analyzing propaganda, communicating across group lines, exercising responsibility to self and others.*

ATTITUDES *of acceptance rather than rejection of people across group lines.*

11

Summary of Methods of Teaching and Learning

UNIT TEACHING REQUIRES MANY AND varied activities on the part of the teacher. These activities differ markedly from those which are ordinarily used in subject-centered, departmentalized classrooms where the use of a textbook largely determines what the teacher does. In many classrooms he assigns study of the text, to be done at home; hears recitations on the text in class; conducts discussions which arise in connection with the questions at the end of the chapters in the text; constructs, administers tests, and marks test papers; and arranges for individuals to do special projects for extra credit.

In unit teaching, instead of concentrating on eight or ten kinds of things noted above, the teacher is called upon to do at least two dozen. Although they have been described in the preceding chapters, the following summary of them will help a teacher to plan his daily work.

Teaching Activities

1. He makes a preplanning survey and plans for daily work.
2. He makes clear to the class the limits of behavior, helps them to set up controls, recognizes and helps to develop emerging leadership, and retains ultimate responsibility for classroom discipline.
3. When necessary he gives information. This may be a formal presentation or the incidental help needed by individuals or committees.

4. He provides materials for classroom use: textbooks and reference and literature books; dictionaries and bibliographies of films; magazines, pamphlets, and newspapers; lists of sources from which to obtain people, materials, and services; pictures, charts, graphs; art supplies, mounting boards; implements and tools.

5. He teaches how to use printed materials to obtain information.

6. He delegates routine matters of distribution and collection of supplies and books to specific pupils and makes sure that they know how to do their jobs and that they fulfill their responsibilities.

7. He arranges time schedules, with the help of committee leaders, so that groups of pupils can meet, class discussions can be held, reports of committees can be given, and films, filmstrips, recordings, and radio and TV programs can be used according to committee plans.

8. He previews audio-visual materials before using them, presents films to the class, and leads discussion after viewing.

9. He meets with committee chairmen for leadership training, with committee recorders for review of their notes, with individual pupils who need individual instruction or help with their work, and with committees to help in their planning, pooling, and preparation of reports.

10. He leads and participates in class planning and evaluation discussions, and he helps the class to identify interests, to set up criteria and goals, to plan content and learning activities, to organize committees for work on the unit, and to find strength and weakness in themselves, their processes, and their products.

11. He demonstrates skills of leadership and discussion.

12. He reviews committee plans for such class activities as trips, speakers, and the use of consultants, and he assists committees in completing and carrying out plans that involve the whole class.

13. He helps the class to understand how to keep records of the unit and checks unit-record books or folders at frequent intervals.

14. He assigns and checks on the completion of work done outside of class (homework).

15. He makes suggestions of subjects for creative writing, sets up minimum requirements, reads and corrects compositions, themes, stories, and other written work.

16. He meets whatever needs for instruction and drill that he identifies. These include spelling, grammar, methods of study, outlining, methods of mobilizing facts from many sources (research), and reading.

17. He assists committees with ideas about collection and display, and helps them report on committee work.

18. He records what pupils say and do in order to detect prejudices, discriminatory behavior, and changes therein.

19. He sets up role-playing and leads discussion about the issues and problems demonstrated.

20. He provides and administers such diagnostic instruments as social distance tests, projective exercises, and discussion of social episode pictures.
21. He constructs, administers, and marks whatever essay and objective tests he needs to determine what learning is taking place, mistaken ideas which need to be corrected, and confusions which need to be clarified.
22. He pulls together the various parts of the unit while it is in progress, and upon its completion, he sees that learnings are integrated and meanings are discovered and understood.
23. In order to lead into action projects, he raises such questions as, "What can you, the individual, do?"
24. He makes daily records of what has been done and a final record of the entire unit. Records include his evaluation of content covered, processes used, and the outcomes in terms of his goals.

Pupil Activities

Unit teaching places responsibility for learning on the pupil. Learning results from many kinds of experiences in which all pupils can participate. However, unit teaching also provides a variety of activities to fit individual abilities.

The following lists should help the teacher to visualize what the students do in response to the many teaching-learning situations which he creates. It also indicates quite conclusively that pupils *do* work in classrooms where there is freedom to live and learn.

Activities in which all pupils can engage:

1. Browse in books and magazines prior to planning sessions.
2. Participate in teacher-pupil planning discussions whenever planning is done by the class or by a committee.
3. Take part in election of leaders.
4. Participate in setting up goals and criteria and in evaluation of self, of process, of products.
5. Accept and fulfill responsibilities for getting facts, doing home assignments, bringing materials and equipment to class.
6. Read newspapers, magazines, pamphlets and books. (The number and reading level will depend on individual abilities.)
7. Keep records of individual work, of facts reported to the class by committees, and of other learning experiences connected with the unit in progress.
8. See and participate in discussion of films; hear and discuss recordings, radio and TV programs, and speakers.

9. Interview parents and other adults in the family and neighborhood.
10. Go on trips with the class.
11. Take part in spontaneous dramatics and role-playing.
12. Do creative writing. (The subject, length, and number will depend upon individual abilities.)
13. Do whatever drill work is assigned: spelling, grammar, and the like.
14. Take tests.

Activities which can be assigned to fit
individual abilities and interests:

(Starred items are especially appropriate for gifted pupils.)

*1. Leadership of committees.
*2. Recording proceedings of committee meetings.
*3. Reporting committee work to the class.
 4. Clipping articles and pictures.
 5. Filing articles and pictures.
*6. Art work: illustrations, murals, maps, graphs, posters, charts.
 7. Making, arranging, displaying collections of pictures, posters, editorials, cartoons, and other items pertinent to the unit being studied.
 8. Setting up bulletin boards.
*9. Writing letters to or telephoning speakers, agencies, organizations, business, and industry to request materials and services and to arrange for interviews and trips.
*10. Attending relevant meetings outside of school hours.
*11. Leading and participating in panel discussions.
*12. Interviewing community leaders and visitors to the school.
*13. Assisting classmates when they need help.
 14. Doing housekeeping tasks.
 15. Distributing and collecting books, other publications, and materials.

REFERENCES

1. Ahmann, John S. and Marvin D. Glock, *Evaluating Pupil Growth*. Rockley, N.J.: Allyn and Bacon, Inc., 1958.

2. Allport, Gordon, *The Nature of Prejudice*. Reading, Mass.: Addison-Wesley Publishing Co., Inc., 1954.

3. Association for Supervision and Curriculum Development, *Learning and the Teacher*. Washington, D.C.: ASCD, 1956.

4. ————, *Perceiving, Behaving, Becoming*. Washington, D.C.: ASCD, 1962.

5. Burton, William H., Ronald B. Kimball, and Richard L. Wing, *Education for Effective Thinking*. New York: Appleton-Century-Crofts, Inc., 1960.

6. Coleman, S. J., *The Adolescent Society*. New York: The Macmillan Co., 1962.

7. *Free and Inexpensive Learning Materials*. Nashville, Tenn.: Division of Services, Peabody College for Teachers, 1962.

8. Getzels, J. W. and P. E. Jackson, *Creativity and Intelligence*. New York: John Wiley & Sons, Inc., 1962.

9. Hall, D. M., *The Dynamics of Group Discussion*. Danville, Ill.: The Interstate Printers and Publishers, Inc., 1950.

10. Havighurst, Robert, *Developmental Tasks and Education*. Chicago: University of Chicago Press, 1948.

11. ———, *Human Development and Education*. New York: Longmans, Green & Co., Inc., 1953.

12. Heaton, Margaret and Helen Lewis, *Reading Ladders for Human Relations*. Washington, D.C.: American Council on Education, 1955.

13. Hoch, L. E. and T. J. Hill, *The General Education Class in the Secondary School*. New York: Holt, Rinehart and Winston, Inc., 1960.

14. Hopkins, L. Thomas, *The Emerging Self*. New York: Harper & Row, 1954.

15. Howell, William S. and Donald K. Smith, *Discussion*. New York: The Macmillan Co., 1956.

16. Hughes, Marie and Associates, *The Assessment of the Quality of Teaching: A Research Report*. Salt Lake City: University of Utah Press, 1959.

17. Jennings, Helen Hall, *et al.*, *Sociometry in Group Relations*, rev. ed. Washington, D.C.: American Council on Education, 1959.

18. Lee, Dorothey, *Freedom and Culture*. Englewood Cliffs, N.J.: Prentice-Hall, Inc., 1959.

19. Lifton, Walter M., *Working With Groups: Group Process and Individual Growth* (Science Research Association). New York: John Wiley & Sons, Inc., 1962.

20. Mallery, David, *New Approaches in Education*. Boston: National Council of Independent Schools (84 State St.), 1961.

21. McCutchen, Samuel P., George L. Fersh, and Nadine Clark, *Goals of Democracy*. New York: The Macmillan Co., 1962.

22. Miel, Alice, ed., *Cooperative Procedures in Learning*. New York: Bureau of Publications, Teachers College, Columbia University, 1952.

23. ———, *Creativity in Teaching*. San Francisco: Wadsworth Publishing Co., Inc., 1961.

24. Murphy, Gardner, *Freeing Intelligence Through Teaching*. New York: Harper & Row, 1961.

25. Musselman, Dayton L., *et al.*, *Improving the High School Curriculum Through Unit Teaching*. Lexington, Ky.: College of Education, University of Ky., 1952.

26. Nelson, Henry B., ed., *The Dynamics of Instructional Groups*, 59th. Yr. Bk., Pt. II. Washington, D.C.: National Society for the Study of Education, 1960.

27. ———, *Individualizing Instruction*, 62nd. Yr. Bk., Pt. I. Washington, D.C.: National Society for the Study of Education, 1962.

28. Noar, Gertrude, *Freedom to Live and Learn*. Philadelphia: Franklin Publishing Co., 1948.

29. ———,*The Junior High School Today and Tomorrow*, 2nd ed. Englewood Cliffs, N.J.: Prentice-Hall, Inc., 1961.

30. Patterson, Franklin, *High Schools for a Free Society*. Glencoe, Ill.: Free Press of Glencoe, Inc., 1960.

31. Rothney, John, *Evaluating and Reporting Pupil Progress*. Washington, D.C.: National Education Association, 1955.

32. Stember, Charles H., *Education and Attitude Change*. New York: Institute of Human Relations Press, 1961.

33. Taba, Hilda, *et al.*, *Diagnosing Human Relations Needs*. Washington, D.C.: American Council on Education, 1951.

34. ———, *Intergroup Education in Public Schools*. Washington, D.C.: American Council on Education, 1952.

35. "Teen Age Culture," *The Annals*. Philadelphia: American Academy of Political and Social Science, Nov., 1961.

36. Thorndike, Robert L. and Elizabeth Hagen, *Measurement and Evaluation in Psychology and Education*, 2nd ed. New York: John Wiley & Sons, Inc., 1961.

37. Warner, Lloyd, Robert J. Havighurst, and Martin B. Loeb, *Who Shall Be Educated?* New York: Harper & Row, 1944.

38. Wrightstone, Wayne J., *Class Organization for Instruction*. Washington, D.C.: National Education Association, 1959.

39. Zapf, Rosalind M., *Democratic Process in the Secondary Classroom*. Englewood Cliffs, N.J.: Prentice-Hall, Inc., 1959.

PART TWO

Ideas, Concepts, and Principles Related to Teaching

12

Facts Teachers Need
to Remember

IMPROVEMENT OF DEMOCRACY AS A way of life for all citizens requires that both the school and the community accept responsibility for intergroup education. However, the school is the place, and for some the only place in which children meet people who differ from themselves in race, religion, ethnic origins, and social class. It is, therefore, the place in which positive attitudes towards human differences can be created. There children can learn from experience which kinds of differences in and of themselves are not valid reasons for rejection. There, too, as the result of experiencing respect for every individual, of finding a place of significance in the mixed group, of deriving satisfaction from democratic group processes, the individual becomes committed to democracy.

Teachers are people of good will. They recognize their responsibility for providing every child with full opportunity to develop his unknown potentialities, to prove himself of ever greater worth, and to learn the way of democratic life. The shortcomings of teachers that most often impede their accomplishments are caused by lack of insight into the nature of emotional needs common to all people, lack of information regarding the culture patterns of the various groups in our society, and lack of awareness of what causes blocks to learning. Professors of teacher-education should devote more time

119

and emphasis to the relationships of people to each other in the learning situation if these shortcomings are to be overcome.

During years of supervising and assisting classroom teachers, and in a decade of meetings with teachers, supervisors, and administrators across the nation, it has been continually demonstrated to the author that teachers need a ready source of facts about the child, about his relationships, and about the society in which he has his being. Although the requisite information, principles, and concepts undoubtedly were included in their college courses on education, psychology, and sociology, facts are easily forgotten, especially in the absence of opportunities to apply them. Once the teacher reaches a classroom, he meets actual situations and problems which involve human relations. Then time and energy are short, and reference books are apt not to be at hand. Moreover, it is difficult to synthesize learnings from the several disciplines quickly enough to meet an immediate need.

The following simplified statements provide summaries of concepts and principles for the teacher. They can also be used at the college level, in methods courses. Some of them are categorical and may seem to be oversimplified. They are neither complete nor exhaustive and, obviously, are not an attempt to state all that is known about the large problem areas they summarize.

Questionnaires returned by teachers in their second year of classroom work to a research committee of the North Central Association of Colleges and Secondary Schools reveal large gaps in their information about the subjects discussed in the following pages.[1] Many had no background of experience with people different from themselves. They were hindered by lack of information about culture patterns. They had little insight into motivations. They were frustrated by lack of skill in teaching children who differed in abilities. Many either did not recognize the nature of tensions and anxieties involved in human relations or, when they did so, lacked the know-how of relieving them. Inservice education must be provided for these teachers. Principals and supervisors entrusted with that responsibility will find that each of the following groups of concepts and principles can be used as the framework upon which to build faculty study and discussion. In schools where teachers

[1] Human Relations in the Classroom, North Central Association, Chicago, Ill., 1963.

embark on the kind of unit teaching described in Part One, all concerned will need to become familiar with this material, which can then be used to motivate and evaluate classroom work.

The professor who is responsible for student teachers will find he frequently faces the necessity of tying together and integrating what has been presented to his students in many other courses. The concepts and principles discussed in this section can give student teachers insight into problems that confront the classroom teacher. In methods courses these concepts and principles will be useful as a framework upon which to structure teaching while the students seek answers to their question, "How shall we teach?"

THE CHILD

Human relations in education center around and in the child. So, in fact, should every aspect of classroom work. In the past fifty years the center of interest in curriculum development has shifted from course content to the child. Teachers have come to regard the school as "child-centered" and have accepted the idea that *all* of him, not just his brain, has to be taken into consideration if he is to learn. Moreover, they know that the child must be regarded as an entity, which nevertheless is influenced by his cultural heritage, his immediate family, and the community in which he lives. They know that what he is and how he relates to people affect the amount and kind of learning he can do.

Unit teaching provides many opportunities for the teacher to see how the child (or teenager) reacts to other people. Moreover, it enables the teacher to arrange many varied learning experiences during which the child (or teenager) can try out various behavior patterns and establish relationships with members of the peer group. When the teacher has the chance to observe these reactions, he can discover both prejudices and positive attitudes. On the basis of such discoveries, he is able to devise corrective groupings and to use units of learning concerned with various aspects of human relations. These will provide what the pupil needs: information, insight, and skills. How much children do need good intergroup understandings and relationships was evident in the answer given by a boy to the question, "What do you like best in school?" He said, "The games because in them even unfriendly friends become friendlier."

The following ideas, principles, and concepts will help the teacher understand and provide for the child.

About the Child

Each child is unique—different from all others.

He is the product of his genes, of his cultural roots and patterns, and of his present environment.

The actual potentialities of a child are not known, nor can they be accurately and fully measured with instruments now available. Intelligence, for example, is known to include more than 61 attributes. Group I.Q. tests now being used in most schools measure possibly 6 or 7 and rely heavily upon verbal ability and memory. Individual I.Q. tests measure about 9 or 10 of the attributes. Moreover, there are many kinds of intellectual abilities.

Research indicates that creative ability is not diagnosed by the commonly used I.Q. tests. Furthermore, evidence shows that those abilities which are required for success in school are not the same as those needed for success on the job.

The child's concept of himself begins to form very early in life. It is the result of what has been said to and about him, done to, about, and for him, and experiences which bring him success. Thus, the child who is loved sees himself to be likeable. Self-acceptance is almost impossible for a child who is rejected by others.

Since the self-image is a factor which heavily influences behavior, it may facilitate or block learning in school. The child who says "I can" rather than "I can't" is motivated and can at least try to do assigned tasks. The child who is successful sees himself as adequate and worthy.

Very few children who are admitted to school are unable to learn. Growth and development are normal and continue, at rates which vary among individuals, both in spite of and because of school and other experiences. When, in school, a child seems to have no desire to learn, or learning seems to have stopped, a search for the causes should be undertaken.

.   .   .

REFERENCES

Allport, Gordon, *Personality and the Social Encounter*. New York: Basic Books, Inc., 1958.

Conant, James B., *The Child, the Parent and the State*. Cambridge, Mass.: Harvard University Press, 1960.

Gesell, Arnold, Frances Ilg, and Louise B. Ames, *Youth: the Years from Ten to Sixteen*. New York: Harper & Row, 1956.

Getzels, Jacob W. and Philip W. Jackson, *Creativity and Intelligence: Explorations With Gifted Students*. New York: John Wiley & Sons, Inc., 1962.

Harris, Irving D., *Emotional Blocks to Learning*. New York: Free Press of Glencoe, Inc., 1962.

Rasey, Marie I. and J. W. Menge, *What We Learn from Children*. New York: Harper & Row, 1956.

Stavsky, W. H., *Using the Insights of Psychotherapy in Teaching*, *Elementary School Journal*, October, 1957, pp. 28-35.

LEARNING

The objective of the classroom teacher is that his pupils learn. Never have the people of this country been entirely satisfied that a sufficient number of the young learn as much as they should, fast enough. This has led to research on the nature of the teaching process and, probably of greater importance, on the nature of learning. Too often, however, the teacher concentrates his attention on what *he* does rather than on what and how the *child learns*. One of the myths about education is that children learn what the teacher teaches.

In unit teaching more emphasis is placed on what the *learner* does. The teacher is responsible for setting up many varied learning situations and activities, with providing the materials and equipment needed by the learner, with helping the individual to understand, to search, to see, to develop the skills of living and learning, and to evaluate.

Unit teaching makes use of processes in which the learner experiences group activities which characterize democratic life. Moreover, it affords maximum opportunities for more children to learn more, about more, more easily because use is made of vicarious and direct learning experiences in addition to learning by word symbol. The teacher does well who keeps in mind the following concepts and principles.

About Learning

Learning results from experience—from direct and vicarious experience and from experience with the use of word symbols. The last of these is the most difficult. Children differ with respect to the way they learn most easily; their rate of learning; what interests them; what is important to them. Learning takes place more easily when the child has identified his own goals and participates in planning how to reach them. Learning should be made pleasurable. It is so when the experience has in it elements that are new and stimulating and when the individual sees in it the possibility of success and growth toward achieving his own purposes.

Learning is motivated by success rather than failure. The reward of knowing that one's effort has produced a good result or the right answer needs to come quickly. The words and facial expression with which the teacher acknowledges the value of a contribution to discussion is a reward. (The word "alright," most frequently used by teachers, is not sufficient.) The reward also is the mark and the comments placed on a test or other written work. Delay in returning such papers to the students, may cancel much of the value of such a reward.

Failure ultimately inhibits initiative and effort, destroys interest, and creates despair. This does not mean that a poor piece of work should be given a good mark or that less gifted children be given only easy work to do. It does mean that the task given to a child must be within the possibility of his accomplishment. Punishment and the threat of failure produce different results at different times and different results with different children. They do not always have the effect the teacher desires.

Some kinds of learnings cannot take place until the individual is sufficiently emotionally, physiologically, socially, or intellectually mature. Some authorities express this by saying that the individual's learning is selective in terms of his own internal organization; that out of each experience he takes only what he is prepared and able to integrate with what he already knows.

Factual material usually is rapidly forgotten unless it is recalled soon and often.

Competition and cooperation in the classroom are processes which motivate learning. Both are important in our society. More and more teamwork is being required of adults in business, industry, science, and the professions. Cooperation in family living is essential.

Achievement and accomplishment are deep-seated emotional needs common to all children. They produce satisfactions which motivate the individual to identify goals in other aspects of his life and to work to achieve them. Deprivation of satisfaction of the need to achieve and accomplish may cause aggression, withdrawal, or psychosomatic illness. Children who have no success in school come to regard themselves as inadequate and unworthy people.

Age-mates often are effective teachers. Teaching classmates or group-mates cements learning for the gifted child, produces a sense of power and satisfaction, and provides both the experience of sharing oneself with others and the joy of service. Gifted children need encouragement and opportunities to become progressively self-directive learners.

.   .   .

REFERENCES

Association for Supervision and Curriculum Development, *Learning and the Teacher* Yr. Bk. Washington, D.C.: ASCD, 1958.

Bettelheim, Bruno, "The Decision to Fail," *School Review*. Winter, 1961, pp. 377-412.

Burton, William H., *The Guidance of Learning Activities*, 3rd. ed. New York: Appleton-Century-Crofts, Inc., 1962.

Dunn, L. M., "The Slow Learner," *N.E.A. Journal*. Oct. 1959, pp. 19-21.

Hopkins, Thomas, *The Emerging Self*. New York: Harper & Row, 1954.

Hullfish, Gordon and P. G. Smith, *Reflective Thinking: The Method of Education*. New York: Dodd, Mead & Co., 1961.

Klausmeier, H. J., *Learning and Human Abilities*. New York: Harper & Row, 1961.

Litcher, Solomon, Elsie Rapien, Frances Seibert, and Morris Sklansky, *The Drop Outs*. New York: The MacMillan Co., 1962.

Mayer, Martin, *The Schools*. New York: Harper & Row, 1961.

Nelson, Henry B., ed., *Learning and Instruction*. Chicago: University of Chicago Press, 1950.

Trow, William Clark, *The Learning Process*. Washington, D.C.: National Education Association, 1954.

BEHAVIOR

Nothing gives the classroom teacher greater concern than what he calls misbehavior. Some young teachers believe that children who do not obey their commands, who do not bring their books to school, who do not learn what, when, and how they are told to learn, who whisper and talk, who quarrel with or tease their classmates, who use bad language and break the Ten Commandments are all maladjusted. The child is often blamed for his misconduct. The fault is said to lie in him or in his parents.

Causes of behavior problems are often neither sought nor understood. They may lie in deprivation of the chance to talk with classmates; in seeing only the backs of classmates' heads; in having to listen to the teacher lecture too much; in having no chance to move around; in seeing no connection between school work and the reality of life; in failing, failing, failing. Some such causes are absent in classrooms where unit teaching is used; therefore, fewer discipline problems are likely to arise.

The methods employed in the unit make use, essentially, of the democratic processes. These require all pupils to share in determining the goals and in deciding who shall do what. When the adolescent student says, "This is what *I want* to do" and "This is what *I will* do," he is much more likely to proceed with learning than when the teacher says, "This is what *I* want you to do." Moreover, the democratic way calls for consent of the participants. Pupils who participate in discussion, consensus, and voting learn to use their privileges and to accept their responsibilities.

Human behavior is essentially a matter of human relationships. The teacher who would deal successfully with all pupils must keep in mind the principles and concepts in the following discussion.

About Behavior

The individual most frequently behaves as he sees and imagines himself to be. His behavior is also affected by his ability to see alternatives, to think about them critically, and to make choices in terms of the consequences he envisions. Obviously, then, both emotional maturity and intellectual development play their respective roles.

When a child or youth has been unsuccessful in school, has been rejected by his peers or his teachers, or has suffered from being treated as the underdog at home, he often leads a fantasy life in which he is the leader to whom others look up and follow. In this daydream he may see himself beating up and destroying someone whom he deems to be of lesser worth than he is. This is likely to be a member of a different race or religion. Then, if an occasion should arise, he may act out his daydream in violence against people and/or property.

Some people are highly suggestible. Thus, a story of one act of violence committed, for example, against a minority group, which is spread across the newspapers and TV screen, replete with pictures and other details, gives to the suggestible person an idea upon which he may then proceed to act.

Feelings of guilt need to be alleviated. A scapegoat provides relief from guilt feelings. Some children and youth are ridden with guilt feelings over such things as their own sex activities and feelings; their school failures; their defiance of parents and teachers; and other actions considered by family, peers, and associates to be socially unacceptable. When feelings of guilt and shame mount up, such a child is apt to commit an overt infraction of rules, such as stealing or destroying property. Moreover, he is likely to do these things in such a way that his detection is easy. The punishment he suffers eases his guilt feelings for the time being.

Excessive anxiety which a child or youth cannot reduce, channel, or control may cause impulsive behavior. Then, for example, as he passes by a synagogue or the school which may represent to him people whom he does not like or whom he has heard his parents blame for their own failure to succeed, he may impulsively seize a stone and throw it at a window, or pick up a paint brush and use it to smear the building with swastikas.

Some persons are blocked in their emotional development and remain at the infantile level. At the age of two or three it is normal for children to destroy things. Ordinarily, as they mature they give up taking things apart and enjoy putting things together. However, should a child be blocked in developing emotional maturity, he may continue to be destructive. Therefore, teachers in school must examine what they can do to remove such blocks and to promote maturity.

Constant failure, suppression, repression, and rejection in school or at home create hostility. The individual so treated often cannot vent his anger and hatred on those who cause it. Instead, he may attack property—especially the kind valued by adults, such as churches, schools, synagogues, and tombstones. School and society help people to release hostility by providing such activities as team sports and interscholastic athletics. The school must also find the way to provide acceptance and success for all the children of all the people.

Some successful and otherwise controlled children, especially in adolescence, may act in terms of a group will. The peer group exerts strong influence upon its members. To be in a gang and, even more, to be its leader is recognition and acceptance deeply desired by many adolescents. Once an individual achieves such a position, he or she may be pushed into behavior known to be wrong in an effort to consolidate a position of strength and leadership or for fear of losing status. Under such circumstances, a "good kid" can act like a sick child.

*   *   *

REFERENCES

Del Castillo, M., *Child of Our Times.* New York: Alfred A. Knopf, Inc., 1958.

Erickson, E. H., *Childhood and Society.* New York: W. W. Norton & Company, Inc., 1953.

Fine, Benjamin, *1,000,000 Delinquents*. New York: The World Publishing Co., 1955.

Kounin, J. and P. Gump, "The Ripple Effect in Discipline," *The Elementary School Journal*, Dec. 1958, pp. 158-162.

Robison, S. M., *Juvenile Delinquency: Its Nature and Control*. New York: Holt, Rinehart & Winston, 1960.

Sheviakov, George and Fritz Redl, *Discipline For Today's Children*. Washington, D.C.: National Education Association, 1958.

Smith, R. P., *"Where Did You Go?" "Out." "What Did You Do?" "Nothing."* W. W. Norton & Company, Inc., 1953.

Snygg, Donald and Arthur Combs, *"Individual Behavior."* New York: Harper & Row, 1959.

Sources of Information on Behavioral Problems of Adolescence. Washington, D.C.: American Psychiatric Association, 1960.

Stone, Joseph L. and Joseph Church, *Childhood and Adolescence.* New York: Random House, Inc., 1957.

ABILITIES

Although for many years teachers have been told by professors, supervisors, and administrators that they must provide for individual differences in abilities of all kinds, except where unit teaching is going on, mass instruction is the most commonly used classroom method. As a result, able students who are not challenged become bored and indifferent. Those who have less complex minds, who cannot learn as much and as rapidly as the so-called average group, fail. They become apathetic and doubtful of their own worth. Pupils with much and with little ability become cynical about the value of education and about the democratic principles and values which the school is responsible for teaching.

Unit teaching calls for a wide range of reading materials to meet the needs of the wide range of reading levels and interests found in most classrooms. It becomes legitimate and respectable for pupils to seek facts from many sources, those that are easy to read as well as those that are difficult, from films, pictures, radio, TV, and from people. Consequently, all the pupils are enabled to participate in discussions. Sharing of facts learned and of work done according to one's abilities and sharing one's abilities and talents with others becomes a way of life—the democratic way. At the same time, each finds satisfaction and reward in doing his best.

Unit teaching uses sub-groups to accomplish many different purposes. Pupils of many kinds of abilities find themselves needed and wanted. The need for leaders for various kinds of work affords many pupils opportunities to develop the skills required to lead the many mixed groups that must function in our democratic society.

Grouping by ability goes on within the classroom when small groups may be needed for very specific purposes which require a special kind of ability. For example a group talented in art will create a mural while another talented in English will write a play.

When pupils are placed in separate classes on the basis of tests and marks, wide differences in many kinds of abilities still remain. Teachers who desire to fulfill the promise of democracy to give equal opportunities for all children to develop their abilities will keep in mind the following concepts and principles.

About Abilities (as related to race, religion, ethnic origins, and social class)

There are no superior races. Individuals can be found in every group who have all kinds of abilities. The ranges are large. There is no point of normality but, rather, a range of normality. People in all races, religions, social classes, and nationality groups vary from the lowest point to the highest in respect to general intelligence (I.Q.), artistic ability, musical genius, mathematical sense, creativity, inventiveness, athletic ability, writing, and all the other mental and physical characteristics of mankind.

The I.Q. test score is not permanent and unchangeable. Research indicates that social-cultural experience, motivation, nutrition, initiative, and aggressiveness affect it.

The lower social classes include two-thirds of the pupils in the elementary schools. Among them are large numbers of gifted children with all kinds and degrees of potentialities and ability including superior intelligence. Many of those who are in the lowest class find school uncomfortable and are neither happy nor successful there.

Development of potentiality depends upon environment. The extent of the opportunity provided by environment plays an important part in intellectual growth. The school may be called upon to supply certain kinds of social and cultural opportunities to children whose environments do not offer these opportunities.

Blocks to learning and development may be created by faulty nutrition; meager cultural opportunities in the home and community; parental indifference to education; rejection by parents, teachers, peers, and society; feelings of inferiority and insecurity owing to second class citizenship in our society; lack of motivation owing to inferior social and civic status; constant failure which creates a self-concept characterized by "I can't" rather than "I can"; and chronically high levels of anxiety.

Pupils vary from one another in their rate of growth and in the timing of developmental changes which affect growth, for example, there are so-called late-bloomers. Much variation also exists in the complexity of mind and in the ultimate level of mental development which the individual may be able to attain. To these factors must also be added the effects of brain damage suffered by many children. This may occur before or at birth or from childhood diseases and head injuries.

Minority-group and lower-class children suffer more than others from inequalities of opportunity in education. For example:

—They often attend physically inferior schools. The school building itself affects learning. Some are new and designed to promote learning; others are old and dilapidated and without the equipment and materials teachers need to do their best work. This is not to deny that fine schools can exist in old buildings, but poor facilities are hardly the cause of good schools. In many places the most inadequate buildings are in old and deteriorated sections of the community where children are also most culturally deprived and in which some minority groups and lower classes tend to cluster.

—Not enough scholarships exist for both high school and college to take care of all the able children of minority groups and the lower classes.

—Minority-group and lower-class children often lack sufficient personal funds to enable them to participate in school functions and activities and in youth groups.

—When teacher judgment determines placement, in many cases, minority-group children and those with lower-class backgrounds are downgraded because of the teacher's conscious or subconscious expectations, prejudices, and stereotypes. If placement is determined by I.Q. score, these children may also be handicapped because I.Q. is in turn affected by cultural experience, nutrition, and motivation.

—The amount of encouragement afforded in the home frequently affects the child's progress and often determines drop out. The home environment of many lower-class and minority-group children does not provide a place to study, books, tools, art equipment, musical instruments, or money to supply extra needs.

. . .

REFERENCES

Bardolph, Richard, *The Negro Vanguard*. New York: Random House, Inc., Vintage Books, 1961.

Ginsberg, Eli, *The Negro Potential*. New York: Columbia University Press, 1956.

Murphy, Gardiner, *Human Potentiality*. Boston: Beacon Press, 1958.

Nelson, Henry B., ed., *Education for the Gifted*, 58th Yr. Bk., Pt. II. Washington, D.C.: National Society for the Study of Education, 1958.

North Research Report, *Intelligence of the American Negro*. New York: Anti-Defamation League of B'nai B'rith, 1957.

THE STRUCTURE OF AMERICAN SOCIETY

Many classroom teachers have not had a single course in sociology. Some more recent graduates have had courses called "School and Society" or "Social Foundations." Nevertheless, large numbers now in service seem to have little information about the class and caste structure of American society. Some prefer to think of it as classless. They lack understanding of lower-class children and of the value patterns that motivate their behavior.

Young teachers, when asked about the human relations problems with which they are confronted, often talk about the difficulty they have in meeting with the parents of their lower-class pupils and of accepting the speech and language habits of those people. Teachers are, for the most part, middle-class people who believe that middle-class values and culture patterns are "normal" and must therefore, be accepted by all their pupils.

When the school population is mixed, teachers are disturbed by the formation of social cliques and by the patterns of rejection and exclusion that develop. Many of them, however, do not have the information or skill required to create better relations across group lines.

Many teachers equate academic ability with socio-economic class. When pupils of the upper-middle class do not succeed, they attribute it to apathy or defiance. When lower-class pupils are bright, they are surprised. They place blame for shortcomings on the student and fail to recognize the results of cultural deprivation. In the lower social classes of all races and ethnic groups, however, are large numbers of high ability people whose talents the nation needs. The philosophy of cultural pluralism emphasizes the values these so-called minority groups have brought to our society. In accordance with it, teachers are developing units of learning which give pupils the chance to explore the realities of economic and social life in America. In such units the principle of social mobility and the use of education to raise one's social class level can be made clear and should add motivation to lower-class students. Learning about work being done by governmental and voluntary human relations and civil rights agencies to remove restrictions that now impede progress for some will help to replace despair with hope for the future.

Basic to all understanding of class and caste should be the democratic principles: the worth and integrity of every human being; the right of every person to share in civic life, responsibility, and policy making; the right of the individual to decide what he shall become. The teacher engaged in units of work on the structure of American society should keep in mind the following concepts and ideas.

About the Structure of American Society

Sociologists have described American society as divided into three main classes—upper, middle and lower. In our society social class differences are both economic and cultural. However, the horizontal lines between the classes are not rigid or completely forbidding. Much more difficult barriers are erected between the races and, to some extent, between religious groups. These vertical walls which tend to prevent free and intimate association are becoming less impenetrable as we learn to implement the principle of the worth, integrity, and dignity of every human being. However, the highest social prestige value is accorded to white, Protestant, Anglo-Saxon lineage.

Social mobility, that is, moving from one class to another, is a powerful force which motivates many but not all children. In our society, people regard upward mobility as a positive good. Children who are downwardly mobile are often regarded as antisocial, even predelinquent. Social mobility makes America an *open-class* society. Economics play a major role in determining to which class a family belongs. Education, marriage, and wealth operate in achieving upward mobility. To belong to the upper-upper class, a family must derive from the founders of the nation and perpetuate its heritage of wealth and prestige.

The American school and many youth agencies emphasize and try to teach middle-class culture and value patterns to all children and they encourage upward mobility. This at times creates confusion, conflict, and rebellion on the part of lower-class pupils.

Social classes differ somewhat in value patterns. For example, they differ with regards to the grammar that is acceptable and the use of profanity; with respect to such traits as cleanliness and promptness; with relation to sex permissiveness. Punishment of children for behavior linked to social-class culture patterns should be avoided. Behavior change will be accomplished most easily if it is linked to the student's own goals.

The philosophy of the melting pot now pertains largely to political ideologies. In other words, newcomers to America are expected to become committed in philosophy, word, and deed to American democracy.

The philosophy of cultural pluralism, which emphasizes the value of difference, operates in other aspects of American life. In accordance with it, the school especially encourages minority group children to be proud of their own cultural, religious, and racial backgrounds and to learn the language, songs, dances, and literature of their ethnic groups. This philosophy instead of emphasizing similarity places value on human differences. The diversity of people is seen as contributing strength to the nation.

．　．　．

REFERENCES

Davis, Allison, *Social Class Influences Upon Learning*. Cambridge: Harvard University Press, 1948.

Gottman, Jean, *Megalopolis*. New York: Twentieth Century Fund, 1961.

Hollingshead, A. B., *Elmtown's Youth*. New York: John Wiley & Sons, Inc., 1949.

Klausner, S. J., "Social Class and Self-Concept," *Journal of Social Psychology*, Nov., 1953, pp. 201-205.

Packard, Vance, *The Status Seekers*. Philadelphia: David McKay Co., Inc., 1957.

Stendler, Celia B., *Children of Brasstown*. Urbana, Ill. University of Illinois Press, 1949.

Warner, Lloyd W., *Social Class in America: A Manual of Procedure for the Measurement of Social Status*. New York: Harper & Row, Torch Books, 1960.

————, Robert Havighurst, and Martin Loeb, *Who Shall Be Educated?* New York: Harper & Row, 1944.

MINORITY GROUP CHILDREN IN SCHOOL

In the large cities of the nation, many teachers must be assigned to classrooms in schools with mixed populations. In New York, Philadelphia, Detroit, Chicago, and Los Angeles, for example, the heart of the city is becoming increasingly nonwhite. Many of the families living there are Negro, Puerto Rican, Chinese, or other orientals. In the Southwest and West, large numbers are Spanish speaking people of Mexican origin and American Indians. Wherever industry and farming require seasonal labor, there are migrant families of several different ethnic origins. All of these people are called minority groups. Although the lower classes constitute roughly one third of the nation, teachers tend to think of these children as a minority group. (To teachers, ours is a middle class society.) Moreover, a large proportion of the racial minority group is also lower class. Because of the similarity of educational problems, we have linked the two for discussion.

Many smaller cities have small but growing concentrations of minorities. In them, as in the large cities, the minority groups are likely to be restricted to certain neighborhoods of inferior housing which undergo constant change and, therefore, deteriorate, as people move into and around in them.

Especially the young and inexperienced teachers in the cities are confronted with children, teenagers, and parents whose ways of life, value systems, and behavior patterns are strange to them. They struggle to teach them the prescribed courses and to maintain standards. They are unaware of the effects of cultural deprivation on tests score, motivations, and effort. They are also unaware of the effect of discrimination and second-class citizenship on the individual's self-concept, which makes him feel and act inferior. Yet all the minority groups which came to these shores contributed to the nation's strength. And by recognizing the value of cultural pluralism, many teachers are helping minority group pupils to identify with their groups, to learn about the cultures from which they stem, and to be proud of themselves and their origins.

Unit teaching of intergroup relations enables the teacher to arrange for pupils to work together across group lines. As, together, they identify common problems, set up goals they want to reach, experience leadership on the basis of qualifications, enjoy cooperative effort, and serve each other, ethnic, racial, religious, and social class differences are forgotten. Equality of status is accorded to all. The worth and significance of the individual is realized.

Units on prejudice, discrimination, race, human rights, interfaith tensions, and other aspects of intergroup relations are close to reality for minority-group pupils. When these units include social action and result in both attitude and behavior change, all who are involved come to see the meaning and value of the democratic way.

The teacher who plans to do something about negative attitudes, group prejudices, stereotypes, name-calling, tensions, hostilities, and the resultant anxieties that block learning will find the following concepts, and principles helpful.

About Minority-group Children in School

Like all others, the children of minority groups need to feel liked, accepted, wanted, needed by their teachers and their peers. The example set by the teacher of acceptance or rejection of minority groups is likely to be followed by the children.

Minority-group children are apt to feel inferior in some ways and at some times unless they are given full opportunity to be accepted as worthy, for themselves alone. Their equality of status must be established and maintained.

These pupils, like all others, behave largely as they perceive themselves to be. Many, because of the status of their groups in our society, believe themselves to be inferior. Feelings of inferiority about color, for example, are likely to be transmitted to four year olds along with the values attached to words. For example, white in our language is better than black; light is better than dark; and brown is apt to be associated with dirty.

Other associations need to be made, and children need to be taught that such meanings do not apply to the color of people. The teacher must never indicate by word or deed, gesture or facial expression, or by the other intangibles that convey attitude that, because of the child's differences or the differences of the groups to which he belongs, any child is of lesser worth to the teacher, to the class, or to society.

Minority group children suffer from name-calling and scapegoating. When there is only one such child in a classroom, he may play a mascot role, be called cute, or be made a pet, or be used as a symbol because of his difference. This may be as unwholesome an experience as being the scapegoat who is blamed for all wrongdoing, who is bullied or punished because of his difference.

An individual child should never be prejudged according to a group stereotype. For example, a child should not be deemed lazy, musical, or mentally inferior (or the reverse) because of his race or religion.

Individual children should not be asked to bear guilt for their group. For example, teachers when reproving a child, should avoid saying to him: "You are bringing shame on your race." Or "Your whole group will suffer from what you have done." Or, "Your family will be disgraced."

Minority-group pupils want the teacher to see and treat them as children, not as Jews or Negroes or Italians or Mexicans. They want to be praised or punished when they deserve it and in the same measure as the other children in the class.

Teachers who understand and appreciate the nature of our pluralistic society will also accept the value of difference. Information about the culture patterns of the minority groups from which their pupils come is helpful to them.

. . .

REFERENCES

Allport, Gordon, *The Resolutions of Intergroup Tensions.* New York: National Conference of Christians and Jews.

Conant, James B., *Slums and Suburbs.* New York: McGraw-Hill Book Co., Inc., 1961.

Educational Policies Commission, *Education and the Disadvantaged American.* Washington, D.C.: National Education Association, 1962.

Gilman, H. L., *Helping Children Accept Themselves and Others.* New York: Teachers College, Columbia University, 1959.

Goodman, Mary Ellen, *Race Awareness in Young Children.* Reading, Mass.: Addison-Wesley Publishing Co., Inc., 1952.

Handlin, Oscar, *Race and Nationality in American Life.* New York: Doubleday, Anchor Books, 1957.

Lee, Rose Hum, *The Chinese in the United States of America.* New York: Oxford University Press, 1960.

Sexton, P. C., *Education and Income: Inequalities of Opportunity in Our Public Schools.* New York: Viking Press, Inc., 1961.

Sherman, Charles B., *The Jew Within American Society: A Study in Ethnic Individuality.* Detroit, Mich.: Wayne State University Press, 1961.

Taba, Hilda, *School Culture.* Washington, D.C.: American Council on Education, 1955.

RACE

Many administrators and teachers in cities and schools which are predominantly white, are very likely to say, "We have no intergroup problems"—meaning, of course, no problems of race relations. They take for granted that absence of overt hostility indicates absence of stereotypic thinking, covert negative attitudes, and prejudice. They assume that where there is no open conflict, there can be no potentiality for exclusion, discrimination, and rejection. They forget that relatively few of the white pupils who are living in such exclusive communities will remain there, that many will move to places in which racially different people do live. About one American family out of five moves every calendar year. And a strong possibility exists that the racial composition of predominantly white communities will change as restrictive housing is outlawed all over the nation.

Many teachers who now teach in all-white communities neglect their responsibility for preparing children to live in the future in a world from which time and space have been practically eliminated and in which two-thirds of the people are nonwhite. Teachers who feel comfortable in all-white schools are also likely to feel justified in omitting the study of minority groups cultures and the problems with which they are confronted in American life. Moreover, they forget the danger of teaching about ideal democracy without presenting the realities of our national life, in which the democratic principles and values are not yet fully implemented.

In all parts of the country, in all kinds of communities, even those now all-white, teachers are being called upon to cooperate in securing desegregation of the schools and neighborhoods. Moreover, they must be prepared to effect integration in their classrooms and school activities once Negro children are admitted. The pupils, too, must be prepared for newcomers. This will require teaching the skills of good interpersonal relations across group lines. In many schools it will also necessitate putting into the classroom curriculum units on race and race relationships. As they plan such teaching-learning experiences, teachers will get help from the unit on race relations outlined in Part Three as well as from the following ideas, concepts, and principles.

About Race

There are several theories of race. The one currently held by many sociologists and anthropologists refers to a common-sense division of people into Negroid, Mongoloid, and Caucasoid groups, but it emphasizes that no one characteristic belongs solely to any one group. For example, skin color in Caucasoids varies from very light to very dark, just as it does in Negroids. Ethnic group is often confused with race. For example, the Jews are not a race. They are a religious-culture group.

No one race is superior. Contrary to the opinion of some people, research in anthropology, sociology, and psychology reveals that such attributes, for example, as high mental ability, good health, and propensity toward delinquency and sex promiscuity are not racially linked. All racial groups have similar wide ranges of differences in these and dozens of other social, physical, and mental characteristics.

Blood does not vary by race. Recent research indicates that blood from different human beings is chemically different in some respects, and that there are different types of blood. However, all types commonly identified are found in people of all races. Any type is transferable to people who have the same type, regardless of race.

Many members of the Negro race in this country are socially conditioned by the fact that their roots began here under a system of slavery. For many families, living conditions are not yet much better than that. Moreover, they do not yet enjoy all the rights and privileges of first-class citizenship. Discrimination against them in housing in all parts of the nation segregates them largely in the deteriorating sections of the community. Even Negro families with sufficient money cannot, in many localities, buy or rent suitable living quarters.

Discrimination in employment restricts many Negroes to menial, unskilled, or semi-skilled jobs and poorly paid occupations. Their average family income is half that of whites.

. . .

REFERENCES

Alpenfels, Ethel, *Sense and Nonsense About Race.* New York: Friendship Press, 1957.

Bontemps, Arno, *100 Years of Negro Freedom.* New York: Dodd, Mead & Co., 1961.

Comas, Juan, *Racial Myths* and *Race and Psychology,* UNESCO. New York: William Morrow and Co., 1956.

Gutman, Jean, *Megalopolis.* New York: Twentieth Century Fund, 1961.

Lincoln, Eric, *The Black Muslims in America.* Boston: Beacon Press, 1961.

McManus, Rev. Eugene P., *Studies in Race Relations*. Baltimore: The Josephite Press, 1961.

Montagu, Ashley, *What We Know About "Race."* Teachers Supp. by Gertrude Noar. New York: Anti-Defamation League of B'nai B'rith, 1958.

Nordholt, Schute J. W., *The People Who Walk in Darkness*. New York: Ballantine Books, 1960.

Putnam, Carleton, *Race and Reason*. Washington, D.C.: Public Affairs Press, 1961.

Race and Science. New York: Columbia University Press, 1961.

UNESCO, *Race*. New York: UNESCO, 1952.

VALUES

From time to time public schools are charged with failure to teach moral and ethical values. Some people believe that teaching spiritual values is also the school's responsibility. Controversy over the subject stems from whether spiritual values can be taught without reference to religious sanctions. The fact that spiritual values are connected with religions is likely to engage the school which attempts to teach them in the church-state controversy. Nevertheless, many school systems have issued teacher guides for programs designed to teach moral and spiritual values. Where a cross-section of community lay and religious leaders have acted as advisory committees to help determine policy and review, religious aspects of the subject are usually avoided.

No school could operate for a day, or even for an hour, without attention to moral values. The teachers inevitably must be concerned about conveying to pupils, at all grade levels, concepts of honesty and honor, of truth and loyalty, of charity and service, of law and order, and of all the other virtues and characteristics upon which civilized life depends. These are conveyed to students by telling about them, by exhortation, by discussion of history, current affairs, and literature, and by the handling of behavior problems and human relations. Values of the good, the true, and the beautiful are more likely to be accepted and adopted by pupils if they have teachers who are motivated by those values and whom they like and respect. There is still greater chance of having students accept and live by these values if they find satisfaction in so doing and are rewarded accordingly by the teacher and classmates.

Values motivate behavior toward others. In other words, the values a person holds affect his relationships. Unit teaching, because it provides so well and so frequently for interpersonal and intergroup action, develops a multitude of situations in which pupils must decide on the basis of their values how to behave toward each other and toward whatever adults may be involved. Frequent opportunities to make decisions in the interest of good human relations afford practice of human relations skills. In the integrated classroom, this results in learning how to talk, to work, and to play across group lines.

Unit teaching also provides practice in the democratic processes. When, during these experiences, the individual pupil has opportunities to prove himself of worth, to be successful, to reach his goals, and to achieve with his group what he might not have been able to do alone, the democratic way becomes a value to him; he sees that it is a way to satisfy needs. The teacher who is striving to produce pupils who are committed to the democratic way rewards them for behavior that is consonant with its values.

When students in college and teachers in service think about the values that govern their personal and professional lives, and those which they want to impart to the students, they will find help from considering the following concepts and principles.

About Values

Values are that which an individual or group or society believe to be good or worth while. They may be objects, qualities, ideas. Values become motivating forces which make the individual strive to attain them and which give a sense of purpose and direction to life. They help the individual to make choices from among alternatives.

Americans have a set of traditional, sacred values which are our ideals. They are associated with democracy and the Judeo-Christian ethic. Among the values which are central to democracy are: the worth and dignity of the individual; the right to equal opportunity and first class citizenship regardless of race, religion, social class, or ethnic origins; freedom of speech, of assembly, and of religion;

universal suffrage; the right to social mobility; social responsibility, that is, concern for the welfare of others; the right to become something of one's own choosing.

Unfortunately, these values do not always govern individual behavior. However, value patterns in our society increasingly support elimination of prejudice and discrimination.

The school demonstrates and inculcates the value of the individual throughout its program by methods of teaching; through reality in the students' organizations; and through open membership and unrestricted participation in school programs of extracurricular or co-curricular activities.

Americans also have a set of traditional, secular values which are in flux. Among these are the values attached to money and possessions, to sex and marital status, to honesty, to cleanliness, to ability and talent, to popularity and social adjustment. The degree of value attached to the above attributes and conditions varies somewhat among the social and sub-culture groups. For example, middle-class people place higher value than do lower-class people on cleanliness and grammatically correct speech free from profanity and obscenity.

Values which operate in American society give superior status to the white race, to the middle class, to the Protestant religion, and to Anglo-Saxon origin. However, the value of difference inherent in our philosophy of cultural pluralism is being accepted by an increasing number of people. Teachers and group leaders need not only to accept difference but to see it as a positive good.

Minority group children, especially Negroes, are likely to internalize inferiority feelings along with words which are value packed; for example, dark and black carry a connotation of bad and inferior; white, on the other hand, is attached to good and superior.

The school has always taught values, but has usually placed heavy emphasis on values which characterize middle-class life. Children learn values by imitation of adults and by identifying with a group and accepting what others in the group feel are good things, good ideas, and good behaviors. The first such group in life is the family. The church represents another group. The school is still another.

Values are both indicated and changed by systems of rewards and punishments and by experiences which have satisfying or damaging outcomes. Reflective thinking operates to change values as the individual matures. Cultural conditioning also affects the values an individual accepts.

.   .   .

REFERENCES

Babcock, Chester and I. James Quillen, *American Problems and Values Today.* New York: Scott, Foresman & Co., 1956.

Educational Policies Commission, *Moral and Spiritual Values in the Public Schools.* Washington, D.C.: National Education Association, 1951.

Getzels, J. W., *The Acquisition of Values in School and Society.* Chicago: University of Chicago Press, 1959.

Hartford, E. F., *Moral Values in Public Education.* New York: Harper & Row, 1958.

Hunt, Mate G., ed., *Values: Resource Guide for the Elementary School Teacher* (grades K to 9). Oneonta, N.Y.: American Association of Colleges for Teacher Education, 1958.

Kilpatrick, William Heard and William Van Til, *Intercultural Attitudes in the Making.* New York: Harper & Row, 1949.

Pfeffer, Leo, *Church, State, and Freedom.* Boston: Beacon Hill Press, 1953.

Thelen, Herbert, *Education and the Human Quest.* New York: Harper & Row, 1960.

PREJUDICE

The statement has been made that four-fifths of the American people suffer from the effects of prejudice.[1] They are people whose relationships are limited and often unwholesome. They include not only those against whom prejudice is directed but also those who harbor antagonistic and hostile feelings.

The school which teaches that democracy is based upon the significance of the individual has no room for irrational prejudice based on race, religion, ethnic origins, or social class.

[1] Benjamin R. Epstein and Arnold Forster, *Some of My Best Friends . . .* (New York: Farrar, Straus and Cudahy, Inc., 1962), p. 50.

Somewhere, possibly at several grade levels, the study of prejudice, what it does to people, how it is learned, and what can be done to decrease it must be included. It can be in hygiene, for prejudice definitely affects mental health. It can be in social studies or history, for the evils of prejudice figured in bringing people to this country and influenced the minds of the great leaders who envisioned a democracy in which all people have equal rights. It can be in guidance or the teaching of moral and ethical values, for brotherhood and equality of opportunity, which do not exist where prejudices abound are fundamental values in democracy as well as in the Judeo-Christian ethic.

The teacher who knows that bad relationships with any child blocks learning, who therefore examines his own attitudes and those of the pupils, who plans teaching-learning experiences to change negative attitudes should keep in mind the following facts, ideas, and concepts.

About Prejudice

Prejudice means a mental set or attitude created by a group of ideas which causes the individual to prejudge another person, group, thing, or situation without having had personal experience or without reference to reality. The term is ordinarily used in connection with negative ideas and attitudes. Degrees of negative prejudice are expressed by such words as bias, dislike, exclusion, rejection, preference, bigotry.

Prejudice against people for reasons of their difference in skin color, race, religion, creed, national origin, or social class has many causes. The following are the most common causes:

— Conscious or unconscious transmission of attitudes by parents, other adults, peers, or the total society
—Fear
—Insecurity
—Ignorance of facts
—An authoritarian type of personality
—A traumatic experience
—A social milieu or situation which fosters intergroup hostility and supports discriminatory behavior.

Negative prejudice is expressed in such behaviors as name-calling, stereotyping, scapegoating, ridiculing, downgrading, exclusion, rejection, discrimination, antagonism, hostility, violence.
Because of prejudice against them, Negroes do not yet have all the rights of first-class citizenship. In many places they and other minority groups do not have equality of opportunity in education, cannot buy or rent houses in some sections of cities and suburbs, are refused employment even though they are qualified, have difficulty in securing advancement, and are apt to be the first ones laid off when employment is slack. Fair employment practices, elimination of discrimination in housing, and equality in the use of public facilities, hotels, restaurants, and recreation are being achieved through social action and legislation. Human relations agencies offer services and produce materials useful in the fight against prejudice and discrimination.

Negative attitudes are affected and may be changed by the use of direct teaching of facts, preaching good will, use of mass media, praise, rewards, and punishments for behavior. The best single method is contact-acquaintance across group lines. This is most effective when people meet to discover common problems and work together to solve them. One element which helps to produce success in such projects is selection of participants who are similar in social class level and/or background of experience and education.

Inter-racial marriage is not the objective of the intergroup agencies nor of any religious or racial group. No evidence exists that integrated housing or integration in education increase intermarriage.

Prejudice against Orientals (Japanese and Chinese), which was rampant before and during World War II, has abated. However, in large cities Chinese, especially, live in segregated districts and are subject to discrimination in employment.

In many parts of the nation, Mexicans are regarded as an inferior "race." However, many have been American citizens for several generations. They are good citizens and have produced many outstanding individuals. Discrimination against them exists in housing, employment, and education. Teachers and group leaders need to become familiar with their cultural backgrounds and values.

Stereotyping can be discouraged by substituting "Americans with Spanish sounding names" for the term "Mexican."
American Indians present problems in acceptance, desegregation, and adjustment in many states.

. . .

REFERENCES

Allport, Gordon, *The Nature of Prejudice.* Reading, Mass.: Addison-Wesley Publishing Co., Inc., 1954.

Davidson, K., *The Children Are Listening.* New York: Family Service Association of America, 1961.

Griffith, B., *American Me.* Boston: Houghton Mifflin Company, 1948.

Myers, Gustavus, *History of Bigotry in the United States,* Henry M. Christman, ed. New York: Capricorn, 1960.

Rabb, Earl and Seymour M. Lipset, *Prejudice and Society.* New York: Anti-Defamation League of B'nai B'rith, 1959.

Taft, Charles and Bruce L. Felknor, *Prejudice and Politics.* New York: Anti-Defamation League of B'nai B'rith, 1960.

Trager, Helen and Marion R. Yarrow, *They Learn What They Live: A Study of Prejudice in Young Children.* New York: Harper & Row, 1952.

Van Til, William, *Prejudiced: How Do We Get That Way?* Teachers Supp. by Gertrude Noar. New York: Anti-Defamation League of B'nai B'rith, 1957.

RELIGION IN EDUCATION

Controversy over separation of church and state in American life is creating increasing tension and hostility in intergroup relations. For school people, this centers in the question may the public school teach religion or engage the pupils in religious practice of any kind. Parents of all denominations vary in the answers they give to that question. Religious leaders and organizations have also varied in their policy statements on this issue. State courts and the Federal Supreme Court have handed down decisions on various aspects of the problem. The latest Supreme Court decision in 1962 barred prayers written and imposed by the state.

Agreement is fairly widespread that the school cannot avoid teaching *about* religions whenever and wherever that is relevant to the subject being studied. For example in history, discussion of the Crusades, the Reformation, and Hitler's use of the myth of racial superiority to exterminate European Jews involve learning about the part religion has played in shaping the course of history.

Art and music are other areas of study from which the great expressions of religious concepts and emotions should not be omitted. In fact, when they are included, pupils learn that great artists and composers have come from all religious groups. A subject like home economics enables that teacher to do some intergroup education as she talks about and the pupils make and eat foods characteristic of various culture groups. This increases empathy and implants the value of differences.

Teachers themselves must know about religious differences and have respect for beliefs and culture patterns different from their own. The example the teacher sets of insight and acceptance lessens the chance of pupils being hurt or rejected by their classmates. The following actual incidents illustrate the dangers of thoughtless action by the ill-informed:

> Just before Christmas an eighth grade teacher was asking each student to tell what presents he or she wanted. One pupil said, "Nothing." After making some side remarks, the teacher asked why. The answer came, "I'm Jewish."
>
> In another class the problem was making breakfast. The teacher included bacon. She reported that a Jewish girl "made a scene" by refusing to eat it.
>
> In a college classroom, the professor did nothing about the laughter and ridicule directed by the students at one who, on Ash Wednesday, bore the mark of his devotions on his forehead.

Problems of interfaith relationships are part of the present and past of American life. The diversity of religious groups is part of the cultural pluralism which has added strength to the nation. In unit teaching, pupils can go beyond the textbook to get the facts and meaning of the American colonial struggles for equality and the right to exercise freedom of worship. Teachers can call in resource persons to help pupils to understand religious-culture patterns. They can develop the kinds of interfaith relationships which characterize democratic life built upon concepts of brotherhood.

The following ideas, concepts, and principles should help teachers to avoid the pitfalls of teaching religion and of creating negative interfaith attitudes.

About Religion in Education

The First Amendment to the Federal Constitution reads, in part:
"Congress shall make no law respecting an establishment of religion, or prohibiting the free exercise thereof."
Four historic cases have been argued in the Supreme Court:
The Everson Case—concerned with use of public funds for transportation of parochial school children, which was declared not a violation.
The McCollum Case—in which released-time classes in the school building were declared unconstitutional.
The Zorach Case—in which a plan for released time was upheld because the classes were held off public school premises.
The New Hyde Park, N.Y., case—Engel v. Vitale, June 25, 1962.

The respondent Board of Education, acting in its official capacity under state law, directed the School District's principal to cause a specified prayer to be said aloud by each class in the presence of a teacher at the beginning of each school day.

This daily procedure was adopted on the recommendation of the State Board of Regents, a governmental agency having broad supervisory, executive and legislative powers over the state's public school system. These state officials composed the prayer which they recommended and published.

The Supreme Court said, "We think that by using its public school system to encourage recitation of the Regent's prayer, the state of New York has adopted a practice wholly inconsistent with the Establishment (of religion) Clause.

Many state laws have been passed on various aspects of the problem. An excellent summary compiled by the Research Division of NEA, called *The State and Sectarian Education*, was published by NEA in 1956.

According to the Federal Constitution, public school teachers may not engage in religious indoctrination or conduct religious exercises. This restricts them from using religious rites and ceremonies, explaining creeds and dogmas, and from discussing the nature of God or how He reveals Himself to man.

When called upon by pupils to answer the question "What is God?" the teacher is wise who says: "People answer that question differently according to their religions. I could tell you only what I believe. For your answer you must go to your parents and your religious leaders." If the child asks, "How does God reveal Himself to man?" a similar answer should be given. Should the pupil ask, "What is the best religion?" the wise teacher will reply: "Each person believes that his religion is best for him and surely your parents believe your religion is best for you. But in any case, we should love and be kind to one another regardless of differences of creed or race."

Discussion, controversy, conflict occur when people try to use the public schools to advance their religious beliefs or disbeliefs. Various aspects of this controversy are concerned with morning or lunch-time devotionals; prayers; Bible reading; Christmas and other religious holiday celebrations; religious symbols and garb; programs involving released time; certain benefits for parochial school children (use of public funds for lunch, transportation, medical examination, and textbooks); teaching moral and spiritual values; teaching *about* religions when relevant in such subjects as history, social studies, art, music, and other aspects of the curriculum.

Some of the controversial issues are: Can moral and spiritual values be taught without reference to religious sanctions? Can the christological content be eliminated from Christmas programs? Should the celebration of Hanukkah be introduced? Can prayers be constructed so as to satisfy all? Is religious instruction in school needed to reduce juvenile delinquency? What about the reduction of school time by dismissed and released time programs? Does teaching *about* religions violate the separation of church and state? Does absence of prayer and Bible reading from the school program make the school Godless? Can public and parochial schools build programs and schedules in which they will share the time of school pupils?

•   •   •

REFERENCES

Boles, Donald E., *The Bible, Religion, and the Public Schools*. Ames: Iowa State University Press, 1961.

Committee on *The Function of the Schools in Dealing with Religion*. Washington, D.C.: American Council on Education, 1953.

Jacobsen, Philip, *Religion in Public Education*. New York: American Jewish Committee, 1960.

NEA Research Bulletin, *The State and Sectarian Education*. Washington, D.C.: Vol. XXXIV, No. 4, 1956.

DISCRIMINATION

Irrational, negative feelings usually are indicative of deeper feelings of insecurity, fear, and possibly guilt and inferiority. Such emotions usually motivate some kind of anti-social behavior directed against the person or group who is disliked or feared by single or large numbers of individuals. The most harmful ways of acting out prejudices are rejection and exclusion, which keep whole groups of people from exercising their rights and from enjoying equality of opportunity in one or more aspects of life. This is discrimination.

In the school organized and operated by the state to teach and, therefore, to maintain democracy, there is no room for discrimination. When it exists there, minority group children are at a disadvantage and are blocked in their development.

If discrimination in housing, employment, education, the use of public facilities, and social life is to be rooted out of our society, at some times and at various grade levels, pupils must learn about it in school. Teachers who plan for such units will be helped if they keep in mind the following facts, ideas and concepts.

About Discrimination

Discrimination refers to denial to an individual or a group of the exercise of their human and/or civil rights.

Areas in which discrimination is most frequently experienced by minority groups are:

—housing—rental and purchase. A powerful force is the belief that values decrease when minority groups move in. Realtors serve to stimulate exodus. Contracts often contain restrictive clauses. Some places use "gentlemen's agreements" which are not in the contracts but seem to be understood by purchasers and owners who refuse to rent or sell to minority groups.

—employment—hiring and advancement.

—public accommodations—hotels, resorts, restaurants.

—social clubs and recreation—swimming pools, bowling alleys, golf courses, tennis courts, and country clubs.

National civil rights legislation is a matter for Congressional action. Fair Employment Practice (FEP) laws and Public Accommodation laws have been passed in 16 states and many cities. Following legislation, in many places, Commissions are constituted by government to enforce the laws.

The Bill of Rights, the first ten Amendments to the Federal Constitution, is violated by discriminatory practice. Teachers, students, and group leaders need to become familiar with this document and dedicated to it as a way of life for themselves and others.

Discrimination still operates in connection with admissions to some colleges and to campus clubs and activities. In some cases there is total exclusion; in others, quotas are set up to limit the number of minority group persons who are admitted. Quotas have been liberalized in many educational institutions, and many national and local fraternities and sororities have eliminated discriminatory clauses from their charters. Action of this kind has been required by administration in some universities.

The type of discrimination claiming national and international attention is segregation in education, which exists, in some measure, all over the country. In many large cities it is so closely tied to housing patterns that little can be done to eliminate it quickly. In some places reduction of segregation can be accomplished by changing zoning lines and by strategic location of new school buildings. Open enrollment is being used in some cities, even though transportation of pupils is required.

Since the Supreme Court decision of 1954, which declared segregation in education to be unconstitutional, many cities and counties have moved toward integration. The process is slow and difficult. Much remains to be accomplished.

. . .

REFERENCES

Douglass, William O., *A Living Bill Of Rights*. New York: Doubleday & Company, Inc., 1961.

Epstein, Benjamin R. and Arnold Forster, *Some of My Best Friends.* . . . New York: Farrar, Straus & Cudahay, Inc., 1962.

Grier, Eunice and George Grier, *Discrimination in Housing*. New York: Anti-Defamation League of B'nai B'rith, 1960.

Hill, Herbert and Jack Greenberg, *Citizen's Guide to Desegregation*. Boston: Beacon Press, 1955.

Javits, Jacob, *Discrimination—U.S.A.* New York: Harcourt, Brace & World, Inc., 1960.

Lee, A. M., *Fraternities Without Brotherhood*. Boston: Beacon Press, 1955.

McIntire, Davis, *Residence and Race*. Berkeley: Univ. of California Press, 1960.

Simpson, George and J. Milton Yinger, *Racial and Cultural Minorities*. New York: Harper & Row, 1953.

U.S. Commission on Civil Rights, *Civil Rights*. Washington, D.C.: U.S. Government Printing Office, 1961.

Weinberger, Andrew D., *Civil Liberties*. San Francisco: Chandler Publishing Co., 1961.

HUMAN RELATIONS SKILLS

Skill in relating warmly and positively to other human beings is needed by every person who wants to enjoy effective and successful living. Teaching and learning the democratic way requires that, in addition to providing for the development of the ordinary human relations skills, the school must also afford opportunities to learn the skills of relating across group lines.

The child begins to learn how to relate to others early in life when he experiences the warmth of loving parents. He begins to develop skills like theirs by responding to them. As he grows older, he observes and then imitates the words, facial expressions, and gestures his parents and siblings use as they relate to him, to each other, to people who come into the house, and to people outside. If members of the family lack skill in human relations, the child will not develop them.

When children come to the school, their behavior patterns indicate the degree or lack of skill already attained by them. The teacher's responsibility is then to provide opportunities for the children to practice the skills already possessed and to develop new ones. For example, in the public school, many children who relate well to others like themselves are unable to use their skill when they meet people who are different in skin color. If the teacher helps such pupils to learn to use the words, facial expressions, and gestures of acceptance rather than rejection, with those of different skin color, the basis of good intergroup relations is established.

Skill in saying and doing the right thing at the right time can be learned in school. It involves learning to predict the effect upon the hearer of one's words and actions and choosing what to say and do accordingly. This is beautifully illustrated in the following incident. A teacher in a university laboratory school was teaching human relations skills to her sixth-grade class. They practiced what they learned when they went to help in the nursery school. One day, while they were there, a four year old went around the room snapping at the children saying, "I'm a rhinoceros." She came to the teacher, who said with annoyance, "I'm a bigger rhinoceros." Whereupon the child ran away.

The sixth-grade teacher, who was standing near-by with two of her pupils, said to them, "What would you have said?" One child answered, "I would say, I'm an elephant. Come play with me." The other child said, "I would say, I'm a little rhinoceros. Will you take care of me?"

About Human Relations Skills

Webster's Unabridged Dictionary defines "skill" as follows: "Ability to use one's knowledge effectively and readily in execution or performance; technical expertness; proficiency; a particular art or science; a power or habit of doing a particular thing completely; a developed or acquired aptitude or ability; an accomplishment."

Synonyms for skill are: adeptness, adroitness, cleverness, deftness, dexterity, finesse, proficiency, facility, readiness, ability, aptness.

Among the most important group of skills to be developed in con-nection with human relations, are the skills of communication. These are talking, listening, gesturing, using facial expressions, writing. The skills of allowing for difference and of differing without anger should also be cultivated in the classroom. Moreover, every indi-vidual needs to learn how to avoid anger-provoking and dangerous words, the derogatory symbols and names applied to minority groups. The skills of language usage help people to prevent con-flict. How to control and resolve conflict in and out of school is equally important.

Another group of skills that the pupil should learn are those included in the overall term "courtesy." This should include how an indi-vidual addresses and responds to people of different status from his own, both lower and higher. It requires learning how to express gratitude, thanks, and the pleasure of meeting people. It includes learning how to say, "I'm sorry" in many different ways and at the right time.

Other skills needed in human relations are those of finding and using relevant information, analyzing, recognizing and using propaganda devices, challenging stereotypes, testing statements for reality, ana-lyzing human behavior in terms of consequences to self and others, helping others to develop adequate self-concepts.

The skills needed for group work are also important. Among these are the skills of leading, recording, reporting, discussing, participat-ing in making decisions, moving from discussion to action.

Teachers require skill in using instruments and devices which reveal pupils' human relations needs. Among these are how to make so-ciograms, how to formulate open-end questions, how to conduct interviews, how to use projective devices, how to formulate and interpret social distance questions, how to set up role-playing ex-periences, and how to conduct discussions.

.   .   .

REFERENCES

Allport, Gordon, *The ABC's of Scapegoating*, rev. ed. New York: Anti-Defamation League, 1959.

Bonney, Merl E., *Mental Health in Education*. Boston: Allyn & Ba-con, Inc., 1961.

Chase, Stuart, *Roads to Agreement*. New York: Harper & Row, 1951.

Jennings, Helen Hall, *et al.*, *Sociometry in Group Relations*, rev. ed. Washington, D.C.: American Council on Education, 1959.

Taba, Hilda, *et al.*, *Diagnosing Human Relations Needs*. Washington, D.C.: American Council on Education, 1951.

PART THREE

Resources for the Teacher

13

Units

IS THE STUDY OF INTERGROUP RELA-
tions a separate discipline? What are its basic principles and its subject matter? What are the skills needed to impart the content and values to students? What materials and other resources are available? Is a separate course needed on the subject, or should various aspects of the subjects be introduced through existing courses of study? Which ones? How? When, Where?

The proponents of intergroup relations education agree that secondary school and even elementary pupils should be confronted with their own prejudices, with the intergroup tensions and conflicts that disrupt neighborhoods and larger communities, with the wastage of manpower that affects the welfare of the nation, and with the struggle for equality of opportunity and for first-class citizenship of minority groups in our society. However, the relevance of these subjects to the central task of the school, namely, the development of responsible citizens committed to the democratic traditions and way of life, is not clearly perceived by many teachers.

Of course, fragments of the large and complex area of intergroup relations are included here and there—more in some school systems than in others. For example, comprehensive guides for teachers have been issued in cities like Cambridge, Massachusetts and by the State Department of Education in Pennsylvania. But much of the teaching tends to be scattered and superficial. One of the reasons is that teachers in general have as yet received little preparation for human relations education in their preservice education and in few places have efforts been made to develop inservice courses and workshops.

In order to meet the teachers' needs for information, for methods of approach, for appropriate teaching-learning activities, and for available materials, the following resource unit outlines have been developed. One of them is on the subject of *race and race relations*, which can be studied in science and in social studies. Another concerns *prejudice and discrimination*, both of which can be regarded as problems of mental health to be studied in hygiene or guidance. They are also problems of society and, therefore, belong in social studies. The several aspects of these social problems might need to be dealt with in separate units. Such units should be studied in the industrial arts shops and be included in the guidance program as part of the study of the working world, of community life, and of education. A fourth unit is on *human rights*, which includes civil rights. This, of course, should always be included in American history and government. Still another has to do with *cultural pluralism*, a fundamental characteristic of our society, which should also be part of both history and social studies.

The unit outlines that follow vary widely. This should help the teacher to understand that there is no one ideal or even best way of presenting and teaching intergroup relations. In all of them, however, emphasis is placed on learning through experience. All of them contain suggestions for a wide range of materials and for very diverse teaching methods and learning activities so that every pupil shall have a maximum number of opportunities to achieve the desired outcomes.

In addition to the unit outlines, a portion of a teacher's log is included to show how he and his class approached and chose a unit on democracy. Another teacher's report is used to show how a class studied about various religions.

Many teachers ask for help with ideas and activities they can use in short units designed to teach brotherhood. Their request has been granted in the following materials.

There is no *single* way to teach human relations and to achieve understanding and commitment to the democratic ideals, values, principles, and processes. Certainly information, that is content, must be an important part of every unit dealing with the many aspects of these complex areas of life and learning. In the following descriptions of units actually done in classrooms, and in the following resource outlines prepared to assist teachers in seeing what the several units involve, both the necessary information and the many sources from which facts can be mobilized are included.

Most important of all is to provide for pupils, who differ in reading abilities by at least four grade levels, the reading materials from which they all can get the facts they need to know. And, because reading is the most difficult way for some, another important factor is to make use of other sources of information: pictures, films, radio, TV, and people. The use of these media is indicated in the following reports and outlines.

However, information alone is not enough to give pupils values and skills and commitment. Reading about how to use the democratic group processes, for example, will not enable most pupils to participate effectively in them. Neither will knowing about human relations enable pupils to relate positively across group lines. Experiences must be provided and with sufficient frequency to afford the practice required to develop skills. Moreover, the experiences must be so constructed and directed as to give all the pupils satisfaction in using them. Only then will boys and girls come to value freedom deeply, to see human differences as good, to respect their own rights, to grant the exercise of rights to all other people, and to accept the responsibilities that accompany the privileges of free men in our society. Those kinds of experiences are included in the reports and outlines that follow.

PREJUDICE AND DISCRIMINATION[1]

Rationale

The American public school is of primary importance to the maintenance and improvement of democracy as a way of life. In it, children and youth learn the basic concepts, principles, and values of

[1] Gertrude Noar, *Prejudice and Discrimination, A Resource Unit for Teachers and Group Leaders*, New York: Anti-Defamation League, 1962. Reprinted, slightly altered, with permission of the Anti-Defamation League of B'nai B'rith.

democracy. There, as the result of experience and practice, they develop the attitudes and skills needed for effective participation in and commitment to democracy in politics and social living.

America is a nation of many kinds of people. Groups which differ in race, religion, national origins, and social class played important roles in creating the traditions and in establishing the greatness of our nation. Yet, among the early settlers, and increasingly as waves of immigration compounded differences, negative attitudes and hatreds resulted in rejections, exclusions, and denial of equality of rights. Now, the struggle for first-class citizenship for Negroes and the problems of church-state relationships, which are major social issues, reveal anew the deep-seated prejudices harbored by many people.

The school, therefore, is confronted with the necessity of teaching about prejudice and discrimination as facts of life, as conditions which prevent the full development of every person, as problems that must be solved if democracy is to be accepted around the world. Through learning experiences in the school, the youth of the land must be confronted with both the truths we hold to be self-evident as well as our failure to implement all of them with respect to minority groups.

Approach

Of the several possible approaches, the one most likely to be used is the need for information which arises when a specific incident of scapegoating or discrimination has occurred in the school or the community and is brought to the attention of the class. However, discussion of current events, a newspaper story, or a magazine article dealing with some aspect of prejudice or discrimination is also a natural approach to a unit.

Objectives

The basic objective of curriculum in intergroup relations is development of the kind of person who can live effectively in a democratic society. Essentially, he is one who understands the pluralistic nature of our society and who not only accepts but values human difference. Such a person knows that differences of race, religion, national origin, and social class are not valid reasons for rejection. He also recognizes the right of every person to first-class citizenship and is willing to work actively to eliminate irrational prejudice in himself and others and to lessen discrimination in American life.

Principles and Values

1. Basic to democracy is recognition and acceptance of the worth and integrity of every human being. (Fascism is based on the theory of superiority of some and the worthlessness of others. Communism regards the individual as worth while only as a tool of the state.)

2. In a democracy all who are to be affected have the right to share in policy making. An example is the Revolutionary War battle cry: "Taxation without representation is tyranny." (In authoritarian societies the people are never consulted. Policy decisions are made at the top and handed down.)

3. In a democracy every individual has the right to become something of his own choosing. (In totalitarian societies, the state decides how much education and for what purposes individuals are to be trained.)

4. Democracy is based upon the intelligent participation of all citizens. All are entitled to firstclass citizenship. (In authoritarian societies an elite group does the deciding and issues orders that the people must obey.)

5. Personal preference and voluntary association are rights. These, however, cannot be used to deny anyone his rights and his "pursuit of happiness."

6. The principle of human similarity and the principle of human difference are both democratic tenets.

7. The value of human difference is established by the strength derived from the culturally pluralistic nature of our population.

Vocabulary

Words and terms which need to be defined, explained, possibly spelled and recognized in reading materials are:

aggression	discrimination	nationality
attitude	ethnic origin	out-group
behavior	exclusion	prejudice
belief	frustration	propaganda
bias	ghetto	quota system
bigot	immigration	race
caste	in-group	rejection
civil liberties	integration	religion
civil rights	majority	scapegoating
class	minority	stereotype
desegregation	national origin	tolerance

Causes of Prejudice

—Dislike of people because of difference from self in race, color, religion, creed, socio-economic class, nationality background, age, sex, political ideology.

—Guilt feelings which begin in childhood over such things as relationship with parents, misdeeds, lies, school failures, social inferiority.

—Fear which arises from feelings of inadequacy and insecurity and is connected with school failure and social situations.

—Ignorance of the facts of self, race, religions, the pluralistic nature of our society, the inaccuracy of stereotypes.

—Rumor which exaggerates and distorts people and events.

—Frustration which comes from lack of personal success and advancement and from excessive punishment.

—Patterns of thought and behavior which are condoned or supported by the family and/or the community. These include name-calling, stereotyping, scapegoating, rejection, exclusion, desecration of property, and aggression against persons.

The Nature of Prejudice

The kind of prejudice about which we are concerned is an unfounded, *negative*, overgeneralized judgment, usually accompanied by an unpleasant feeling tone toward a person or a whole group, formed without benefit of facts. It may be based upon a projection: an individual tends to attribute to others what he hates most in himself. It may or may not be based on actual experience.

The feeling tone includes scorn, dislike, fear, aversion. There may, however, be thoughts apart from feeling. It is not necessarily attended by a sense of moral outrage.

The ideas, feelings, and values which are included in the complex called prejudice constitute a *hostile attitude*. It is usually directed toward a person who belongs to a group and simply because he does so he is presumed to have the objectionable qualities ascribed to that group. Such a group of qualities and characteristics form a *stereotype*. A truly prejudiced person is often unwilling or unable to subject this stereotype and his prejudgment to reality testing. If he knows a particular individual who differs from the stereotype, he calls that person an exception to the rule.

People are, of course, also prejudiced *for* or in favor of the group to which they belong. This preference may be based upon satisfying experiences. On the other hand it, too, may be an emotional reaction to one's in-group, for which there cannot be factual evidence of superior character, intelligence, or culture of all the members of the group.

Prejudices vary in intensity. The words which indicate intensity are *preference, bias, dislike, hostility, hatred, bigotry*.

Sources and Forms of Prejudice in Children

Prejudice is not instinctive. Children are not born with specific hatreds. These they learn as they grow up. They observe and hear how parents, teachers, and other adults and peers behave and talk. Because the child likes and admires individuals, he wants to be like them and to do as they do.

Dislikes, biases, hostility, and hatred reveal themselves in fantasy, which may be the precursor to action. Much behavior which reveals prejudice is in the form of verbal aggression. This includes rumors, jokes, doggerel, accusations, teasing, threats, name-calling. Coercive action, scapegoating, exclusion, rejection, and discrimination also are behaviors caused by prejudice.

The most frequent victims of prejudicial behavior are usually those who have high visibility because of color, who cannot retaliate, who are weak because previous attack has undermined them, who are accessible (easily reached or at hand), or who personify a hated idea (e.g., Roosevelt personified progressivism).

Effect of Prejudice on the Individual

The person who harbors prejudices based upon differences of race, color, religion, creed, nationality backgrounds, or social class, restricts his associates and thereby impoverishes his own life. His negative feelings, which may become as intense as hatreds, engender anger which, in turn, causes feelings of guilt. Acute emotions of that kind may affect the person's physical well-being and cause psychosomatic illnesses. The accompanying anxiety often serves to block learning.

Minority group persons suffer from feelings of insecurity, of inferiority, of guilt, of frustration, and of anger as the result of the treatment they receive in our society. In many such children, learning is blocked and aspirations killed, and they are unable to develop their potentialities. Many drop out of school. Moreover, those who do continue their education are often unable to find suitable employment; they suffer from despair and become apathetic and unproductive.

Minority groups suffer from discrimination in housing, employment, education, the use of recreational facilities, and public accommodations. Negroes and Jews especially, in some localities, are unable to buy or rent suitable houses or apartments. The sections of a community to which they are restricted are often spoken of as "ghettoes." If a minority group family succeeds in getting a house in a previously homogeneous neighborhood, violence may erupt unless community leaders help the residents to think through the problem and make plans to welcome newcomers. Prejudiced people often move away from a neighborhood because they are told that property values will go down. Much evidence exists to prove the fallacy of that rumor.

Discrimination

Minority group persons are refused employment in some communities and in some kinds of business and industry. When they are employed, they often are refused advancement. When times are bad, they are often the first to lose their jobs. Negroes, Puerto Ricans, and Mexican-Americans are often able to find only menial work opportunities at low pay. The average income of Negroes is about half that of white families of similar social levels.

The youth of minority groups still find themselves educationally blocked, some more so than others. Although there has been great progress in eliminating *race* and *religion* from college application blanks, and photographs are often no longer required, the number of Jews and Negroes admitted to some colleges and universities is limited. Quotas, though enlarged, probably are still used. Much progress has also been made in eliminating restrictions on admission of minority groups to college sororities and fraternities.

In 1954 the Supreme Court decided that segregation in education is unconstitutional and that it harms the individual child. All communities were ordered to desegregate their public schools. Progress in enforcing the law has been slow. Many states have refused to act without further court action. In some places, when the first schools were desegregated, violence erupted. In other communities, where public officials were firm, law and order were maintained. Segregated schools exist in the North as well as the South, and efforts must be made all over the country to eliminate discrimination in education at all levels.

In many communities, nonwhite people are excluded from the use of public parks, beaches, swimming pools, bowling alleys, skating rinks, horseback riding facilities, golf and tennis clubs. Sit-in, nonviolent protest demonstrations are being used successfully to open such recreational facilities to all people. Public transportation, notably buses and terminals, are also slowly being desegregated.

Many hotels and restaurants in cities and towns and in summer resorts across the nation still exclude nonwhites and Jews or restrict their numbers by establishing quotas. Sit-in protests are helping to open restaurants. The efforts of government and private human relations agencies are being successfully used to open hotels to all people.

All American citizens are entitled to vote in public elections. However, in many southern communities this right is denied to Negroes.

Effects of Discrimination

Discrimination in any aspect of life deprives the individual of the human and civil rights which are granted to him by the Federal Constitution and the Bill of Rights. This affects his personal development and his social and civic effectiveness. Many citizens are thus prevented from attaining a standard of living commensurate with their desires and abilities.

Discrimination results in economic loss to the locality, the state, and the nation. The cost of discrimination is high.

Foreign relations are also affected by the practice of discrimination in America. The violence which has frequently accompanied school desegregation and the failure of nonwhites to receive equal treatment in hotels, restaurants, and transportation facilities are told in large headlines in the Asian and African press. The uncommitted peoples find it hard to believe in the principles and values of democracy when we fail to implement them in the United States.

Racial and Religious Bigotry

Bigotry has led to the formation of "hate groups." These are usually organized by one person or a small group who find the enrollment of members and the sale of its publications to be profitable. Possibly the most notorious group is the Ku Klux Klan (KKK), organized to persecute Negroes, Jews, and Catholics. In some places the KKK is outlawed, and now members are not permitted to conceal their identities behind masks. There are a number of anti-Semitic groups in the nation which print and distribute obscene literature blaming the Jews for all the country's ills. Anti-Catholicism, while not so well-organized, flared up during the 1960 election.

Corrective Measures

Education is required to eliminate the dangers to our society which come from prejudice and discrimination. The requisite principles, values, and information must be added to preservice and inservice teacher education and to the many elementary and secondary school courses in which the subject is relevant.

The mass media are increasingly devoting time and space to various aspects of intergroup relations. Newspaper and magazine pictures, articles, editorials, and news reports tell of relevant events, problems, and issues. TV and radio programs feature speakers, panel discussions, and interviews with educational, political, social, and civic leaders.

Plays on TV and Broadway and movies portray the human relations problems which grow out of racial and religious prejudice and discrimination.

Public meetings are being held frequently and in many places to present the problems to the people and to give them opportunities for discussion.

Intergroup activities are increasingly popular. These include exchange of pulpits by religious leaders, sharing holiday celebrations across group lines, interchurch visits, interracial education activities, interracial community activities.

Many international, national, state and local, public and private human relations agencies exist. Among them are:

United Nations
United Nations Educational, Scientific, and
    Cultural Organization (UNESCO)
Anti-Defamation League of B'nai B'rith
American Friends Service Committee
United Nations Commission on Human Rights
American Jewish Committee
National Conference of Christians and Jews
Catholic Interracial Council
Urban League
National Council of Churches
National Association for the Advancement of
    Colored People
University Human Relations Centers
Governors' Commissions on Civil Rights
Mayors' committees against discrimination
City committees on human relations

Legislation has proven to be an extremely effective means of eliminating discrimination. The Federal Bill of Rights and the Amendments to the Federal Constitution are the bases for city, state, and national laws. After laws are passed, enforcement agencies must be authorized before corrective action can be undertaken.

The most commonly used legislative commission is known as FEPC (Fair Employment Practice Commission). Another example is the law on Public Accommodation and Facilities. Supreme Court decisions on segregation and religion in public education are also very important.

What the Teacher Does

As soon as the class decides to embark on a unit, the teacher must have before him a general survey of the subject. This resource unit is, in fact, the survey he needs. In it the teacher will find more materials and learning activities than he can use. He must, therefore, decide what, in the light of his own situation, are the possibilities and limitations of the unit.

After making a preplanning survey, the teacher is ready to lead the class in pupil-teacher planning to determine goals, content, learning activities, and evaluation devices. As the unit develops, daily planning is needed.

Unit teaching requires the teacher to do many things. He must relate the following activities to the specific content and experiences needed to accomplish the purposes of the unit. *The objectives are to give students information about prejudice and discrimination, to develop positive attitudes toward human differences, and to encourage democratic behavior across group lines.*

No significance should be attached to the order in which the activities are listed.

—When necessary, he gives information. This may be a formal presentation or the incidental help needed by individuals or committees. It may be necessary, for example, to help students to understand what they read about the causes of prejudice and the dynamics of discrimination.

—The teacher provides materials for use in and out of the classroom. These should include whatever text, reference, and literature books are required to supply the information needed to answer questions raised by the students and himself during planning and discussion sessions. He will also need to secure and provide dictionaries, bibliographies of literature, catalogues of films and publications, and lists of resource agencies.

Other materials the class will need from time to time are magazines, newspapers, pamphlets, art supplies, pictures, mounting boards, implements, and tools.

—Organization of committees may be done in several different ways. The teacher helps the class to use appropriate methods. He also makes sure that membership is not determined on the basis of race, religion, ethnic origin, or social class but that as far as possible, each group has a cross-section of the student population.

—The teacher delegates routine matters of distribution and collection of supplies and books to pupils, makes sure that they know how to do their jobs, and helps them to fulfill their responsibilities. He also encourages able pupils to help their less able classmates. He makes sure that minority group pupils are never slighted or omitted.

—Arrangement of time schedules for committee meetings, committee reports, class discussions, viewing of films and filmstrips, seeing TV programs, and listening to records and radio programs is an important teacher activity in which pupils should participate to some extent.

—The teacher announces subjects for discussion, indicates where and how information can be obtained, and when the entire class is involved, he acts as discussion leader.

—Previewing audio-visual materials on prejudice and discrimination is an essential teacher activity. Presentation and follow-up discussion of an audio-visual aid are important teaching activities. These may be delegated to or shared with pupils of high ability.

—The teacher makes sure that group leaders are selected without reference to race, religion, ethnic origin, or social class. He must train and assist committee chairmen, reporters, and recorders. All sub-groups (committees) are likely to require teacher help in planning, pooling, preparing reports, and evaluating their progress and products. Discussion group and committee roles may need to be demonstrated by the teacher.

—Individuals require help from the teacher.

—Plans made by committees for trips, speakers, and the use of consultants must be reviewed by the teacher, who will need to assist the class in carrying on such activities.

—The teacher explains the need for keeping records of personal work, committee reports, learning activities, and factual material. He helps pupils to set up their unit-record books and, from time to time, checks on them.

—Completion of homework assignments and drill exercises needs to be checked by the teacher.

—The teacher makes suggestions for creative writing (skits, plays, descriptions, poems, open-end questions), establishes minimum requirements, and indicates time schedules for their completion.

—When he identifies the need for instruction and drill, the teacher tells, shows, demonstrates, directs, reads to and with, and in other ways teaches whatever is required in spelling, grammar, methods of study, outlining, ways of mobilizing facts from many sources (research), and reading; and thus, he enables the students to succeed.

—The teacher acts as a source of ideas and inspiration, helping pupils to make and display collections, design illustrations and murals, produce dramatic presentations, and make varied and interesting reports.

—As he requires information about what pupils think and say and the direction of change in their attitudes and behaviors, the teacher devises, administers, and analyzes short and long essay and objective tests, inventories of social attitudes, and opinion polls.

—The teacher sets up role-playing experiences to help pupils to understand human motivations and behavior and to develop empathy.

—The various parts of the unit will need to be integrated by the teacher, who must make sure that meanings are understood and fundamental concepts and principles are established.

—At the close of the unit, the teacher helps the class to evaluate it in terms of their goals. He also evaluates his methods and procedures and the outcomes in terms of his goals. He adds this to the daily record he has kept and files it for reference.

Learning Activities

In unit teaching, responsibility for learning is placed upon the pupils. Their activities in and out of the classroom are envisioned by the teacher when he analyzes for himself his teaching activities. Although the following pupil activities are itemized, several of them may go on simultaneously because all pupils do not do the same thing at the same time. Moreover, a number of them will probably be included in the plans for any one classroom period.

The sequential order of pupil activities is not to be inferred from the following list.

For all Pupils

—Participation in pupil-teacher planning:
  1. Discussion of and making decisions with respect to the choice of subject to be studied.
  2. Setting up goals to be achieved by the group and the individual.
  3. Determining content—what information will be needed to answer the questions raised and the problems encountered.
  4. Determining the learning experiences required.
  5. Allocating and accepting responsibilities.
  6. Taking part in sub-group (committee) work.

—Evaluating self, the group, leadership, processes used, and products of both committee and class work.

—Reading, both to gather facts and for enjoyment. The quality and difficulty of the materials read will depend upon individual abilities. The materials to be read will include textbooks, dictionaries, reference and literature books, magazines, pamphlets, and newspapers.

—Recording in unit-record books individual work, factual material from committee reports, speakers listened to, films seen, radio and television programs.

—Writing, which may be only a few sentences for some pupils but more extensive and creative for others. Writing should be done on open-end questions such as "People I Like" (or do not like), "Why I feel inferior (superior) to others in the class," "What makes me happy" (unhappy), "The kind of person I would like to be." The understanding should always be that these will not be read to the class. They will provide the teacher with much information about the attitudes and problems of his students.

—Learning to spell and use new words.

—Seeing and discussing films and TV programs, listening to speakers, radio programs, and recordings provided by either the teacher or committees for the entire class.

—Participating in preparation of questions for speakers.

—Taking part in dramatics and role-playing.

—Interviewing adults in the family and neighborhood about problems of discrimination in employment and social class.

—Taking trips planned by the teacher and committees for the entire class. These should include visits to housing developments, slum areas, various kinds of religious institutions and community centers, the center of government for the locality, art and historical museums.

—Participating in general discussions on such subjects as the propaganda techniques used by hate groups, when and how children learn to hate people different from themselves, the value of human differences in our society, the implications of the Bill of Rights, the meaning of cultural pluralism, the responsibility of the individual for the maintenance and improvement of democracy.

For Some Pupils

*—Writing dramatic skits, poems, original stories.

*—Leadership of sub-groups.

*—Recording class and committee activities (secretary).

—Reporting individual and committee work.

*—Art work—illustrations, murals, posters, charts.

—Clipping news items, articles, and pictures from magazines and newspapers.

 * Recommended for high ability pupils.

—Filing materials for use by all committees.

—Collecting, classifying, organizing, and displaying: pictures, pamphlets, charts, items of interest about culture groups, relevant editorials, news stories, and cartoons.

—Securing films, projects, and other equipment and making all necessary arrangements for viewing films, seeing television programs, listening to recordings and radio programs.

*—Writing letters of invitation and thanks to speakers, consultants, and resource persons who may be secured to help the class with such subjects as intergroup relations in the community, discrimination in housing, employment, the use of public facilities and education in the community and the nation, the effect of prejudice in the United States on international relations, the nature and genesis of prejudice.

—Making telephone calls in connection with plans for speakers, interviews, and trips.

—Collecting and analyzing resort hotel advertisements, real estate ads, employment ads to discover devices used to indicate discriminatory practices.

—Visiting the offices of human relations agencies to secure material and information. Among them are the National Conference of Christians and Jews, the Anti-Defamation League of B'nai B'rith, the Urban League, state or local committees on human relations or even the United Nations Commission on Human Rights.

—Interviewing civic and social leaders, educators, and visitors to the school.

*—Conducting and participating in panel discussions.

*—Administering and analyzing opinion polls in the school. These may include items of social distance, such as: "I would like (dislike, not sure I want) having as a guest in my house a Negro, a Jew, a Catholic, a Japanese."

*—Reading and analyzing historical documents and individual laws relating to civil rights.

Culminating Activities

—Prepare assembly programs for special events.

—Conduct panel discussions in assembly and/or at PTA and community meetings.

—Prepare and present appropriate dramatization to report the unit to the entire student body.

—Present accumulated materials to library.

* Recommended for high ability pupils.

—Organize a social action project; for example, to secure use of a public facility for all the pupils in the school.

—Work with student council in a project to survey intergroup tensions and to develop a human relations program for the school.

Action Outcomes

Learning is evident in behavior. Among the things pupils should be encouraged to do are:

1. Develop a personal code.
2. Make a new friend across group lines.
3. Write letters praising TV and radio programs which promote good intergroup relations.
4. Challenge stereotypes when they hear them.
5. Discourage and never tell stories which present unfavorable images of minority groups.

REFERENCES

Grades 1-8

Books

Eskie, Sunny, *A Land Full of Freedom.* New York: Friendly House, 1962. Text and illustrations combine to teach the child the basic elements of American freedom and democracy. (Grades 2-3), Teacher guide.

Evans, Eva Knox, *All About Us.* New York: Capitol Publishing Co., Inc., 1947. Story of how people over the centuries changed in skin color, custom, and language. (Grades 5-8)

Hall, Gordon Langley, *Peter Jumping Horse.* New York: Holt, Rinehart & Winston, Inc., 1961. A warm, humorous picture of a modern Indian boy's life on a reservation in Canada. (Grades 3-4)

Lerner, Marguerite Rush, *Red Man, White Man, African Chief.* Minneapolis: Medical Books for Children, 1961. Winner of the 1961 Brotherhood Award, this book explains skin pigmentation to children in simple, everyday language and in relation to objects familiar to any child. (Grades 5-8)

Wilson, Bettye, *We Are All Americans.* New York: Friendly House, 1959. Illustrated book teaches children the values of diversity. (Grades 1-2), Teacher guide.

Pamphlets

Kraus, Robert, *The Rabbit Brothers*. New York: ADL.[1] Humorous cartoon pamphlet that tells the story of twin rabbits—one dislikes other rabbits who are different while the other tries to find some good in all rabbits. (Elem. and Jr. H.), Teacher guide.

Films[2]

The Toymaker. 15 min., color, black and white, ADL. Two hand puppets are friends until they discover they are different.

Junior High School

Books

Bond, Gladys Baker, *Little Stories on Big Subjects*. New York: ADL. A box of seven short stories providing children with vicarious experiences in solving problems of human relations. Teacher guide.

Fisher, Lois J., *Bill and His Neighbors*. Boston: Houghton Mifflin Co., 1950. A boy's view of racial and religious prejudices and the problems they create in junior high school.

Harmon, Sidney, *Hand in Hand*. New York: Whittlesey House, 1961. Based on the prize-winning motion picture, this is the deeply moving story of two children who challenge the barriers society has set up between their faiths.

Pamphlets

F.E.P.C. and the Cost of Discrimination. New York: ADL. Graphic presentation of the results of the Elmo Roper Poll indicating that discrimination in employment is costly to the entire American economy.

Montagu, Ashley, *What We Know About "Race."* New York: 1958. Definitive presentation of scientific knowledge about races of mankind. Teacher guide. (Useful in Sr. H.)

Van Till, William, *Prejudiced—How Do People Get That Way?* New York: ADL, 1957. Explains why people become prejudiced, and what can be done about it. Teacher guide. (Useful in Sr. H.)

Plays

Bond, Gladys Baker, *Mission Accomplished*. New York: ADL. Depicts harmful social effects of anti-Semitic prejudice.

[1] ADL—Anti-Defamation League of B'nai B'rith, 515 Madison Ave., N.Y.C.
[2] All films listed in this bibliography are 16mm.

Julian, Joseph, *The Devil and the Dream*. New York: ADL. How the devil tries to inject the seeds of prejudice into the minds of teenagers but is thwarted by the spirit of American freedom.

Films

Heritage. 10 min., ADL. An animated color cartoon on human rights, moral values, and the relationship between rights and responsibilities.

Propaganda Techniques. 10 min., Coronet Films, Chicago, Ill. Informative approach to propaganda and its detection. Also good for senior high school. Explains techniques and gives examples.

Filmstrip

Rumor Clinic. 35mm., silent, ADL. With audience participation, shows how rumors develop.

Senior High School

Books

Abrams, Charles, *Forbidden Neighbors*. New York: Harper & Row, 1955. Study of prejudice in housing.

Colman, Hila, *The Girl from Puerto Rico*. New York: William Morrow and Company, 1961. The trials of a family newly arrived from Puerto Rico.

Decter, Moshe, ed., *The Profile of Communism: A Fact-by-Fact Primer*, rev. ed. New York: Collier Books, 1961. Analyzes Communist program, strategy, inconsistencies, in question and answer form.

Lee, Alfred M., *Fraternities Without Brotherhood*. Boston: Beacon Press, 1955. Study of prejudice on the American campus.

Powdermaker, Hortense, *Probing Our Prejudices*. New York: Harper & Row, 1944. Explores the nature, origin, and effect of emotionally based prejudices. Helps high school students become aware of their own prejudices and suggests school activities.

Senior, Clarence, *Strangers—Then Neighbors: From Pilgrims to Puerto Ricans*. New York, ADL, 1961. Examines the pattern of immigration to the United States with emphasis on the most recent immigrants—the Puerto Ricans.

Waltrip, Lela and Rufus, *Quiet Boy*. New York: Longmans, Green & Co., Inc., 1961. Tale of a Navajo torn between the world of the white man and the Indian.

Pamphlets

Allport, Gordon, *ABC's of Scapegoating*, rev. ed. New York: ADL, 1959. Popular study of the psychological mechanism behind scapegoating.

Alpenfels, Ethel, *Sense and Nonsense About Race*, rev. ed. New York: Friendship Press, 1957. The concept of race and racial problems in simple anthropological terms.

Berger, Monroe, *Racial Equality and the Law*. New York: UNESCO, 1954. The effects of anti-discrimination legislation on prejudiced attitudes and practices.

Douglas, William O., *A Living Bill of Rights*. New York: ADL, 1961. Shows how the Bill of Rights protects the American citizen.

Handlin, Oscar and Mary, *Danger in Discord*. New York: ADL, 1959. Origins and history of anti-Semitism in the United States.

Hartman, Paul, *Civil Rights and Minorities*, 5th rev. New York, ADL, 1962. Report of survey of the status of civil rights in the 50 states as revealed through an analysis of state laws.

Lee, Irving J., *How Do You Talk About People?* New York: ADL, 1950. A discussion of semantics and prejudice.

Merit Employment—Why and How. Phila.: AFSC,[3] 1956. A survey of the progress made toward job equality.

Tead, Diana, *What is Race?* New York: UNESCO,[4] 1952. Illustrated discussion on race, clarifying facts as against fallacies.

Films

Boundary Lines. 10 min., color, ADL. Cartoon treatment illustrates the harmful effects of the artificial barriers man erects.

Make Way For Youth. 32 min., ADL. How teenagers shelved racial prejudice in favor of cooperative recreational and civic projects.

Picture in Your Mind. 16 min., color, ADL. Traces the roots of prejudice, and how and why man continues to have prejudices and fears.

Which Way For Human Rights? 7½ min., ADL. One of *The Challenge* series of discussion films emphasizing that violation of human rights anywhere concerns everyone.

The Challenge. 30 min., ADL. Based on the President's Committee on Civil Rights' report, a photographer-writer team makes a nationwide search to discover what people are doing to safeguard democracy.

[3] AFSC—American Friends Service Committee, 160 North 15th St., Philadelphia 2, Pa.
[4] UNESCO—152 West 42nd St., N.Y.C.

The Chosen People. 30 min., ADL.   One of a series on prejudice sponsored by the National Council of Catholic Men; this film is a sensitive discussion of the problem of anti-Semitism.

The High Wall. 32 min., ADL. The case study of a bigot and how he got that way.

To Live Together. 30 min., ADL. Tells about the experiences and difficulties encountered by a group of children at an interracial summer camp.

Teacher Reference

Books

Allport, Gordon, *The Nature of Prejudice.* Cambridge: Addison Wesley Press, 1954; New York: Anchor Books, 1958. Discussion of the legal, social, and economic aspects of group prejudice with special emphasis on the deeper psychological causes of hatred and conflict.

Belth, Nathan C., ed., Harold Braverman and Morton Puner, *Barriers.* New York: ADL, 1958. Graphic, comprehensive description of anti-Semitism and how it affects Jews.

Epstein, Benjamin R. and Arnold Forster, *Some of My Best Friends* . . . New York: Farrar, Straus & Cudahy, Inc., 1962. Tells how discrimination operates in the fields of education, employment, housing, and other aspects of American social life.

Forster, Arnold, *A Measure of Freedom.* New York: Doubleday & Company, Inc., 1950. A report of the 1949 survey on anti-Semitism in the United States.

——, and Benjamin Epstein, *The Troublemakers.* New York: Doubleday & Company, Inc., 1952. A report of the individuals and organizations active in fomenting racial and religious dissension.

Goodman, Mary E., *Race Awareness in Young Children.* Cambridge: Addison-Wesley Press, 1952; New York: Collier Books, 1962. A study of nursery school children—what they think and feel about race and how they learned it.

Noar, Gertrude, *Freedom to Live and Learn.* Philadelphia: Franklin Publishing Co., 1948. Methods and techniques of unit teaching and using the human relations approach to content and learning activities.

——, *The Junior High School—Today and Tomorrow,* 2nd ed. Englewood Cliffs, N.J.: Prentice-Hall, Inc., 1961. Teaching and organizing procedures for the development of a junior high school curriculum based on meeting the needs of early adolescents.

Taba, Hilda, *et al., Reading Ladders For Human Relations.* Washington, D.C.: American Council on Education, 1949. Bibliography arranged according to interest areas.

Trager, Helen G. and Marian Radke Yarrow, *They Learn What They Live: A Study of Prejudice in Young Children*. New York: Harper & Row, 1952. In-service education programs and experimental work with children are documented, interpreted, and evaluated in an attempt to discover and understand the genesis and growth of prejudice.

Pamphlets

Allport, Gordon, *The Resolution of Intergroup Tensions*. New York: NCCJ.[5] Examination of the various methods used in efforts to reduce intergroup tensions.

Books For Friendship (rev. ed. of *Books are Bridges*). New York: ADL and AFSC, 1962. Annotated list of books graded from kindergarten to upper junior high which depict fairly and sympathetically people of all religious, racial, regional, national, and economic groups.

Noar, Gertrude, *Information Is Not Enough*, rev. ed. New York: ADL, 1961. Indicates that the student needs more than facts about races and nationalities to help him overcome prejudice.

Rose, Arnold, *The Roots of Prejudice*. New York: UNESCO, 1951. Surveys some of the main factors producing prejudice.

Valien, Bonita, *The St. Louis Story*. New York: ADL, 1956. A study of the successful desegregation of the St. Louis schools and the factors behind it.

HUMAN RIGHTS

Rationale

The American Bill of Rights, which includes the first ten and the 13th, 14th, 15th, and 19th Amendments to the Constitution, the Universal Declaration of Human Rights, and other similarly motivated documents are the results of man's age-old longing to be free. They were created while man struggled to mold society in his best interests. Like all great universal expressions, these declarations of man's aspirations must find application in the personal life and behavior of the individual. Thus, these great concepts fall within the realm of activity and comprehension for all people from early childhood through life.

Adolescents will understand that they, as well as those with whom

[5] NCCJ—National Conference of Christians and Jews, 43 West 57th St., N.Y.C.

they live, work, and play, have rights which should not be infringed upon. This concept grows in depth as they develop values out of their experiences at home, in the community, and at school. If in the classroom they share in planning, decision-making, and evaluating, they begin to experience the exercise of rights through democratic processes. In adolescence, they reach for independence, asserting themselves as individuals. They spend considerable time and thought examining their rights. Adolescents are sharply aware of and concerned with interpersonal and intergroup relations, with tensions and conflicts, and with the operation of law and order.

Research questionnaires, opinion polls, and examinations administered in school and college classrooms have revealed an appalling lack of understanding of the meaning of the provisions of the Bill of Rights. Interviews and discussions with students have revealed also a widespread unwillingness to accept the provisions of the first ten Amendments to the Federal Constitution. Many of the youth of the land seem to be unwilling to behave or to permit others to behave in consonance with this document, which is so basic to American life.

In view of this lack of information, understanding, and commitment, and of the current threat to freedom, a unit of study on the general subject of human rights, or one on the American Bill of Rights, seems to be mandatory for secondary schools.

Basic to an understanding of democracy and preparation for participation in it is the recognition of man's desire for liberty and his spiritual urge to attain dignity, self-respect, and security. The student who is on his way to active and intelligent participation in our democracy must come to realize his own value and importance as an individual—in relation to himself, to others, and to the world around him. Teachers have the responsibility, therefore, to help the student to find meaning in his own life, to understand the values of the American way of life, and to instill in him commitment to the ideals and principles of our democratic society.

Basic Democratic Principles

Every individual, because he is a human being, in his own right has worth, dignity, and significance.

Every person in the United States is entitled to first-class citizenship.

Democracy endows all people with the rights included in the American Bill of Rights and later Amendments.

The rights guaranteed to the people must be respected by the government and its officials.

"Freedom is the way we think about and treat a non-conforming neighbor, a dissenter, the holder of a minority view among us, and the liberty he actually enjoys."[1]

Content Outline

1. Historical backgrounds—some highlights:

Magna Carta, 1215. "To none will we sell . . . deny . . . delay right or justice."

The Mayflower Compact, 1620. ". . . to exact . . . just and equal laws . . . for the general good of the colony. . . ."

The Petition of Right, 1628. ". . . no . . . tax . . . without common consent by act of Parliament. . . ."

The English Bill of Rights, 1689. ". . . suspending of laws . . . without consent of Parliament is illegal. . . ."

Patrick Henry's speech before the Virginia Convention, 1775. ". . . give me liberty or give me death!"

The Declaration of Independence, 1776. ". . . all men are created equal . . . [and are] endowed by [their] Creator with certain inalienable rights . . . life, liberty, and the pursuit of happiness . . ."

The Constitution of the United States and the Amendments, 1787. "This Constitution . . . shall be the supreme Law of the Land."

The Emancipation Proclamation, 1863. ". . . All persons held as slaves within any state . . . shall be . . . forever free. . . ."

Lincoln's Gettysburg Address, 1863. ". . . government of the people, by the people, for the people shall not perish from the earth."

Supreme Court of the United States, May 17, 1954. Brown v. Board of Education—347 U.S. 483, 98 L.Ed. 873, 74 S.Ct. 686 ". . . in the field of public education the doctrine of 'separate but equal' has no place."

2. Great leaders who have fought for the principles of human rights belong to all races and all religious and nationality groups. Their lives and contributions are of interest:

1 William O. Douglas, *A Living Bill of Rights* (N.Y.: ADL, 1961), p. 25.

Susan B. Anthony
Carrie Chapman Catt
William O. Douglas
Frederick Douglass
William L. Garrison
Samuel Gompers
Andrew Hamilton
Justice Oliver Wendell Holmes
Thomas Jefferson
John F. Kennedy

Asser Levy
Abraham Lincoln
James Madison
Thomas Paine
Eleanor Roosevelt
Franklin Delano Roosevelt
Earl Warren
Roger Williams
John Peter Zenger

3. Basic concepts pupils need to understand:

authority and the rule of law and order
equality before the law
freedom within the law
human worth and dignity
morality and moral duty
representative government
individual and collective responsibility
civil rights and civil liberties
social mobility
social class

4. Words pupils need to learn to spell and comprehend:

amendment, authority, citizen, constitution, declaration, discrimination, executive, freedom, grievance, independent, indictment, judiciary, jury, legislative, moral, principle, redress, responsibility, security, seizure, trial, universal

5. The provisions of the Bill of Rights and the Declaration of Human Rights:

Freedoms and rights guaranteed: of thought, belief, and expression; to safety and security of person; to trial; to property; to equality of opportunity; to vote; to peaceable assembly; to the privileges and immunities of citizenship.

6. Governmental institutions that protect citizens' rights:

Courts—local, federal, superior, supreme.
State legislatures, city councils, Federal Congress.

Governors' and Mayors' official commissions on human relations, civil
  rights, or intergroup relations.
Fair employment commissions and agencies.
Fire, Health, Police Departments.
United Nations.
Committees and commissions against discriminations.

7. Nongovernmental agencies that work to safeguard civil rights:

Students should learn to appreciate that in a democracy, in con-
trast to other forms of government, the people create and voluntarily
support organizations that give assistance to the individual in time of
need. They should learn which of the following organizations exist in
their own communities and how to get help from them.

American Civil Liberties Union
American Friends Service
  Committee
American Jewish Committee
Anti-Defamation League
Catholic Interracial Council
Governors' commissions on human
  relations

Mayors' commissions and
  committees on human relations
National Association for the
  Advancement of Colored People
National Civil Liberties Clearing
  House
National Conference of Christians
  and Jews
Public Affairs Committee
Urban League

8. Other documents (besides those listed under 1 and 5 above) which
   have influenced man's age-long struggle for freedom. Among them
   are the Bible, the French Declaration of the Rights of Man, the
   United Nations Charter, state constitutions.

9. Threats to our democratic heritage and international status:
     Maintenance and strengthening of our freedoms require vigi-
   lance and positive action. Students need inspiration and information that they may as adults commit themselves to the task of
   eliminating:

—discrimination in housing, education, employment, political and social
  life
—restrictions in immigration laws based on national and racial origins
—segregation in schools, housing, public facilities
—disregard for law and the use of violence in intergroup conflicts

—encroachment of religion on public education
—dissemination of "hate literature"
—curtailment of academic freedom
—guilt by association
—incitement to suspicion, fear, and divisiveness.

Outcomes To Be Evaluated

Recognition of the rights of pupils in the classroom to speak, to differ without anger, to be heard.

Acceptance on the part of all pupils of their obligations and responsibilities for individual effort, learning, and acceptable behavior; for sharing in the work to be done; for contributing to group efforts, to the common welfare, and to the solution of common problems.

Participation of all in making decisions which affect the individual and the group.

Applications to Daily Lives of Students:

Every person is endowed with certain rights.

Every pupil has certain rights and obligations in his class, school, home, and community. Along with these, he has responsibilities.

Every person has the right to participate in making decisions that affect him and the responsibility for being informed so that he can do so.

In a democratic organization (classroom, school, or club) problems are solved by cooperative action of leaders and people.

Every young person has citizenship obligations which increase as they move toward adulthood.

Teacher Responsibilities

Provide dictionaries, books, and other reference materials, such as pamphlets, magazines, newspapers, and copies of the documents being studied, and explain and interpret content.

Direct students to set up unit-record books and examine them at intervals.

Teach spelling, meaning, and usage of words.

Conduct planning sessions.

Assist pupils to organize committees on various aspects of the content, to plan and report.

Participate in planning and pooling sessions of all committees.

Direct and assist with the accumulation of factual and creative materials.

Secure speakers, consultants, and resource persons to meet the needs of the class.

Require and allocate time for committee progress reports.

Require all pupils to record in unit-record books factual materials and principles developed and reported by committees.

Assist in the integration of committee reports into a meaningful whole.

Arrange for trips to historical museums or government buildings to see originals or copies of documents.

Assist in preparation of scripts and dramatizations based on the lives of the persons being studied.

Select, show, and lead discussions on films.

Encourage individuals to begin collections. Provide time for them to exhibit them to the class.

Read and evaluate written reports and creative work done by individuals.

Arrange conversation circles to discuss books being read by members of the class.

Suggest various ways for individuals to write reports of and reactions to books.

Facilitate administrative procedure for securing and exhibiting material for a mobile museum.

Arrange for class and committee visits to local branches of national agencies.

Conduct tests or quizzes on facts which students should know.

Assist in securing foreign-born persons to participate in round-table discussions.

Arrange for class or committee trips to museums or exhibitions that are pertinent.

Assign, according to interests and abilities, writing of themes, compositions, codes of behavior, stories, radio scripts, personal experiences, anecdotes.

Discuss the role people play in groups; what factors make a group effective; the large number of groups to which an individual usually belongs.

Conduct role-playing (socio-dramas) when occasion permits.

Learning Activities

All pupils can engage in many of the following activities. Some should be accepted and/or assigned on the basis of individual abilities and interests.

Participate in planning the content and learning activities.

Participate in planning and organizing committees and in committee meetings and activities.

Do research for facts in dictionaries and other reference books.

Set up individual unit-record books and keep them up-to-date.

Participate in drills and tests.

Read references, texts, newspapers, magazines, pamphlets, documents, historical novels, and biographies according to individual abilities and interests.

Collect and catalogue for classroom use books and other reference materials.

Organize and participate in panel discussions on the concepts to be learned.

Plan and give progress reports of committee work.

Write brief stories or pages from a pupil's diary that would reflect the application of any one of the listed concepts to the characters or plot of the story; for example, incidents of exclusion or discrimination.

Take trips; evaluate them; crystallize learning in some form, such as letter to a friend, original story, poem, or skit. Record relevant data in unit-record books.

Set up criteria to be used in selection of class and school leaders; present them to the student government organization; use them in selecting committee leaders.

Evaluate leadership activities of committee and class officers and of other members of the group

Read one or more biographies and make relevant records of them in unit-record books.

Write and if possible, illustrate short biographies of people being discussed.

Write and produce dramatization of an event in the life of the person being studied that reflects his concern for human rights.

Write letters of invitation and thanks to speakers and other resource persons.

Write letters, telephone, and communicate in other ways with people regarding arrangements for interviews and trips.

See and discuss films.

Individuals may begin collections of relevant biographies, portraits, famous sayings, documentary items in the news, songs.

Take part in conversations about books.

Collect documents, books, illustrations, replicas, postcards that are in some way connected with the Bill of Rights in American life for a mobile museum.

Participate in surveys administered by the teacher or a committee to obtain information and opinion regarding the provisions in the Bill of Rights.

Listen to speakers from government agencies speak on the relationship of that agency to human rights.

Prepare questions for speakers.

Prepare and give speeches of introduction and thanks for speeches.

Organize and participate in panels to discuss such questions as:

—How do our internal conflicts regarding human rights affect our international status?
—How can the American people best promote democracy in the world?
—Is our own community a testing ground for democracy?

Prepare, individually or with a small group, a radio script on human rights suitable for broadcasting.

Examine the student government with respect to the extent of student representation, use of student taxes, authority vested in it, responsibilities.

Participate in evaluation of committee work, group discussions, election and appointment of officers.

Evaluate self.

Suggested Activities

Reading

Newspapers, pamphlets, magazine articles, reference books, text-books, documents, novels, and plays. See References at the end of this unit for titles.

Discussion

Discuss in class, committees, and panels such subjects as:

Problems and progress of desegregation of public schools in the North and the South.

Meaning of provisions in the Bill of Rights and the Declaration of Human Rights.

Current nonviolence movement; sit-in demonstrations and Free-dom Riders.

Techniques used by political extremists.

The meaning of "separation of church and state" and its relation-ship to religion in public education.

Reactions around the world to newspaper items which describe our failure to secure first-class citizenship for all our people.

Evaluation of committee work, of individuals, of processes used, of the unit itself.

Time lines

Construct time lines for man's struggle for liberty through the ages; America's progress toward universal first-class citizenship.

Committees

Set up Committees for the following purposes:

research for facts
clipping and filing pictures and articles of interest
securing and using audio-visual aids
housekeeping
interviewing people
maintaining library to catalogue, issue, and check return of books and
  pamphlets

securing and preparing for speakers, consultants, and resource persons
planning for trips
securing, scanning, classifying, and filing free and inexpensive materials.

Art work

Study great artists who devoted their talents to human rights and
their pictures; for example, Kaethe Kollwitz, Orozco, and Rivera.
Produce illustrations, murals, posters.
Collect relevant pictures from newspapers and magazines.
Draw and collect cartoons.

Music

Listen to recordings and sing some of the "songs of protest." These
can be obtained from Folkway Records, 117 W. 46th Street, N.Y.,
N.Y., and the Library of Congress, Washington, D.C. (The teacher
should hear these before using in the classroom.)

Dramatics

Stage dramatic readings of such plays as *Purlie Victorious*, Ossie
Davis; *A Raisin in the Sun*, Lorraine Hansberry; *Waiting for Lefty*,
Clifford Odets; *The Male Animal*, Elliot Nugent and James Thurber.
Produce programs for radio written by pupils in the class.
Produce original plays.

Trips

Visit one or more of the following:

historical museums to see original documents
Washington, D.C.
historic section of Philadelphia
Williamsburg, Virginia
local places of historical interest
New York City and the United Nations
local seats of government
state capitols

Speakers, consultants, and resource persons

Local governmental officials
Visiting teachers and students from other countries

Veterans who served in armies of occupation in various countries
Directors of civic and human relations agencies
Local judges and lawyers

Writing

Letters of invitation and thanks to speakers, consultants, and resource persons.

Stories and plays and poems based upon historical and current events that grow out of the exercise or denial of civil rights.

Radio programs: interviews, quizzes, plays.

Committee reports and research papers.

Essay questions in tests.

Role-playing

Act out social episodes in which individuals are denied civil rights.

Attempt to explain civil rights to a visitor from Russia, from Germany, from China.

Pretend to be a speaker faced with a hostile audience using the techniques of the political extremists and demagogues.

TV and radio

Listen to, see, discuss, and evaluate relevant programs.

Films

See, discuss, and evaluate such films and filmstrips as:

Almanac of Liberty. 55 min., b&w, ADL. A kinescope of the CBS *Studio One* production, inspired by the book of the same name by Supreme Court Justice William O. Douglas.

An American Girl. 28 min., b&w, ADL. Tells the story of an American teenager who stands up for her right to be different.

Crisis in Levittown. 30 min., b&w, ADL. A series of interviews with residents, both for and against the integration of the first Negro family to move into Levittown, Pa.

Defining Democracy. 17 min., b&w, Encyclopaedia Britannica Films. An outline to help students differentiate between a democracy and a totalitarian form of government.

Discussion in a Democracy. 10 min., b&w, Coronet Film. Through expert advice and their own experience, a typical group of students learn the importance of discussion in a democracy.

Freedom to Learn. 28 min., b&w and color, ADL. A high school teacher, charged with teaching communism, is called before the school board and expresses her confidence in the traditional American right of freedom to learn.

Freedom to Read. 14 min., b&w, ADL. A film in the Challenge series that deals with a conflict over the kinds of books to be kept in the community library.

Great American Series, *Statesmen of America.* Encyclopaedia Britannica Films, 10 films. Dramatic presentations of episodes in the lives of ten famous American political leaders: Adams, Calhoun, Franklin, Hamilton, Jackson, Lincoln, Marshall, Washington, and Webster.

Which Way for Human Rights? 9 min., b&w, ADL. Deals with the Universal Declaration of Human Rights and is designed to stimulate discussion about the violation of those rights. Employs open-end technique.

Filmstrips

Anatomy of Nazism. 50 frame color filmstrip, ADL. Vivid analysis of 20th century totalitarianism. Documentary photographs of Nazis in Germany.

A U.S. Citizen and His Governments. Series of 4 filmstrips, color, 220 frames, American Council on Education, Washington, D.C. Part IV of this series, called *Securing the Blessings of Liberty,* examines the basic concepts underlying U.S. government.

Let's Live Democracy. 43 frames, b&w, ADL. Analysis of social and economic factors which gave rise to discrimination against minority groups. A plea for equal rights and opportunities for all men.

Our Constitution, The Bill of Rights and Other Amendments. 45 frames, McGraw-Hill Book Co., N.Y. Through cartoons, this filmstrip discusses the rights guaranteed to all citizens. Accompanying pamphlet suggests points to be emphasized.

To Secure These Rights. 50 frames, b&w, silent with script, ADL. Graphic story of the report of the President's Committee on Civil Rights. Contrasts American ideals in U.S. Constitution with actual practices.

Recordings

Listen to, discuss and evaluate recordings as:

"Human Rights," Folkways Records Album No. FH-5524. A documentary on the Declaration of Human Rights featuring an interview with Mrs. Eleanor Roosevelt. Accompanied by script and complete document.

"No Man Is an Island," Decca Records Album No. A-349. Consists of a collection of famous speeches (by Pericles, Paine, Webster, Lincoln, and so forth) dealing with the theme of brotherhood and the dignity of man. They are read by Orson Welles.

"The Signing of the Magna Carta," Columbia Records, New York, N.Y., 1949. 12″ LP. CBS is broadcasting: "This is John Daly at Runny-mede, England. The hour has come and gone, on this 10th day of June, 1215, the hour when King John agreed to sign the Magna Carta . . ."

Evaluation

Use discussions of process and products, information tests, and essay questions to evaluate unit.

Culminating Activities

In many cases a unit ends with two important learning sessions which involve the entire class. The first of these is devoted to pulling all threads together, examining facts, weighing them for relative values, integrating them, crystallizing meanings, drawing some conclusions, noting information still lacking, and considering how the learnings can be applied to the life of the individual and the group. The final session of a unit is devoted to evaluation of information learned, of group process, of leadership skills, and of ability to follow.

Toward the close of other units, however, the teacher should raise the questions: Is what we learned of sufficient value to pass on to others? If so, to whom? How shall we do that? In such a situation, the class can then move into planning and carrying out a culminating activity. Following are suggestions for such projects:

1. Plan and hold an exhibition of documents and the other materials created by the class. Write letters of invitation to other classes, faculty, principal, superintendent, PTA to come and see the exhibition. Assign posts to members of the class and hold them responsible for explaining exhibits to visitors.

2. Plan and produce an assembly program. This could be a panel discussion, a most important speaker, a presentation of collected materials to the library, a dramatic production of an original play.

3. Conduct a poll of the student body to determine the extent of agreement with the provisions of the Bill of Rights. Present and explain the results through the medium of the school newspaper and/or assembly platform.

4. Plan and take a trip to Washington, D.C. or to the United Nations in New York City. (This, of course, depends upon the distance and costs involved.)

REFERENCES

Books

Bontemps, Arna, *The Story of the Negro.* New York: Alfred A. Knopf, Inc., 1948. A history of the American Negro, emphasizing the role of Negro leaders who fought for the complete emancipation of their people.

Brown, F. J. and J. S. Roucek, eds., *One America.* Englewood Cliffs, N.J.: Prentice-Hall, Inc., 1952. History, contributions, and problems of important religious, ethnic, and racial groups in America.

Brown, H. and J. Guadagnolo, *America Is My Country.* Boston: Houghton Mifflin Co., 1955. A book to tell young people about the high ideals of our nation's founding, and to teach them what their rights and freedoms are.

Brown, S. G., ed., *We Hold These Truths.* New York: Harper & Row, 1948. A source book. A collection of 56 documents that express our democratic ideals and methods from the Mayflower Compact to the report of the President's Committee on Civil Rights in 1947.

Decter, Moshe, ed., *The Profile of Communism: A Fact-by-Fact Primer,* rev. ed. New York: Collier Books, 1961. Analyzes Communist program, strategy, and inconsistencies, in question and answer form.

MacIver, Robert M., *Great Expressions of Human Rights,* Institute for Religious and Social Studies. New York: Harper & Row, 1950. Fourteen great historical documents are interpreted by noted authorities for practical application today.

Morgan, Joy E., ed., *An American Citizen's Handbook.* Washington, D.C.: National Education Association, 1947. This handbook consists of essays, documents, poetry, and songs connected with American history and brief biographies of certain great figures in the past. Also included are nine great charters of democracy from Magna Carta to the U.N. Charter, thumbnail sketches of each state of the U.S., and statistical sketches on each of the nations belonging to the UN.

Pfeffer, Leo, *The Liberties of an American: The Supreme Court Speaks.* Boston: Beacon Press, 1956. The rulings of the Supreme Court in historical setting are comprehensively set forth in this book for the general reader.

They Made a Nation, Tufts Civic Education Center, Living Democracy Series. Washington, D.C.: National Council for the Social Studies, 1948. An effective recreation of the people and times of the American Revolution with an account of the writing of the Constitution and thumbnail sketches of the men who signed.

To Secure These Rights, President's Committee on Civil Rights. New York: Simon and Schuster, Inc., 1947. The report investigates the problems of discrimination in the U.S., points up the gap between American ideals and practices, and indicates a plan of action.

Pamphlets

Baldwin, R., *Human Rights—World Declaration and American Practice.* New York: Public Affairs Committee (22 E. 38th St.), 1950. An explanation of the articles of the UN Declaration of Human Rights and a summary of the related American practices.

Civic Education Foundation, *And Crown Thy Good.* Medford, Mass.: Tufts University, 1952. A graphically written pamphlet for junior high school, on the concepts of our rights and their application in daily living.

Community Relations Service, *You, Your Town, Your World and Human Rights.* New York: Community Relations Service (165 E. 56th St.), 1955. A practical guide for the community leader on the meaning of our rights and what can be done to secure appreciation and practice.

Douglas, William O., *A Living Bill of Rights.* New York: ADL, 1961. Describes how the Bill of Rights protects the American citizen.

Leskes, Theodore, *The Civil Rights Story.* New York: American Jewish Committee, yearly summary. Gives background and interpretation of two major civil rights events: the enactment by the 85th Congress of civil rights legislation, and the developments in Little Rock, Arkansas.

Mack, Robert W., *Do We Really Believe in the Bill of Rights?* Reprint from *Social Problems* (Northwestern University, Evanston, Ill.), April 1956. A report on the study made by Professor Mack of university students and their belief or disbelief in the basic principles of the Bill of Rights.

Raab, Earl, *The Anatomy of Nazism.* New York: ADL, 1961. Brief basic history of Nazism—its origin, techniques and philosophy.

Sparling, Edward, *Civil Rights—Barometer of Democracy.* New York:

ADL, 1949. Examination of the status of civil rights in the United States.

United Nations, *The United Nations and What You Should Know About It*. New York: UN Department of Public Information, 1962. A UN source book with illustrations and descriptions of the organization, services, programs, and specialized agencies around the world.

Fiction

Bryan, Florence H., *Susan B. Anthony*. New York: Julian Messner, Inc., 1947. Fictionalized biography of the pioneer suffragette who, as early as 1850, demanded that all people, regardless of color and sex, enjoy the same basic citizenship rights and privileges.

Eaton, Jeanette, *Lone Journey: The Life of Roger Williams*. New York: Harcourt, Brace & Co., 1944. A fictionalized biography which portrays the historical setting of the life of this fighter for religious freedom.

Frank, Anne, *Diary of a Young Girl*. New York: Doubleday & Co., Inc., 1950. (Also available in Pocket Books, N.Y., 1952.) A young girl's account dramatically shows how a totalitarian government runs rough-shod over the liberties and rights of an individual.

Lee, Harper, *To Kill a Mockingbird*. Philadelphia: J. B. Lippincott Co., 1960. Vivid story of children growing up in the midst of hatred and injustice in the South, with a father willing, not only to stand up and be counted, but to fight, in the courtroom, for the rights of all men.

Hawthorne, Hildegarde, *His Country Was the World: A Life of Thomas Paine*. New York: Longmans, Green & Co., Inc., 1949. The story of a fighter for freedom of the human race and a philosopher of the American Revolution.

Lewis, Sinclair, *It Can't Happen Here*. New York, Doubleday & Co., Inc., 1935. The novelist projects a dictatorship in America and shows what could happen to our traditional rights and privileges.

Smith, Lillian E., *Killers of the Dream*. New York: W. W. Norton & Co., 1949. A most sympathetic picture of the mores and values of the South comes through essentially biographical material. It sheds light in dark places.

RACE AND RACE RELATIONS

Rationale

A satirical column written by James A. Wechsler in *The New York Post* of July 25, 1962 begins with the following imaginary report quoted as coming from *The Insider's Newsletter*. "A unique solution to the world's racial tension may be developed by the end of the century—and it will come in a bottle.

"Scientists say they will be able to produce a pill in the next 50 years which would control skin color."

Wechsler then gives dispatches supposedly transmitted by the Associated Press early in 1963 from foreign capitals and major American cities, and statements made by prominent political figures in the North and South. They differed widely, according to the thought patterns of the areas they represented and of the individuals speaking.

Is skin color the major issue that confronts America along with the rest of the world? Not really, for no one group of people has a monopoly on any one color. They are all shades, from light to dark. For example, Caucasians, the so-called white race, vary from the light skin of some Scandinavians to very dark people in India. Negroes, on the other hand, vary from the almost black skinned Africans to some Americans who have very fair skins.

The problem is deeper and much more serious than skin color. To understand it and to move constructively toward its solution, people need not pills, but large doses of information to correct myths and superstitions; new experiences to rid them of prejudice, fear, insecurity, and guilt; and a positive climate of public opinion and laws to wipe out racial discrimination. If children now in school are to be equipped for the tasks they face in adulthood, teachers must mobilize for them the necessary facts about race from biology and anthropology, and the required understandings about race relations from sociology, political science, and economics.

The study of race and race relations must begin early. By the time children are four and five they absorb the values which are attached to words denoting color. For example, in the English language, light means better than dark, brown is associated with soil and thus with dirt. The kindergarten and first grade teachers therefore face the task of adding other associations and values to colors, and of dissociating the *value* from the *person* whose skin color is light or dark. Moreover, difference itself should be established as good and beautiful.

In the primary grades, along with the study of community helpers and the various occupations of their fathers, children can learn that *race* does not determine ability to *become*. They must be helped to see that some persons of all races become doctors, lawyers, and teachers, and that all the other jobs in our society are also done by persons of all racial groups.

As early as the fourth grade many children can learn the scientific facts about race, and all of them can learn the cause of variation in skin color. They will also ask many questions about race relations that are reflected in the newspaper headlines they read and the radio and TV news broadcasts they see and hear. By the time boys and girls are in the junior high school, they are ready for a unit on the subject.

This resource outline presents a review of the information to be included in units on race or race relations or on both aspects of the problem. Since many students drop out after the ninth grade, a unit in the junior high school should be as comprehensive as possible. What it will contain must be decided in light of the maturity of the pupils, the questions they raise, and the nature of the local situation. Senior high school students should be encouraged to explore the issues in depth.

In all units on race and race relations, teachers must make clear to students and, if necessary, to their parents, that democratic values and principles are involved; that the values of the Judaeo-Christian ethic are at stake; that the failure of Americans to solve the problems endangers both the nation's internal welfare and international relations. Democracy is on trial around the world, and the public school cannot dodge the issue.

Textbooks

Because books suitable for upper elementary and secondary school use are not generally available, the following pamphlets are recommended for use in place of textbooks.

Alpenfels, Ethel, *Sense and Nonsense About Race*, rev. ed. New York: Friendly House Press, 1959.

Montagu, Ashley, *What We Know About "Race."* New York: ADL, 1958. (Teacher guide)

Tead, Diana, *What Is Race?* New York, UNESCO, 1952.

Presentation of content in graphic form makes the UNESCO publication particularly valuable for all school levels and for both verbally gifted and slow readers.

Approaches

The one to be used must be selected on the basis of maturity of pupils and the local situation.

Discussion of an interracial incident such as name calling, scapegoating, rejection, exclusion, discrimination or violence occurring in the classroom, the cafeteria, the play area, or the community, or reported in the news media.

A trip into the community during which its racial composition is observed.

A film or TV broadcast dealing with problems of race relations.

A speaker on the implications of race relations for the survival of democracy.

Objectives

To give secondary school students information.

To correct widespread misinformation and superstitions.

To counteract rumors which create tensions and conflict.

To develop positive attitudes toward racial differences.

To develop democratic values and implement democratic principles.

Content

Definition: A race is "a group of people which shares in common a certain set of innate physical characters and a geographical origin within a certain area."[1]

Major races: Anthropologists classify people as Mongoloid, Negroid, and Caucasoid. Ethnic groups (Italian or English) and culture-religious groups (Jews) are not races.

Origin of races: The theory most widely accepted today ascribes race to the role played by the genes in inheritance, mutation, accidental loss or fixation of genes and to the role of natural selection, adaptation, migration, and geographical isolation.[2] Students should also learn about evolution.

The myth of racial superiority: There is no conclusive evidence that

[1] J. B. S. Haldane, in *What Is Race?*, page 36.
[2] See Diana Tead, *What Is Race?* (N.Y.: UNESCO, 1952).

any one race is better than others with respect to intelligence, physical or athletic ability, musical or artistic talent, mechanical or scientific inventiveness, or any of the other intellectual, physical, or emotional characteristics shared by all mankind.

The cause of skin color: The quantity and dispersion of melanin causes differences in skin color.

History

Negro participation in explorations of America
Slavery
Emancipation
"Jim Crowism"
American Indians
Integration and assimilation
Progress
Orientals on the West Coast during World War II, after World War II
Desegregation movements

Leaders and contributors to civilization

A wide variety of people from such fields as history, literature, music, art, science, governmental and social service can be selected. They should be whites, Negroes, and Orientals. Those who are living as well as those from the past should be included.

Problems of race relations in America

The nature and genesis of prejudice
Discrimination in employment, housing, public facilities, social clubs, and education
Stereotypes to be recognized, tested for reality, and challenged at all times
Current movements to secure full civil rights for Negroes: Freedom Riders, sit-in demonstrations, Black Muslims (Negro Nationalism)
Segregation
Desegregation in public schools, colleges, and universities
Social class and caste
Intermarriage

Legislation

National Civil Rights Acts of 1957, 1960
State laws for and against segregation
Laws affecting the status of Orientals

Learning Activities

Study of words and concepts

Students should learn to read, spell, use, and define such words and concepts as the following:

anthropology	genes	Oriental
assimilation	geographic isolation	preference
attitude	inheritance	prejudice
Caucasoid	integration	race
conflict	legislation	segregation
culture patterns	Mongoloid	sociology
desegregation	mutation	stereotype
ethnic origins	myth	tension
evolution	Negroid	voluntary association

Identification of prejudices, stereotypes, and misinformation

Corrective teaching cannot begin until the teacher knows what his pupils think and feel. This will be facilitated by the use of the following devices:

1. Open-end questions.

The open-end question or statement stimulates highly thoughtful creative writing which, under ordinary circumstances, will reveal negative attitudes based upon prejudicial stereotypes. Preliminary to writing, ten or fifteen minutes should be used as "warm-up." During this time the teacher tells of his own experiences and feelings and encourages many pupils to talk about themselves. He then develops with the pupils, and places on the board, a number of open-end sentences. He stresses freedom of choice as to which one each student shall use in his own writing. Students must be assured that what they write will be read only by the teacher. Examples of such sentences are:

To my mind, races (or religions) should be segregated (desegregated) because . . .

When I think about Negroes (or Chinese), I see . . .

I am afraid (not afraid) of people whose skin color is not white because . . .

I went to an intergroup party which turned out to be a bad (good) experience because . . .

2. Checklists of characteristics, such as:

Choose one or more words from the list of characteristics, on the right, which, to your mind, describes each of the groups of people listed on the left:

People	Characteristics	
White	superior	intelligent
Negro	inferior	aggressive
Yellow	cultured	servile
Indian	mercenary	undemocratic
Puerto Rican	uncivilized	literary
Mexican	smart	musical
Aryan	educable	indolent
Anglo-Saxon	democratic	energetic
American	reserved	dark skinned
French	artistic	aristocratic
Italian		
English		

3. Social distance inventory, such as:

—If you had a party, which kinds of people (white, Negro, Oriental, Mexican, and so forth) would you exclude? invite?
—Name three kinds of people (races) you would like to have as neighbors.

4. Short answer tests (true and false or completion), such as:

—All people in the same race are of the same color.
—The white race is superior to all others.
—Negroes have less mental ability than whites.
—Three races of mankind are . . . ., ..., ...
—Negro blood is the same as (different from) white blood.

Reading

Textbooks and reference books, newspapers, pamphlets, and magazines that discuss racial problems will provide factual material. Novels and plays will provide opportunities to study human relations. (See References for titles.)

Conversation circles

Conversation circles consisting of a cross-section of the class can be used to exchange experiences, ideas, and factual information gained from research.

Committee work

Committees can be formed to cover such parts of the content as concepts of race; history of Negroes, of Orientals, of Indians in America; the theory of evolution; effects of environment; discrimination in various aspects of American life.

Speakers, consultants and resource persons

Such persons can be obtained from organizations, such as the Urban League, National Association for the Advancement of Colored People, Committee on Racial Equality, Anti-Defamation League, American Civil Liberties Union, from local government departments, business, industry, and the professions.

Trips

—to historical museums and libraries
—to business, industry, government offices, to investigate discrimination
—to various sections of a city to investigate housing and living conditions

Films[3]

Boundary Lines. 10 min., color. Modern art and music intensify a dramatic cartoon showing the fallacy of artificial boundary lines separating people and nations.

Man—One Family. 17 min., b&w. Emphasizes the principle that there is no master race and no distinct racial groups among human beings.

Picture In Your Mind. 16 min., color. Earliest roots of prejudice and the reasons why any group, tribe, or nation thinks its way of life is superior to all others.

[3] All the above films are 16 mm. and are available from ADL.

One People. 12 min., color. Portrays by cartoon characters superimposed upon a map of the United States the various nationalities that have come to this country.

The High Wall. 32 min., b&w. A boy's hatred of people who are racially, religiously, and culturally different is traced back to his early childhood. His hostilities are found to be a contagious infection, communicable from parent to child.

Crisis in Levittown, Pa. 30 min., b&w. Dr. Dan Dodson of the N.Y.U. Center for Human Relations interviews residents about their feelings and actions when a Negro family moves into the community.

Wanted—A Place to Live. 15 min., b&w. This discussion film on the subject of minority group discrimination in housing raises very serious questions, the solutions of which are left to the audience.

The Story of Sammy Lee. 30 min., b&w. An Olympic swimming champion meets prejudice and discrimination when he tries to buy a home. Interviews with many people show that all Americans are not bigoted.

Radio and TV

Relevant programs should be seen and heard both at home and in school where they should be discussed and evaluated.

REFERENCES

Books

Baldwin, James, *Nobody Knows My Name.* N.Y.: Dial Press, 1961. The author confronts himself in this six year log of his experiences abroad. He writes about others, too—Mailer, Wright, Faulkner. He calls upon America, to which he returns, to take a new look at committment to freedom.

Barnett, Anthony, *The Human Species.* N.Y.: W. W. Norton & Company, Inc., 1950. A study of the biology of man. Good treatment of diversity.

Boyd, W.C., *Genetics and the Races of Man.* Boston: Little, Brown & Co., 1950. Clear presentation of recent trends in biological study of race.

Brown, J. Francis and Joseph S. Roucek, *One America.* Englewood Cliffs, N.J.: Prentice-Hall, Inc., 1952. The history, contributions, and present problems of religious, ethnic, and racial groups in America.

Dexter, Harriet H., *What's Right With Race Relations.* N.Y.: Harper & Row, 1958. A nationwide account of American accomplishments based on study of education, employment, housing, transportation, recreation, churches, voting, the press, the courts, and the armed forces.

Greenberg, Jack, *Race Relations and American Law*. N.Y.: Columbia University Press, 1959. A treatise on the law of race relations as it exists today. Draws the conclusion that law does make a difference. Study is broadly conceived and well researched.

Hughes, Langston, *A Pictorial History of the Negro in America*. N.Y.: Crown Publishers, Inc., 1956. Photographs, drawings and brief lucid articles.

Lerner, Marguerite R., *Red Man, White Man, African Chief*. Minneapolis, Minn.: Medical Books for Children, 1961. An illustrated, simplified discussion of the cause of skin color. Suitable for grades 4 to 7.

Montague, Ashley, *Man's Most Dangerous Myth: The Fallacy of Race*. 3rd ed. N.Y.: Harper & Row, 1952. False beliefs are exploded with scientific facts and principles.

Race and Science. N.Y.: UNESCO, 1961. Based on *Race and Psychology, Race and Culture,* and *Race and Biology*. Illustrated in color. Discussion guide.

Rose, Arnold, *The Negro in America*. Boston: Beacon Press, 1948, Chap. ii, xiii, xiv.

Rowan, Carl T., *Go South to Sorrow*. N.Y.: Random House, Inc., 1957. A vivid description of events in the south during the years immediately following the Supreme Court's decision on segregation in education.

Woodward, C. V., *The Strange Career of Jim Crow*. New York: Oxford Univ. Press, 1955. Traces the practice of segregation in the South, from its beginnings after the Civil War.

Pamphlets

American Friends Service Committee, *Race and Conscience in America*. Norman: University of Oklahoma Press, 1959. States the basic issues, attitudes toward slavery, the doctrine of separate but equal, the impact of segregation, and the responsibility of the individual.

Courlander, Harold, *On Recognizing the Human Species*. New York: ADL, 1960. Shows that social divergencies cannot disguise the basic unity of human traditions and customs.

Hartman, Paul, *Civil Rights and Minorities*. New York: ADL, 1962. Report of survey of the status of civil rights in the 50 states as revealed through an analysis of state laws.

Klineberg, Otto, *Race and Psychology*. New York: UNESCO, 1951. Provides evidence that there are no inherent racial differences in intelligence and that differences are due to environment and opportunity.

North, Robert D., *Research Report Bulletin—The Intelligence of the*

American Negro. New York: ADL, 1956. Evidence is presented to re-affirm the conclusion that intelligence is not based on racial differences.

Van Til, William, *Prejudiced—How Do People Get That Way?* New York: ADL, 1957. Teacher guide. Illustrated text provides easy reading on a complex subject. Guide gives suggestions for additional learning activities.

Novels

D'Usseau, Arnaud, *Deep Are the Roots.* New York: Charles Scribner's Sons, 1946.

Lee, Harper, *To Kill A Mockingbird.* Philadelphia: J. B. Lippincott Co., 1960

Paton, Alan, *Cry the Beloved Country.* New York: Charles Scribner's Sons, 1948.

Peterson, Louis S., *Take A Giant Step.* New York: Samuel French, Inc., 1954.

Plays, Musicals and Moving Pictures

Flower Drum Song
Madame Butterfly
Othello
Porgy and Bess
Purlie Victorious

Raisin in the Sun
South Pacific
The King and I
West Side Story
Winged Victory

AMERICAN CULTURAL PLURALISM

Rationale

Study of American society includes the philosophy of cultural pluralism which now dominates sociological and educational thought and, to a great extent, planning for intergroup education. Its principles and values derive from the nature of the peoples who settled and developed the nation and from their intergroup relationships. Numbers of people came to this country at different times in waves of immigration from all parts of the world. They brought some problems with them and found new ones waiting for them. This resource unit outline deals with the problem of immigration in the United States. The issues involved in the movement and resettlement of people are of concern to all nations, but in the United States it is particularly important to understand not only those who came in the past, but also the new immigrant—who he is, why he comes here, and what he does here.

Presidents of the United States, many members of the Congress, and religious and civic group leaders have publicly opposed the current immigration policy, which is, in many ways, inconsistent with the democratic ideals we proclaim. For example, in his State of the Union message on January 1, 1957, President Eisenhower said:

... in the four and one-half years that have elapsed since the enactment of the Immigration and Nationality Act, the practical application of that law has demonstrated certain provisions which operate inequitably and others which are outmoded in the world of today. Prompt action by the Congress is needed looking toward the revision and improvement of that law.

The present immigration law is both a serious threat to the maintenance of good international relationships and a discriminatory weapon which can be used unjustly against those who consider themselves good American citizens. Those potential citizens who never gain entry into this country might also be listed as victims of a discriminatory immigration law. The continuing use of racial criteria as a basis for entrance, the imposition of a "second-class" citizenship on those Americans who have become naturalized citizens, and the restrictive nationality quotas are some of its objectionable features.

Since one of the major responsibilities of the schools is to prepare students for active and intelligent participation in a democracy, the classroom should provide them with many opportunities to become familiar with the problems that confront the nation. The development of fair and practical immigration programs has been a major concern throughout our history. In a unit dealing with the pluralistic nature and needs of our society, the past and present problems should be surveyed and the naturalization and the integration of new Americans should be studied. The teacher must determine and select whatever content material is suitable to the needs of his pupils from the variety of suggestions for learning activities, which include a wide range of experiences and materials for pupils of varied age levels. All materials suggested have been graded and annotated. Depending upon the group and the goals desired, however, many materials can be used successfully with several age groups.

This unit deals essentially with history, present social problems, and intergroup relations. It can, therefore, be used in courses on American history, problems of democracy, and in general education classes.

Principles To Be Established

Abilities of all kinds exist in all nationality groups.

Contributions of people from all nationality groups have developed and strengthened America as a nation.

The integrity of the individual depends in large measure on his ability to accept himself and the facts of his origin. Teachers assist him when they help him to be proud of himself and his cultural heritage and do not ask him to forget the language and customs which are part of it.

Equality of status is established when the leaders, contributions, and past and present problems of the various culture groups are included in the study of American history and current affairs, and in problems of democracy courses.

The philosophy of cultural pluralism emphasizes the value of difference.

The location of one or two highly creative people may change the course of history. For example, the fact that Einstein was in the United States instead of Germany gave the U.S. primacy in developing the atom bomb.

American immigration policy and laws affect international relationships and have an effect upon the extent to which uncommitted peoples accept the reality of American democracy.

Content

1. Words and terms to be recognized, understood, and spelled:

immigrant, emigrant, quota system, religion, race, prejudice, ethnic group, ethnic origins, naturalization, citizen, refugee, alien, visa, passport, "open-door policy," open-class society.

2. Waves of immigration:

What people were involved; what they hoped to find in America: political and religious freedom, economic opportunities, an open-class society, political asylum, freedom of thought.

What people brought and continue to bring with them: culture patterns, languages, music, art, creativity, industrial skills, personal vigor and ambitions, knowledge and skills in medicine and science.

Where they came from and now come from: Scandinavia, Ireland, Germany, China, Japan, Southern, Eastern and Central European countries, Puerto Rico.

3. Discriminatory legislation:

Alien and Sedition Acts—1798
Chinese Exclusion Act—1882
Quota Law—1921
The Immigration Act—1924
Immigration and Naturalization Act—1952

4. Reasons underlying discriminatory laws:

—Regarding of immigrants as threats to economic security. (For example, unskilled workers are afraid of being replaced by Puerto Rican newcomers willing to work for less money. American doctors were afraid of competition from doctors who came as refugees from Germany during the Hitler period.)
—Religious, racial, ethnic, and social prejudice.
—Political threat of foreign ideologies, notably communism and fascism.

5. Effects of exclusion:

—Loss of opportunity for international cooperation in seeking solutions of population problems.
—Decrease in international good will.
—Manpower shortages.
—Possible loss of highly creative individuals.

6. Problems immigrants meet:

—Immediate adjustment upon arrival.
—Adjustment to and integration into American life and society:
language, customs, political ideologies, intergroup prejudices, and hostilities.

—Discrimination in housing, employment, education.
—Antagonism of super-patriotic groups.

Teacher Activities

—Provide dictionaries and materials for reference—magazines, books, poems, pamphlets, pictures.
—Assist pupils in planning unit-record books, and inspect them as pupils make notations in them.
—Provide for study and testing of spelling and meaning of new words.
—Conduct class planning discussions to set up goals and content.
—Assist pupils in organizing committees.
—Meet with committees to assist them with planning, pooling, discussing, and reporting.
—Provide art materials.
—Assist pupils in creative writing: stories, plays, poems, autobiographies.
—Help pupils to produce plays.
—Secure and show audio-visual aids, preview those selected for use, conduct discussion of them.
—Plan time for class to hear committees' reports. Conduct discussion of them.
—Assist committees to plan field trips.
—Provide information about possible speakers and consultants.
—Assist pupil committee to formulate questions for interviews and for speakers; for presentation and thank-you remarks.
—Maintain classroom library with appropriate books: nonfiction, novels, plays, poems, stories, biographies.
—Provide time for reading aloud and discussion of poems.
—Plan with class for sharing readings—conversation circles about books.
—Plan and conduct role-playing experiences.
—Use projective techniques (social preference tests, matching traits and nationalities) to help pupils determine their prejudices and recognize stereotypes.
—Initiate discussion of and help pupils to plan a culminating activity.

Pupil Activities

Use dictionaries to find spelling and meaning of new words and take spelling tests.
Write sentences and paragraphs using words learned.
Browse, read, and discuss in order to clarify concepts.
Participate in planning goals, content, and activities.

Organize committees, formulate objectives, plan work. Hold committee meetings to pool findings, to plan progress and final reports.

Clip news items, articles, and pictures relevant to the unit.

Obtain information from printed sources; from books and newspapers; from people, radio, TV.

Keep unit-record book up-to-date.

Study maps.

Make original drawings, charts, maps, graphs, murals.

Set up bulletin board displays.

Make and exhibit dolls (paper, character, papier mâché).

Write original stories, plays, poems, autobiographies, family histories.

Plan and participate in dramatic activities.

See and discuss films.

Draw family tree.

Participate in panel discussions.

Write letters to Division of Public Documents, U.S. Govt. Printing Office, Washington, D.C., for copies of laws and naturalization requirements and procedures.

Obtain, discuss, and display old visas and passports from friends and relatives.

Find out from UNESCO how other countries handle problems of immigration.

Read Emma Lazarus poem; discuss in terms of present immigration policy.

Analyze and discuss the American self-concept and its effect upon international relationships.

Visit, in committees, those neighborhoods in which immigrants have settled in large numbers to determine housing conditions, recreational facilities.

Invite speaker to discuss employment opportunities for immigrants.

Invite a recent immigrant to talk about his personal experiences.

Obtain information about movements aimed at discrediting aliens.

Role-play problem situations.

Take tests on social preferences and matching of traits and nationalities to determine own personal stereotypes and prejudices.

Discuss stereotypes and prejudice.

Invite representatives from agencies, ethnic and social groups, editors of foreign language newspapers, and writers as speakers, consultants, and resource persons.

Visit (as individuals or committees) various agencies; report to class.

Visit court to witness naturalization proceedings.

Participate in "I Am An American Day" (also called Citizenship Day).

Study the influence of various groups of immigrants on language, food habits, popular music, dancing, and other phases of the American culture.

Read biographies and report on immigrants who made outstanding contributions.

Summary Outline of Teaching-learning Process

1. Preplanning survey of possible content, learning activities, available materials.

2. Preparation for, keynoting, and introduction by teacher.

3. Pupil-teacher planning of unit: determining purposes and goals, setting up content, learning activities and sources of information, allocating and accepting responsibilities.

4. Committee and sub-group work:

planning
pooling facts
preparing and making reports
art projects
securing speakers, consultants, and resource people
planning and taking field trips
securing films and projectors
writing
setting up bulletin board displays and other exhibits.

5. Individual work:

learning new words, terms, concepts
securing facts from reading, films, TV, people
art work
creative writing
reporting for a group
leading a group
going on trips
keeping a record book
evaluating self.

6. Class work:

planning together
discussions
seeing films

listening to visitors
evaluating.

7. Planning and producing a culminating activity.

Culminating Activities

—Prepare and conduct an assembly program such as a play, a panel discussion, a pageant to share ideas and information with others.
—Set up and man an exhibit of material collected: original drawings, maps, charts.
—Present material to library in an appropriate assembly program.
—Prepare a dinner party, inviting PTA, community leaders, resource people. Have a menu of different national dishes prepared by parents and students. After dinner, present program summarizing the work of the class.
—Write, mimeograph, and distribute a booklet on one or more aspects or problems in which the pupils are most interested: for example, "What the New American Should Know," "The Real American," "Welcome?" "Cultural Pluralism—Its Meaning and Values."

Behavior Outcomes

Decrease in use of stereotypes, name-calling, rejection, and exclusion because of differences in ethnic backgrounds.
Evidence of new friendships across group lines.
Increased leadership skills.
Increased desire and ability to participate in group processes.

REFERENCES

Books

Adamic, Louis, *Nation of Nations*. New York: Harper & Row, 1945. (Junior and Senior High) The story of American history, stressing the part played by groups other than the Anglo-Saxon.

Auerbach, F. L., *Immigration Laws of the United States*. Indianapolis: The Bobbs-Merrill Co., 1955. Statutes, regulations, administrative practices, and leading decisions regarding U.S. immigration law.

Baruch, Dorothy W., *Glass House of Prejudice*. New York: William Morrow & Co., Inc., 1946. A discussion of the causes and the results of prejudice against minority groups.

Bernard, William S., ed., *American Immigration Policy: A Reappraisal.* New York: Harper & Row, 1950. Although this precedes the present immigration law, it examines quota laws, the economic effects of immigration, the process of immigrant adjustment, and the relationship of American immigration policy to international scene.

Brown, F. J. and J. S. Roucek, eds., *One America.* Englewood Cliffs, N.J.: Prentice-Hall, Inc., 1952. (Junior and Senior High) History, contributions, and problems of important religious, ethnic, and racial groups in America.

Bruce, J. Campbell, *The Golden Door.* New York: Random House, Inc., 1954. Case studies of the effects of present immigration and deportation policies.

Cavanah, Frances, ed., *We Came to America.* Philadelphia: Macrae Smith Co., 1954. (Junior and Senior High) Anthology—stories of 26 immigrants from Europe, Asia, the Near East, and West Africa. Each country is represented by a brief account of the history of immigration from that country.

Cirtautas, K. C., *The Refugee.* Boston: Meador, 1957. A psychological study of the refugee describing typical feelings and experiences.

Corsi, Edward, *In the Shadow of Liberty.* New York: The Macmillan Co., 1935. The story of Ellis Island and American immigration.

Davie, M. R., *et al.*, *Refugees in America.* New York: Harper & Row, 1947. A comprehensive account of the pre-World War II refugee immigration.

Handlin, Oscar, *The Uprooted.* Boston: Little, Brown & Co., 1951. Epic story of the great migrations that made the American people.

Jaworski, Irene D., *Becoming American.* New York: Harper & Row, 1950. (Junior and Senior High) Describes the difficulties of the immigrant in adjusting to life in this country.

Mills, C. Wright, Clarence Senior, and Rose Kohn Goldsen, *The Puerto Rican Journey.* New York: Harper & Row, 1950. Report of how Puerto Ricans have reacted to life in New York City.

Schibsby, Marian and Lewis, *How To Become A Citizen of the United States.* New York: Common Council for American Unity, 1954. (Junior and Senior High) Detailed information on each step of the naturalization process.

Senior, Clarence, *Strangers—Then Neighbors: From Pilgrims to Puerto Ricans.* New York: ADL, 1960. Examines the pattern of immigration to the United States with emphasis on the most recent immigrants—the Puerto Ricans.

Stewart, George R., *American Ways of Life.* New York: Doubleday & Company, Inc., 1954. How America has been formed from the many emigrants and exiles who have come here.

Stewart, Marguerite, *We, the American People.* New York: The John Day Co., Inc., 1951. Story of immigration, including an analysis of damage done by prejudice.

Tyler, Poyntz, ed., *Immigration and the United States.* New York: H. H. Wilson, 1956. Articles on the historical background of immigration and present policy.

Whom We Shall Welcome, President's Commission on Immigration and Naturalization. Washington, D.C.: U.S. Government Printing Office, 1953. Report of the immigration and naturalization policies of the United States with recommendations for a revised policy.

Pamphlets

Allport, Gordon W., *ABC's of Scapegoating,* rev. ed. New York: ADL,[*1] 1959. Study of psychological mechanism behind scapegoating.

A Song in a Strange Land, Lutheran Refugee Service.* New York: The Service, 1956. Handbook for those interested in assisting immigrants to become integrated into American life.

Corsi, Edward, *Paths to the New World.* New York: ADL, 1956. Traces the history of our immigration laws and presents suggestions for changes in the current laws.

F.E.P.C. and the Cost of Discrimination. New York: ADL. Illustrated summary of results of Elmo Roper poll.

Hall, Margaret E., *How To Become a Citizen of the United States.* Legal Almanac Series, No. 8. New York: Oceana Publications, 1953. How a person may become a citizen according to the Immigration and Naturalization Act of 1952.

Humphrey, Hubert H., *Stranger at Our Gate,* Public Affairs Committee.* New York: The Committee, 1954. The factors behind our present immigration laws and their injustices.

I Lift My Lamp, Women's Division of Christian Service, Methodist Church.* New York: The Division, 1954. Summary of the arguments in favor of revising the current immigration law, with specific recommendations offered.

In Quest of Freedom, U.S. Office of Information Service. Washington, D.C.: U.S. Government Printing Office. Short account of twenty famous migrants from different countries who made notable contributions.

Van Til, William, *Prejudiced—How Do People Get That Way?* New York: ADL, 1957. Illustrated pamphlet explaining how people become prejudiced and how it can be avoided. Teacher guide.

[1] See Resource Agencies below for complete address of agencies with (*).

Films

Answer For Anne. 40 min., Religious Film Assoc., 45 Astor Place, N.Y. (Junior and Senior high school) A high school girl learns about the problems of D.P.'s.

Music in America. 17 min., McGraw-Hill Text-Film Dept., 330 W. 42nd St., N.Y. (J,S). A "March of Time" production giving a view of our musical culture and the groups that have contributed to it.

New Americans. 17 min., ADL (J,S). Stresses contributions refugees make to their adopted country through the story of one refugee.

One People. 11 min., color, ADL (S). A study of the racial and ethnic groups which comprise America today.

Story of an Immigrant. 30 min., Teaching Film Custodians, 25 W. 43rd St., N.Y. (J,S). A Russian immigrant succeeds in America.

The Cummington Story. 20 min., United World Films, 1445 Park Ave., N.Y. (S). The struggle against intolerance when a group of refugees is settled in New England.

The Greenie. 11 min., Teaching Film Custodians, N.Y. (J). A little Polish boy comes to America and finds problems until he is accepted.

The Toymaker. 15 min., ADL (J). Two hand puppets are friends until they discover they are "different." Provides for discussion of cultural differences, causes of tension and conflict, and what to do about them.

Who Are the People of America? 10 min., Coronet (J,S). Story of how America grew and was built by immigrants and their descendants.

Teacher References

Books

Allport, Gordon, *The Nature of Prejudice.* Cambridge: Addison-Wesley Publishing Co., Inc., 1954. Discussion of the legal, social, and economic aspects of group prejudice with special emphasis on the deeper psychological causes of hatred and conflict.

Handlin, Oscar, *Race and Nationality in American Life.* Boston: Little, Brown & Co., 1957. The history of race and ethnic relations in the United States.

Marden, Charles, *Minorities in American Society.* New York: American Book Co., 1952. Describes minority group characteristics and relationships between dominant-minority groups.

Murphy, H. B. M., *et al., Flight and Resettlement.* New York: UNESCO,* 1955. A symposium on the mental health, psychology, and resettlement problems of refugees.

Noar, Gertrude, *The Junior High School—Today and Tomorrow,* 2nd ed. Englewood Cliffs, N.J.: Prentice-Hall, Inc., 1961. Teaching and organizing procedures for the development of a junior high school curriculum based on the needs of early adolescents; Chap. iii, "Human Relations Education," particularly relevant.

Riessman, Frank, *The Culturally Deprived Child.* New York: Harper & Row, 1962. The deprivation of children because of conditions imposed upon them by society results in human wastage when the school fails to recognize potential and provide an adequate program. Concrete proposals are included.

Schermerhorn, R. A., *These Our People: Minorities in American Culture.* Boston: D. C. Heath and Co., 1949. One-chapter treatment of each of five immigrant groups: Italians, Poles, Czechs and Slovaks, Hungarians, Yugoslavs; also chapters on Spanish-speaking and Japanese Americans.

The Positive Contributions by Immigrants. New York: UNESCO, 1955. A symposium answering the questions: how, when, and under what conditions can successful adaptations be made by immigrants.

Ziegler, Benjamin M., ed., *Immigration, An American Dilemma.* Boston: D. C. Heath and Co., 1953. Historical background and the effect of immigration policies on the welfare of the United States.

Bibliographies of Reading Materials on immigration and intergroup relations

Immigration and Citizenship. New York: ADL, 1956.

Immigration to the United States. New York: American Jewish Committee,* 1953.

Storen, Helen, ed., *Readings in Intergroup Relations.* New York: National Conference of Christians and Jews,* 1951.

The Integration of Immigrants. A periodical digest of source material. New York: National Council on Naturalization and Citizenship, 1957, 1958, 1961.

The Pen Is Mightier. New York: American Jewish Committee, 1950. (supplements 1951-1954).

Trager, Helen, ed., *Reading Ladders for Human Relations.* Washington, D.C.: American Council on Education, 1949.

Resource agencies

American Immigration Conference, 509 Madison Ave., New York 22, N.Y.

American Jewish Committee, 165 East 56th St., New York 22, N.Y.

Anti-Defamation League of B'nai B'rith, 515 Madison Ave., New York 22, N.Y.

Lutheran Refugee Service, 15 East 26th Street, New York, N.Y.

National Conference of Christians and Jews, 43 West 57th St., New York 19, N.Y.

National Council of Churches of Christ in the USA, 475 Riverside Drive, New York, N.Y.

National Council on Naturalization and Citizenship, 509 Madison Ave., New York 22, N.Y.

Public Affairs Committee, 22 East 38th St., New York 16, N.Y.

Science Research Associates, 57 West Grand Ave., Chicago 10, Ill.

UNESCO Publications Center, 152 West 42nd St., New York 36, N.Y.

U.S. Government Printing Office, Div. of Public Documents, Washington 25, D.C.

Women's Division of Christian Service, Methodist Church, 150 Fifth Ave., New York, N.Y.

THE MAJOR RELIGIONS
OF THE WORLD

A TEACHER'S REPORT

Ohio State University's Laboratory School has operated a core curriculum and used unit teaching methods for the past twenty-five years. During that time, high quality has been the characteristic of classroom instruction. Mrs. Trudora Harshman, teacher of a tenth-grade core in the Laboratory School, during 1961, graciously permitted the use of the following summary of a unit done by her class.

Objective

To better understand other peoples and the reasons for intercultural misunderstanding and conflict.

Content

Developed in answer to three main questions:

1. What, in 1961, seems to be the place or role of religion in the world at large?
2. How, in what ways, do you (the individual student) draw upon religion in your own life? Why?[1]

---

[1] *Author's note.* This question would be inappropriate in a *public* school. Discussion of personal religious experience would be an infraction of the First Amendment to the Federal Constitution.

3. What experiences and understandings are needed to extend your knowledge about world religions?

In pursuit of answers to the questions, the class studied similarities and differences of Christian beliefs in Protestantism, Restoration and Catholicism, Judaism, Mohammedanism, Hinduism, Buddhism, and primitive religions. Each student was responsible for a "major research project" to be presented in a term paper. Among the topics chosen by individual pupils were "Life of Confucius," "Comparison of Jewish and Christian Holidays," "Religious Beliefs in Ancient Egypt," "Christianity vs. Communism," "Aztec-Mayan Sacrifice."

Activities

Committee work: Seven sub-groups were formed. They were responsible for bringing to the class information, speakers, and films and for planning trips.

Films: The class saw and discussed *Boundary Lines, Picture in Your Mind, Aztec and Mayan Life, UNESCO, The Loon's Necklace, Life of Martin Luther.*

Filmstrips were also used and discussed: *Great Religions of the World* and *Epic of Man*, both of which are produced by *Life Magazine*.

Resource speakers presented the following subjects: "Music in the World's Religions," "Architecture and Religion," "Why I Am A Moslem," "My Hindu Beliefs," "Diet and Judaism," "Episcopalian Beliefs," "Amish Beliefs," "Religious Values and Judaism," "Reorganized Latter Day Saints," "Catholicism," "Science and/or Religion," "Buddhism," "The Common Denominator in Religious Values."

Field trips were taken to see a campus production of *Amahl and the Nite Visitor*, to hear *The Messiah*, to visit a synagogue, the oldest cathedral in the city, and the newest Episcopal church.

Records were kept:

Books read: title, author, date of publication, theme or plot, impressions, what was learned, liked or disliked, change in thought created by reading the book, new ideas.

Learnings from experiences: general impressions and generalizations derived from each experience.

Committee plans: names of committee members, time required to do the work, reading done, speakers secured and heard, field trip planned, films for the class, facts gathered, reports given (individual, panel, debates).

Evaluation

Throughout the unit time was taken for evaluation discussions. Instruments such as those below were used to evaluate single experiences.

Evaluation of visual aids: title, what I learned, what I liked most in it, what I did not like, how the film helped me, how the film could be improved, I would (would not) like to see it again, because. . . .

Evaluation of committee work: subject, purpose, kinds of activities, contributions to purposes of the class, concepts presented, adequacy of information presented, additional information needed, relationship to the total unit, general rating for the committee.

At the end of the unit a final evaluation was made of it as a unit and as a learning experience.

Culmination

A list of generalizations gathered from the pupils' records was drawn up. Each pupil selected three or more statements from the list and wrote for at least an hour about them.

CHOOSING A CENTER OF INTEREST[1]

Approach to the Unit

The class was a typical tenth grade. Many boys and girls were already large, and all seemed to be growing fast. The girls had new permanents and wore lip rouge in the prevailing manner. They were still likely to gather in groups to giggle and whisper. Many of the

[1] Adapted from a teacher's log. Gertrude Noar, *Freedom to Live and Learn,* Phila.: Franklin Pub. Co., pp. 123-134.

boys were still awkward and shy. Sometimes one boy got a violent push and landed squarely into the middle of a girl group. They traveled in gangs and were not averse to using "wolf-whistles."

But all of them were eager to get on with the job of growing up. They often were wide-eyed as they caught glimpses of the rapidity and meaning of social change and the pending world-wide catastrophe which imperiled their future lives.

School was fun. Here they met the "gang." Here they had the chance to dance, to have parties, to chat and laugh in the lunch room. Here they did not have to care about what parents thought of their looks and behavior.

Half the class were newcomers in the senior high school. The others, having come from traditional eight-year elementary schools, had spent the previous year in the senior high school. They had heard about planning experiences, trips, and such, but were not too sure it would work. "After all," said one, "what was the teacher for, anyhow, if the kids did all the work!"

The teacher knew that the students must first have the chance to get acquainted, then to experience different ways of learning and to see him as a friend and guide. His plan was to lead with the question: "What are some of the things you learned in the past two years?" The first few who responded were brief, using single words or short, often incomplete statements. Then a few, with encouragement and helpful questions, began to describe their previous class work. Soon the teacher was able to say: "Some of you are telling us not only what you learned but how you worked. Suppose we all try to get that in." Those whose previous teachers had used unit teaching talked about planning, dramatics, art work, and clipping files.

The teacher shifted the focus of attention from the *how* of learning, to the *why* and wrote on the board, as the students mentioned them, a list of the purposes of education. In answering the questions, "Why did you do all these things?" "Why are you here?" "What is school for anyway?", students said, first, "We have to learn so we can make a living." Then the following list emerged:

Education prepares the young to:

1. make a living.
2. take part in civic affairs such as voting, helping others to make good

neighborhoods, holding office, keeping law and order.
3. live in peace in our homes, in the nation, and in the world.

Through education the young learn to:

1. read and write.
2. have self-control.
3. respect others.
4. work and study.
5. get information about themselves, all kinds of subjects, people, politics, and government.

The period closed with the suggestion that each student examine himself to determine how far he had come on the road to being an educated citizen.

SECOND DAY

Goals Determined

The teacher opened discussion by reminding the class that their home assignment was to do some self-examination. He said he was sure that all of the pupils found gaps in their learning experiences and wished for opportunities to do something about them. He suggested that a good way to talk about these might be to begin with one of the following three statements: "I wish," "I wish I knew," "I wish I knew more about."

After a few minutes of thoughtful silence, Margaret began: "I wish I knew more about being a secretary." Others followed quickly with their own desires for information about jobs and job opportunities. These included nursing, airplane pilots and hostesses, and beauticians. It was evident that many of the boys and girls had needs in the area of vocational information and that was placed on the board as the subject of a possible unit.

Then a boy said: "I wish I knew *more about* farming." This began a new series of informational needs. Students wanted to know more about the Navy, automobiles, department stores and building skyscrapers. Again a need was indicated, to know about various industries, and it was placed on the board as a possible unit.

The teacher's attention was attracted by James who looked ready to speak and, when encouraged, said: "Do you really want me to tell what I want to know?" The teacher assured him of interest so he replied: "What I want to know is about girls." Those who had not yet learned to talk freely were somewhat stunned. However, James' need was recognized as legitimate by the teacher. The facial expressions and some side remarks from other boys, showed that James was not alone in this matter. A new trend of thought had begun which led the next few students to express personal problems, such as: "I wish I didn't get stage fright." "I wish I would get taller." "I wish I had more friends." These were discussed briefly and personal problems was placed on the board as a third possible unit.

Then came some wishes for the future: "I wish I would never be let down." "I wish I knew whether or not I'll be drafted when I'm eighteen." "I wish Mary, Sally, and I would become famous singers." These were so individual and so in the realm of fantasy and speculation that the class decided they could not make a unit of them. With "I wish I knew more about history," and "I wish I knew more about other countries—especially France because my mother came from there," the period came to a close. The teacher asked that at home each student write about his wishes and bring the paper in the next day.

THIRD DAY

Common Concerns Emerge

The period began with the reading of papers written at home the previous night. Analysis showed some of them to be purely personal matters about which individuals had to do something but which did not affect others. Other papers did concern a few of the group; still others were of common concern. Expressed needs and interests were sorted into the three lists. The class agreed to center its attention on the following list which held the promise of satisfying some need or interest for everyone.

1. Study of foreign countries: We live in "one world"; all of our families originated elsewhere. We need to know in order to understand people different from ourselves.

2. Study of our own government: We may be called upon to make it better. We need to know about law and how it is made. Some of us may get government jobs. We need to know why our government is better than other forms of governments, such as communism and other kinds of totalitarianism.
3. Citizenship: We are Americans. We do not know enough about what it means to be a good citizen.
4. Getting along with people: some of our classmates and neighbors are different from us. We need to live with people of different nationalities, religions, and races without fighting. We also need to know how to live with our families.
5. How democracy began and grew: Our men fought to have it and we may have to also.
6. Living within the law: Many people, young and old, get into trouble. Juvenile delinquency and crime are increasing. This costs the community much money. Human beings are wasted.

The discussion had been animated and interesting. Thought processes had been pushed. The level of maturity was considerably beyond that evidenced by the expression of wishes on the previous day. The suggestions were recorded in notebooks. Before the class was dismissed, the teacher asked the students to discuss the subjects with their parents and each other in order to crystallize their thoughts and move closer to decision-making.

FOURTH DAY

Sources of Information Explored

The previous day's work disclosed the need for much information on a wide variety of subjects. The teacher opened discussion with reference to that fact and asked, "Where and how is information obtained?" The first answer, of course, was reading books, newspapers, pamphlets, and magazines at home, in school, in libraries, in stores, and elsewhere. Students then suggested that talking and listening to people would help. People listed as sources of information were: teachers, parents, classmates, doctors, lawyers, businessmen, neighbors, service personnel, and laborers. Next they suggested informative places and things and that this meant looking, handling, making, and doing.

Attention was then turned to the previous day's list of interests and after discussion, two more subjects were added: (7) peace, and (8) atomic warfare.

Browsing Begins

The teacher had brought to class as much material as he could find in the school library on the topics listed. He reviewed them for the pupils and suggested the importance for each student of browsing through material on subjects about which he or she knew little or in which he or she felt no present interest. He then directed the pupils to rearrange themselves into interest groups so as to facilitate the handling of the reading matter which had been sorted accordingly. Chairs were moved, and the boys and girls spent the period absorbed in reading, in leafing through books, and in looking at pictures.

FIFTH DAY

Criteria Set Up

When the class assembled, students said they wanted to continue examining the materials. To give this more direction, the teacher suggested that first some of them might tell the class about the interesting discoveries they had made while browsing the previous day. Ten or fifteen minutes of this stirred up new interests, and pupils moved into different parts of the room to see the materials they had not previously seen.

Half an hour elapsed before the teacher called a halt to browsing. The next step was to set up the criteria to be used in reaching a decision. The following list was placed upon the board as students identified the standards they would use.

Criteria for Selecting a Center of Interest

Many sources of information should be available.
It shouldn't be too long, too hard, too short, too easy.
It should be interesting to all.
It must have value for the future.
It should present possibilities for taking trips, hearing speakers, seeing

films and other pictures, making collections, doing meaningful creative writing, doing art work, working in committees.

SIXTH DAY

Exploration of Interest Areas

Each of the suggestions for units was reexamined in the light of questions raised by various students. For example, with reference to foreign countries, pupils asked: "Is the development of backward countries of importance to us?" "Why do groups of people have different customs?" "Can people live together peacefully?" "If not, why not?"

Time did not permit completion of the list, so the teacher asked the class to write questions at home for as many of the topics as they could.

SEVENTH AND EIGHTH DAYS

Formulation of Problems

The plan that was carried out this day was exciting to both the children and the teacher. As questions were formulated, beginning with rather simple, immature ideas, gradually accumulating depth and meaning, more and more pupils participated and obviously enjoyed the experience of successful thinking and expression of ideas. A set of questions was written on the board for each area. These were carefully examined for overlapping and similarities. Elimination was done, then combining. Finally, after critical evaluation, a choice was made. The following outline of the unit finally chosen illustrates how the process was carried out.

Subject—Democracy: Ours to Keep and Cherish

Big ideas to be explored:

Basic values on which democracy is based.
Human rights and liberties.
Law and order.

Areas of interest to be explored:

History.
Politics.
Government.
Community life.
Individual responsibilities.
Basic documents.
Threats to democracy.
Comparison of democracy with totalitarianism.

14

Brotherhood Celebrations

AMONG THE GREAT MOTIVATING PRIN-
ciples of civilized life is the brotherhood of man. It provides both
social and moral guidance in human relations. It has its roots in the
Judeo-Christian ethic as well as in the philosophy of democracy. In
an effort to promote the study of intergroup relations in schools, colleges, and the community, the National Conference of Christians
and Jews originated the celebration of Brotherhood Week.

Many schools do not confine their efforts to the one week in which
Washington's birthday falls but spread them out over the entire
month of February. The danger of regularly concentrating on any
subject during a short period of the school year lies in surfeit. When
this happens both teachers and pupils say: "I'm sick of brotherhood!
I do not want to hear of it again for the next year." Such feelings
indicate failure to accomplish the purposes of activities designed to
better human relations.

Intergroup relations content and learning activities should be used
whenever they are relevant to the needs of the pupils, to conditions
in the school or community, and to national and international events.
The material which follows suggests a number of approaches to activities that are appropriate during Brotherhood Week or Month.
They can also be used whenever occasion arises for study of intergroup relations.

SUGGESTIONS FOR STUDY AND LEARNING ACTIVITIES

Subject—Brotherhood and Race

Great leaders have said:

Louis D. Brandeis: "America has believed that in differentiation, not in uniformity, lies the path of progress."

Jacques Maritain: ". . . the race question in America is the spectacle of a nation which struggles . . . in order to free itself of abuses which are repellent to its own spirit, and to raise its entire practical behavior to the level of the tenets and principles in which it believes and in the strength of which it was born."[1]

Ralph Bunche: "This has always been and today remains, man's greatest challenge—how to teach the peoples of the world the elemental lesson of the essential kinship of mankind and man's identity of interest."

Pupil activities

Find and memorize other quotations on the same theme.

Discuss in class or use a panel for such questions as: What is the meaning of race; how many are there in the world? Is any one race superior to others?

Invite a speaker to discuss racial discrimination in the United States.

See and discuss the film: *A Morning for Jimmy* (N.Y.: ADL).

Read Ashley Montagu, *What We Know About "Race"* (N.Y.: ADL, 1958).

Subject—Brotherhood and Ethnic Groups

Great leaders have said:

Dwight D. Eisenhower: "Where brotherhood is ignored, there liberty, too, is ignored. Where liberty is to be defended, there brotherhood must impose its greatest influence."

Albert Schweitzer: "No man is ever completely and permanently a

[1] Jacques Maritain, "Reflections on America" (New York: Charles Scribner's Sons, 1958).

stranger to his fellow-man. Man belongs to man. Man has claims on man."[2]

Franklin D. Roosevelt: "We are rich in the elements from which to weave a culture. In blending these elements into a national fabric of beauty and strength, let us keep the original fibers so intact that the fineness of each will show in the completed handiwork."

Pupil activities

Find and memorize other quotations on the same theme.

Discuss in class, or use a panel for such questions as: What claims does one man have on another? What claims do you make on others? What are your community and society doing to break down barriers and eliminate prejudice?

Invite a speaker to discuss immigration.

Hold a costume party to which pupils come dressed in the folk-costumes of the nation from which their families came.

Read: John F. Kennedy, *A Nation of Immigrants* (N.Y.: ADL) or Eva Knox Evans, *All About Us* (N.Y.: Capitol Pub. Co.).

See and discuss the film: *All the Way Home* (29½ min., b.&w. ADL.) The problem is neighborhood integration. (Secondary school.)

Boundary Lines. (11½ min., col. ADL.) Dramatic use of color cartoons, art and music (secondary school).

Subject—Brotherhood and Religion

Great leaders have said:

Thomas Paine: "The Rights of Man": "Toleration is not the opposite of intoleration, but it is the counterfeit of it. Both are despotisms. The one assumes to itself the right of withholding liberty of conscience, and the other of granting it."

Mohandas K. Gandhi: "The need of the moment is not one religion, but mutual respect and tolerance of the devotees of the different religions."

Eleanor Roosevelt: "All of us can encourage cooperation among the citizens of this country by our attitudes in our daily lives, and if we value peace, we will do all we can."

[2] Albert Schweitzer, "Memoirs of Childhood and Youth" (New York: The Macmillan Co., 1949).

Pupil activities

Find and memorize other quotations on the same theme.

Discuss in class, or use a panel for such questions as: What do we hold in common with people of other religious backgrounds? How can we develop stronger brotherhood despite our differences?

Invite a speaker to discuss religious discrimination in employment, housing, education.

Role-play a problem situation in which religious prejudice is evident. Re-do the scene showing an alternative attitude and behavior pattern.

See and discuss the film: *Chosen People*. (27 min., b.&w. Presented on NBC–TV by the National Council of Catholic Men. Available ADL.)

Read: Florence Mary Fitch, *One God* (N.Y.: Lothrop, Lee & Shepard Co., 1944).

Your Neighbor Celebrates, Arthur Gilbert and Oscar Tarcov (N.Y.: ADL, 1957).

Subject—Political Freedom and the Meaning of Democracy

Basic principle to be developed:

Communism and other totalitarian forms of government stifle the ideals of self-expression and the real meaning of brotherhood. In an atmosphere of political freedom, implementation of the principles of brotherhood can help the nation to realize its best potential.

Pupil activities

Discuss such topics as: the danger of political extremism on both the left and the right, freedom of speech, civil rights for all citizens.

Write a letter to a Senator or Representative on the subject of civil rights legislation.

Collect and display on bulletin boards relevant articles, editorials, and pictures.

Draw a map of the world showing the free nations and those under Communist domination.

See and discuss the film: *Date With Liberty* (20 min., b.&w. ADL). Based on *Almanac of Liberty* by Justice William O. Douglas.

Subject—Responsible Citizenship

PRINCIPLE: Brotherhood depends upon man's willingness to know his neighbors—at home and in distant places.

Everyone belongs to many groups. He is a member of a family, a school, a neighborhood, a city, a state, a nation, and ultimately of the international community toward which civilization is moving. Today children and youth must be informed about the battles being waged by groups at home and abroad as men take giant steps in the age-long struggle for freedom.

Aspects of the problem

1. Effective participation is required of all.
   "That government is the strongest of which every man feels himself a part." . . . *Jefferson*
   The unique quality of a democracy lies in the close relationship that exists between the governed and the government.
2. Moral values are involved.
   "Nothing which lacks justice can be morally right." . . . *Cicero*
   Freedom in a democracy is based upon a moral conviction—the acceptance of the worth and integrity of every human being. Insofar as any human being is hurt because of prejudice owing to his color, religious belief, ethnic origins, or social class, the potentials of a democracy are weakened, and all of its citizens suffer.
3. Understanding must be established that racial superiority is a myth.
   "After all there is but one race—humanity." . . . *George Moore*
   The educated citizen in a democracy must integrate two basic concepts: a realization of himself with all his unique attributes, and an understanding of the common humanity he shares with all people everywhere.

Pupil activities

Read: Douglas, Wm. O., *A Living Bill of Rights*. New York: ADL, 1961; Tead, Diana, *What Is Race?* New York: UNESCO, 1952; The Declaration of Independence.

Write a paper on: The meaning of first class citizenship; What we can do in our school (town, nation) to strengthen commitment to democracy.

See a film: *Divided We Stand*, 28 min., b.&w., produced by the National Council of Catholic Men. New York: ADL. Deals with anti-Catholicism; *The Chosen People*, 27 min., b.&w.; Deals with anti-Semitism.

Make a chart or diagram of the structure of the government of the United States.

Discuss: The decisions of the Supreme Court on the subject of desegregation in education and prayer in the schools; Law and Order —how to observe and preserve them under all conditions.

Subject—The People of America

Basic principle to be developed is: The promise of America is the possibility of a richer and more abundant life for all people, regardless of differences in race, creed, or national origin.

The founders of our nation made a commitment to history that here would be a proving ground for the ideals of democracy advanced by philosophers and statesmen through the ages. If the promise is to be fulfilled, then citizens young and old must know and care about each other; must believe that human differences are a potential source of good; and must understand and deal intelligently with the conflicts that arise in a culturally pluralistic society.

Education from elementary school to adulthood must, perforce, provide opportunities to learn more about the values of the sub-culture groups which have helped to direct the nation's growth.

Aspects of the problem

1. The people of America.
   The contributions of people now called minority groups have made America strong.
2. The existing paradox.
   Although cultural pluralism offers great opportunities for rich and varied national growth, it also provides situations in which lack of information and prejudice give rise to intergroup conflict. The object is to help people understand that human resources are wasted because of ignorance and hate.
3. The struggle for first-class citizenship for all.

Democratic values that stress the worth, and integrity of the individual are steadily winning the battle against bigotry and unfair practices. Students need to understand the nature of the conflict and the challenge that faces the nation.

Pupil activities

Read the biographies of great Americans of all races and ethnic groups who have made significant contributions to civilization in art, music, literature, poetry, politics, statesmanship, sports, civic welfare, science, invention, world peace.

Dramatize episodes in the lives of new immigrants of the past and the present.

Visit the court in which citizenship is being granted to those who have qualified.

Invite a speaker to discuss immigration laws.

Appendix

BIBLIOGRAPHIES OF MATERIALS ON HUMAN RELATIONS

Title	Source
About 100 Books: A Gateway to Better Intergroup Understanding, Ann G. Wolfe, 1959. Books published in 1957-58 grouped for pupils from 5 to 8 years, 8 to 12, and 12 to 16. 36 pp. 25 cents.	American Jewish Committee, 165 E. 56th St., New York 22, N.Y.
Books About Negro Life for Children, rev. ed., Augusta Baker, 1961. Contribute to "unbiased, accurate, well-rounded picture of Negro life in all parts of the world." 21 pp. 25 cents.	New York Public Library, Public Relations Dept., 5th Ave. & 42nd St., New York 19, N.Y.
Books for Friendship, rev. ed., M. E. McWhirter, ed., 1962. Over 1000 titles arranged in groups such as, "friends in our land," "friends in other lands." It also contains songs, games, and foods. 94 pp. 50 cents.	Anti-Defamation League of B'nai B'rith, 515 Madison Ave., New York 22, N.Y. and American Friends Service Committee, 160 No. 15th St., Phila. 7, Pa.
Books for Junior High School and *Books for Senior High School.* 900 old and new titles. Free.	The Library, Phila. Fellowship Commission, 260 So. 15th St., Phila. 2, Pa.

Free and Inexpensive Learning Materials, 10th ed., 1960. Over 3000 items listed, classified as to subject area, described, and evaluated. 252 pp. $1.50.

George Peabody College for Teachers, Division of Surveys and Field Services, Nashville 5, Tenn.

Gateways to Readable Books, 3rd ed. Ruth Strang, Ethlyne Phelps, and Dorothy Withrow, 1958. Annotated and graded. Selected especially for those with reading difficulties. Also lists magazines and newspapers. 181 pp. $3.00.

H. H. Wilson Co., 950 University Ave., New York 52, N.Y.

Reading Ladders for Human Relations, rev. ed., Heaton and Lewis, 1955. 657 books on family life, growing up, belonging to groups, socio-economic differences, and adjusting to new situations. 215 pp. $1.75.

American Council on Education, 1785 Massachusetts Ave., N.W., Washington 6, D.C.

Social Understanding Through Literature, Carlsen and Alm, 1954. 475 secondary school books on social and political problems. The difficulty and maturity level of each book is indicated.

National Council for the Social Studies, 1201 16th St., N.W., Washington 6, D.C.

One Nation Library Series

Courlander, Harold, *On Recognizing the Human Species*. 48 pp.

Douglas, William O., *A Living Bill of Rights*. 72 pp.

Handlin, Oscar, *American Jews: Their Story*. 48 pp. Teacher guide.

Kennedy, John F., *A Nation of Immigrants*. 40 pp. Ethnic distribution map and teacher guide.

Montagu, Ashley, *What We Know About "Race."* 40 pp. Teacher guide.

Anti-Defamation League of B'nai B'rith, 515 Madison Ave., New York 22, N.Y.

Van Til, William, *Prejudiced—How Do People Get That Way?* 32 pp. Teacher guide.

Freedom Pamphlets

Belth, Nathan, Harold Braverman and Morton Puner, *Barriers: Patterns of Discrimination.* Discussion guide. 121 pp.

Grier, George and Eunice, *Discrimination in Housing: A Handbook of Facts.* 68 pp.

Raab, Earl and Seymour Lipset, *Prejudice and Society.* 40 pp.

Taft, Charles and Bruce Felknor, *Prejudice and Politics.* 56 pp.

Anti-Defamation League of B'nai B'rith, 515 Madison Ave., New York 22, N.Y.

Freedom Books

Race Awareness in Young Children, rev. ed., Mary E. Goodman, 1962. 95 cents.

The Profile of Communism: A Fact-by-Fact Primer, rev. ed., Moshe Decter, ed., 1961. 160 pp. 95 cents.

Collier Books, 60 Fifth Ave., New York 11, N.Y.

Other agencies from which materials may be obtained

American Civil Liberties Union, 170 Fifth Ave., New York, N.Y.

National Association for the Advancement of Colored People, 20 West 40th Street, New York 18, N.Y.

National Conference of Christians and Jews, 43 West 57th Street, New York 19, N.Y.

National Urban League, 14 East 48th Street, New York, N.Y.

Public Affairs Committee, 22 East 38th Street, New York, N.Y.

UNESCO Publications Center, 152 West 42nd Street, New York 36, N.Y.

Index

Abilities, pupil, 129-132
Academic freedom, 185
Activity committee, 56, 72 (*see also* Committees)
Adolescent development:
fatigue levels, 50
group influence, 128
human rights understandings, 180-181
patterns, 11-12, 17, 23-24, 220-221
American Civil Liberties Union, 184, 203, 237
American Friends Service Committee, 94, 169, 184, 235
American history (*see* Social studies)
American Immigration Conference, 217
American Jewish Committee, 184, 217, 235
American society, structure of, 132-134
Anti-Defamation League, 94, 95, 96, 97, 169, 174, 184, 203, 217, 235, 236, 237
Art activities, 91-92, 190, 193, 231
Attitudes:
changing, 121, 136, 145, 146, 172
evaluating, 99, 104-108
hostility, 165
Audio-visual aids, 85, 171, 220 (*see also* Films; Materials)

Behavior (*see also* Human relations)
adolescents (*see* Adolescent development)
changing, 121, 134, 136, 172, 213
discrimination, 151-153, 164
evaluating, 99, 104-108
requisite teaching information, 126-128
values, teaching, 141-142
Bill of Rights, 180, 181, 182, 183, 188, 189
Books, 74-75 (*see also* Materials; References)
Brandeis, Louis D., 229
Brotherhood celebrations, 160, 228-234
Browsing periods, 32, 34, 37, 40, 112, 210, 225-227
Bunche, Ralph, 229

Catholic Interracial Council, 184
Child, concepts about, 121-122
Civics (*see* Social studies)
Civil rights (*see* Human relations)
Classes, social, 132-134 (*see also* Socio-economic status)
Co-curricular activities, 143
College discrimination, 152, 167
Committee Against Discrimination, 95, 97
Committee on Racial Equality, 203
Committees:
community resources, 92
critical skill development, 99
cultural pluralism, 211
Detroit plan, 11
discussion, 78
field trip planning, 89
interviews, 87
marking factor, 101
materials, selecting, 76
operation, 49, 50, 53-73, 170, 212
pupil activity, 113, 172, 187, 189-190
race relations unit, 203
radio and television programs, 86
religion unit, 219, 220
selecting unit, 43-44
speakers, 86
teacher's role, 111, 171, 186, 210
Communications media:
attitudes, changing, 146
committee work, 57, 60, 72
criteria of good unit, 35
freedom study, 5
interest, stimulating, 32-33, 34
learning experience, 85-86, 92, 94, 96
prejudice, combating, 168-169
pupil activities, 112, 113, 173, 174, 188, 191
race relations unit, 204
records, 67
resource outlines, 161
teaching method, 111
Community resources, 92-93, 94-95
Consensus, 37-38, 45, 78, 109, 126
Content:
cultural pluralism, 207, 208-210

238